André Laurendeau:
Witness for Quebec

André Laurendeau: Witness for Quebec

Essays Selected and Translated by
Philip Stratford

INTRODUCTION BY
CLAUDE RYAN

Macmillan of Canada
Toronto

ISBN 0-7705-1002-7 cloth
0-7705-1013-2 paper

The Conscription Crisis, 1942, was originally published as
La Crise de la conscription, 1942, © Éditions du Jour, 1962.
The original selections from *Le Devoir* are
© the estate of André Laurendeau.
The selections from *Le Magazine Maclean* have been
collected in the volume *Ces choses qui nous arrivent*,
© Éditions H.M.H. Ltée, 1970.

*Grateful acknowledgment is made
to the Canada Council for a grant in aid
of the translation and publication
of this book.*

Printed in Canada

CONTENTS

from *Le Devoir*

from *Le Magazine Maclean*

ANDRÉ LAURENDEAU

To capture the complex personality of the man and the variety of his works would require much more than the collection of essays published in this volume. André Laurendeau was active for thirty-five years in widely differing capacities: as editor of a review and animator of a youth movement; as political activist, member of Parliament, and party leader; as a journalist; as a television commentator, writer, and dramatist; as co-chairman of a royal commission. There was no form of commitment that did not, at one stage or another in his career, command his support. Nothing short of an exhaustive biography and a complete edition of his works could really do him justice.

Compared to such a definitive study, which I hope will tempt some scholar in the near future, Professor Stratford's selection can be considered only an introduction. It is a pleasure to note, however, that the three main sections under which he has grouped these essays by Laurendeau faithfully represent, in varying forms, the themes and tensions that were at the heart of his experience.

Born into a family that was deeply nationalist, formed at Collège Sainte-Marie by Jesuits of the same stripe, familiar from youth with the nationalist leaders of the time, completely caught up in the aspirations of his own people, and himself a richly talented person, André Laurendeau was destined by nature and by history to play a leading role in the nationalist movement in French Canada.

Unlike a Pierre Elliott Trudeau who quickly grew aloof from the traditional élite in Québec, Laurendeau adopted the goals of French-Canadian nationalism at an early age and then set out to serve them to the best of his abilities.

He remained faithful to this first commitment all his life, whatever role he assumed. Although he was often very harsh with the bourgeois élite who led French-Canadian nationalism, he was always conscious of belonging to the same group. He was always careful to examine the behaviour, attitudes, plans, flaws, and failures of his compatriots as a man who was one with them, as a man who bore his own share of responsibility, even when he was denouncing a fault. He always took care never to accept important commitments except in this light.

I remember the day he was invited by federal authorities to join the inquiry into biculturalism and bilingualism. At first the thought of participating in this project, which had been his own idea, did not particularly attract him. When he finally accepted, it was only after he had consulted thirty or so people from different walks of life whose judgement he respected. When the majority of them advised him to accept, he plunged in, as he wrote at the time, without a glance behind or to either side. But his own instinct would probably have prompted him to decline the invitation.

Fernand Dumont has written that Laurendeau was essentially "a witness for ourselves", that is, a witness for the French-Canadian way of life. If one wishes to understand the full sense of this expression and the different forms this role assumed in Laurendeau's experience, there is no better way than to compare the articles that he published in *Le Devoir* between 1947 and 1963 with those he wrote for *Le Magazine Maclean* from 1961 to 1966.

The *Devoir* articles are, to my mind, the better. In them Laurendeau has already begun to put into perspective the forces and institutions which vie for the allegiance of every French Canadian. But he still defines himself with reference to them as a man who knows them from the inside and who, without necessarily accepting all their tenets, is nevertheless always ready to treat them with understanding and sympathy.

Like all those who have assumed key positions of responsibility on *Le Devoir*, Laurendeau's main preoccupation was politics. He spoke more volubly on this subject than on any other. But he was also interested in the intellectual, social, and spiritual life of French Canada. If a new book or a new personality broke the surface, if, occasioned by a strike, a public debate, or a simple letter-to-the-editor, a new problem came to light, Laurendeau was generally one of the first to turn his attention to this new form of life and to examine its possible implications for the future. A reality which had previously been private would suddenly become public because of the interest he brought to bear on it. He had the gift of being able to show that the simplest things and happenings are often heavy with significance for the future life of the community.

How interesting in this respect are the three articles he wrote in 1956 on Pierre Trudeau's important essay published in *The Asbestos Strike* on the evolution of French-Canadian social thought between 1900 and 1950. In this virulent diatribe Trudeau had laid severe charges against the generation which, in the name of Catholic social philosophy and nationalism, had dominated French-Canadian life for half a century. Trudeau had bitterly reproached this generation with having fed on abstract and conservative ideas, and above all with having obscured behind a cloud of sterile nationalism those political, economic, and social goals which should have been pursued in their own right.

The men whom Trudeau was criticizing were for the most part familiar figures to Laurendeau. Trudeau had known them too late, only through the institutions they had founded or the the writings they had left behind them. Laurendeau had heard their names used as household words since his childhood. He had known almost all of them personally. Trudeau's charges seemed to him unjust. He spoke his mind in three articles which show better than any others his concept of the role he was playing at this time as witness for and critic of French-Canadian society. Laurendeau certainly shared Trudeau's ideal of objectivity. He subscribed to many of his criticisms. But he refused to brook the attitude of the polemicist who in the name of absolute values borrows a stranger's mask and judges men and institutions as though he has not been born in their midst and as though he does not owe a great deal to them, notwithstanding their limitations.

"Mr. Trudeau," writes Laurendeau, "rarely allows us to measure the decades that are necessary for a society, any human society, to reorient itself, to discover and assimilate one tiny truth. The tempo of a social milieu is not that of an intellectual, and to clearly establish the effectiveness or ineffectiveness of any political or social system one must carefully mark the point of departure and the point of arrival." Because Trudeau situated himself outside French-Canadian time, he saw nothing but failure in the attempts made between 1900 and 1950 to give our society the institutions it needed. Laurendeau, on the other hand, saw everywhere seeds, beginnings, promise, at the very least experiments that should never be condemned in an off-hand manner. He could not admit the haughty outsider's attitude that had inspired Trudeau's diatribe. Yet because there was nothing in his nature of the jealous custodian of some brand of orthodoxy who refuses criticism of any kind, he was quite ready to recognize the great positive value of Trudeau's essay and closed his reply to it with these words: "The best part of Trudeau, besides his technical competence, is his love of liberty: he is prepared to run its risks as well as claim its advantages. A remarkable personality has been revealed."

The whole of Laurendeau lies in that sense of nuance which permitted him to criticize a speech or an article very severely without becoming blind to the riches it concealed. He held a high opinion of the French-Canadian nation. He believed profoundly in its originality. He shared its historical memories, its characteristic traits, its aspirations, and its frustations. Though he was as aware as anyone of its weaknesses and shortcomings, it never occurred to him to dissect them like some anthropologist or UNESCO expert. No one was more demanding than he with regard to the educational system, political parties, public administration, and social élites. But unless he was dealing with outright cretinism, dishonesty, or pure incompetence, it never occurred to him to set himself up as judge over people whose origins he shared and whose weaknesses and limitations he knew he shared too.

Laurendeau's concept of the originality of French-Canadian society and the open-mindedness he wished to bring to every subject explain his stand on the question of Canadian unity.

He was, without a doubt a strong upholder of the "two nation" thesis. He believed firmly in the existence of two distinct nations in Canada. On this particular point his thinking undoubtedly expressed itself in different ways at different stages in his career. But basically it never changed. The Laurendeau of the anti-conscription fight in 1942 was fundamentally the same as the one who, under the reign of Duplessis and Saint-Laurent, never tired of proclaiming the original vocation of the State of Quebec. And it was the same Laurendeau who prepared those too often neglected "blue pages" on the theme of the "two societies" for the Laurendeau-Dunton Report.

Laurendeau, like the nationalists of his time, had started from the idea of "two races" as propounded by Henri Bourassa. Schooled by Lionel Groulx, he had learned to discern the capital importance of the vocation of Quebec for the future of French Canadians. In turn he became one of the great sources of inspiration for that movement of self-affirmation in Quebec which was to make its first dynamic showing under Jean Lesage and then to give birth to the separatist movement.

There can be no doubt that Laurendeau refused the separatist option up to the time of his nomination as co-chairman of the Royal Commission on Bilingualism and Biculturalism. This volume contains certain articles, written a few years before that date, which deal with this theme. By 1967 or 1968 he had begun to add appreciable nuances to his affirmations of ten years earlier. But as far as the main question was concerned, I do not think one can say that he had modified his views in any fundamental way.

Laurendeau had, however, followed the political career and personal development of René Lévesque with great interest. When Lévesque opted for sovereignty in the autumn of 1967, Laurendeau, who still admired him, was deeply impressed by his action. I do not remember his ever mentioning that Lévesque's choice tempted him personally. I do recall, however, the many times he repeated his conviction that unless major changes were made in the structures of the country, it would be difficult for Canada to survive.

Laurendeau had had little experience of English Canada before 1955. Until then, like most French-Canadian nationalists, he had based his impressions on bitter memories drawn from the history of the first hundred years of Confederation. In 1955 he went on a trip through western Canada for the CBC, and thereafter he seemed to speak of the rest of the country with the same concern for interiorizing it as he applied to the study of his own milieu.

Whenever Laurendeau came into contact with a reality it ceased to be exterior to him. From then on it became part of his experience. He was incapable of remaining indifferent to it, of speaking of it coldly. The more English Canadians he got to know, the more he began to think that there existed among them a greater understanding and friendship towards French Canadians than he had at first believed. He was also very interested in the growing concern among English Canadians to defend their cultural values against the invasion of American values.

But while this new Canadian nationalism led many English Canadians, quite justifiably, to entrust the central government with a wider and wider role in many domains, Laurendeau, though he understood the tendency, refused to associate Quebec with it. "Thanks to Confederation," he wrote as early as 1949, "we have a state within which we are a majority and where we can take the political initiatives which best correspond to our own ideas and interests. Whenever the State of Quebec is diminished, to that extent we lose the possibility of autonomy. Quebec is the political reality to which our destiny as a people is fixed."

It is perhaps this declaration that best contains Laurendeau's message on Canadian unity. For many reasons—historical, psychological, economic, and political—Laurendeau wished to see the Canadian experiment pushed further. In no way did he wish a rupture. But he placed above this ideal that of the inalienable liberty of French Canadians. In his eyes it became more and more important to assure that goal first. As long as it could be reconciled with the preservation of the Canadian federation, he remained open to the idea of continuing the experiment begun in 1867. In 1967 in the "blue pages" of the B and B report which the Trudeau government hastily relegated to the dungeons, Laurendeau expressed the same convictions in different terms, clearly suggesting that more concrete proposals would be forthcoming at a later date. Owing to his premature death, the concrete proposals he announced in 1967 never saw the light of day. And yet it was toward this end that he was tending when he made his decision to accept Ottawa's invitation in 1963. When the B and B Commission decided to terminate its work without following up on the proposals that Laurendeau had promised, many people spoke sadly of "the betrayal of Laurendeau's dream". History will confirm the validity of this harsh verdict.

At the same time as he devoted himself in many public roles to the service of his fellow citizens, André Laurendeau never ceased to progress in a long private development which may forever remain secret.

Most men, when they reach adulthood, settle into a profession, a way of life, a social class. They allow themselves to be shaped by such externals, or at least accept the measurement of their own values by those of their colleagues or their professional or social milieu. The lawyer, the businessman, the politician, or the magistrate nearly all let themsélves be taken in by the logic of the positions they hold. In the end they become living incarnations of that logic in their attitudes and in their lives.

This was not the case for André Laurendeau. As he progressed he distanced himself more and more from certain of the traditional values of the milieu to which he belonged. First and foremost he wanted to be a free man and one who was always available to take in new experience. The very thought that someone might consider him locked into certain rigid attitudes put him on edge.

It is interesting in this connection to read the article on "The Churchwarden" that he wrote for *Le Magazine Maclean*. In this disbelieving warden who was obliged "to operate under two different systems: the orthodox one which he knew better than most of his fellow Catholics, and the other, his own, the one that spoke from his innermost heart," I find something of the Laurendeau of the last years.

He remained, I believe, a religious man. Until the very end he was spontaneously moved by truly evangelical attitudes like those of a John XXIII, or by historical events of great spiritual significance like Pope Paul's pilgrimage to the Holy Land. He always reserved for Saint Francis of Assisi the same admiration that he had felt in his youth.

But there must have been days when, like his atheistic churchwarden, he felt himself to be "the choice victim of a closed society". I have noted over and over again that he admired French-Canadian society unstintingly, because of the richness of life he had found in it since his own childhood and because of the remarkable originality of its culture and its institutions. But he could not help finding the many constraints it imposed on its members heavy and suffocating.

Among these constraints none were more painful in Laurendeau's opinion than those which were too easily carried over from the realm of faith and applied to social behaviour and social institutions. In this formidable correlation between the faith of French Canadians and the social structures they had created for themselves, Laurendeau was quick to discern seeds of hypocrisy which eventually grew to flagrant self-contradiction. Without having sought the role, Laurendeau was something of a prophet in this regard. The phenomenon of rejection he had predicted for a relatively distant future declared itself much earlier than he had anticipated.

The kind of spirituality that seemed to attract him towards the end of his life was not one of structures and systems. He rejected the dogmatism, the excessive sense of discipline and authority, and "the extreme pressure towards conformity" inherent in such narrow belief. His seemed rather that smiling, understanding, indulgent, frequently sceptical, often disabusing, but never despairing kind of wisdom that one finds in the *Maclean* articles. The columnist for the most part holds the same fundamental ideas as the editor-in-chief of *Le Devoir*. But the style is different. The militant gives way, most of the time, to the teacher trying himself to understand and then trying to make the reader understand the basic elements of their collective experience. The most striking thing in these admirably written pages is the perfect limpidity of the style and the total absence of hate, bitterness, or fanaticism. Also his new detachment differs from the embattled tone that we had become used to from the journalist on *Le Devoir*.

"Evening falls and the snow with it. Winter becomes intimate. It holds out the invitation of home and hearth and of sitting in front of a wood fire watching the flames constantly changing, like the sea." When Laurendeau wrote these lines in 1966 he was still chairman of the Commission on Bilingualism and Biculturalism. But he was no longer consumed as he had been with a passionate urge for results. He was thinking of other things at the same time, as he always did. Perhaps he was thinking of the literary career which he had always carried within him but which the demands of a life given over to the service of others never permitted him to realize to the full. Or perhaps he was thinking of those profound questions about the meaning of life and death, about liberty and the dignity of man, about war and peace, which, as countless passages in his work testify, were always present to his mind.

March 1973   *Claude Ryan*

EDITOR'S NOTE

There are three sources for the essays contained in this volume. The first is a long memoir published in 1962, *La Crise de la conscription, 1942*, which comes as close to concerted autobiography as anything Laurendeau ever wrote. Ramsay Cook has called it a document of capital importance for understanding French-Canadian attitudes, then and now. I am pleased to make it available in translation, for it not only introduces the man who is the subject of this collection but also many of the themes which haunt his later work and crop up time and again in the last thirty years of Quebec's history. To take only one example, perhaps the most obvious one, Laurendeau's account of the 1942 conscription crisis is an illuminating gloss on the attitudes and events surrounding that other crisis in October 1970.

This first long essay takes us up to the time when Laurendeau left politics and began his career as editorialist on *Le Devoir*. The second main source I have used is that copious body of work represented in almost twenty years of almost daily contributions to Quebec's leading French-language newspaper. The problem was what to choose when one could only include so little from so much. The sample is taken at roughly yearly intervals over the span of Laurendeau's work as a journalist. It aims to represent the variety of his interests as well as the continuity of his political and social concerns. The selection of some twenty pieces from over two thousand is inevitably inadequate, but this is the first time that any of the *Devoir* material has been collected, in either French or English.

The third source is more concentrated and homogeneous. From March 1961 to November 1966, just a year and half before his death, Laurendeau wrote a monthly column for *Le Magazine Maclean*, and these were collected in 1970 in a volume entitled *Ces choses qui nous arrivent*. These essays, as Claude Ryan points out in his preface, were more relaxed, more meditative, less directed to immediate problems than the editorials in *Le Devoir*. They provide added elements of autobiography, give more insights into Quebec politics, and illustrate Laurendeau's views on more global issues.

I had originally hoped to include examples of some of Laurendeau's other writings — some of his evocations of childhood from the book *Voyage au pays de l'enfance*, perhaps one of his plays or television dramas, a passage from his novel *Une vie d'enfer*, some early tracts or late interviews, but the scope of a one-volume edition would simply not permit the wider representation. Still, the important thing to grasp is the quality of his restless intelligence, his deep sense of justice, his quick compassion, and his fluid imagination, and these are clearly apparent in the essays and editorials collected here.

I do have one outstanding regret: that his work will be such a belated revelation to many English Canadians. His voice and his message should have been familiar to all of us from the start. I am proud to pay tribute to his memory with this translation, but I hope to see the day when the best that is thought and written in Quebec will become immediately available in English in the rest of the country as a matter of course.

March 1973   *Philip Stratford*

André Laurendeau:
Witness for Quebec

The Conscription Crisis, 1942

INTRODUCTION

When Hitler threw his armoured legions into Poland on the morning of September 1, 1939, he plunged us into a catastrophe whose consequences were to be universal. The same stroke set off thousands of regional crises. In Quebec we lived through one of them.

To give an exact and complete account of this crisis one would have to retrace the history of the war, or at least closely follow the story of Canadian participation in it from 1939 to 1945.

I am no historian. I am not writing a fat history text. But I did actively and intimately live out the conscription crisis. I will tell what I knew of it. Call it a history of our feelings.

The crisis went deep. It shook us up. It changed some of our ideas. Then it seemed to have blown over. By common consent we stopped talking about it, as though we weren't too proud of what we had done, on one side or the other. And yet, in a certain way, was it anything else but an unusually acute manifestation of the difficulties that French Canadians and English Canadians have always experienced in living together?

In one sense the subject is closed. I have trouble imagining what contingency could exactly revive the circumstances and feelings of those times. But feelings, especially when they go so deep, don't disappear without leaving scars; and they well up again where one least expects them.

So we stopped thinking about the war. But when it was over, French Canadians gave clearer and more fervent support to the idea of provincial autonomy than ever before. And separatism broke out again.

On the whole, the conscription crisis underlined once again

1

the fact that Canadians are two nations. The evidence was made unmistakably clear at the time of the Riel affair, then again over certain school problems, then in 1917 at the time of the first conscription. It is only when two nations confront each other with intense feeling that one can measure to what degree they really exist. To think that these clashes could have been created by politicians is a superficial way of explaining them. Politicians use feelings and passions, they do not invent them.

The 1942 crisis could possibly be described in purely rational terms. That's a trap I will try to avoid. Certainly the nationalists' attitude was logical enough; it was even rigorously logical; it forced the government into self-contradictory positions. It has been said before that in politics French Canadians have feelings but no ideas. The same could be said of any people. So the question remains, how was it that in 1942 such simple logic could have swayed the French-Canadian nation, almost to a man?

One might also claim that French Canadians are a backward race and that they were victimized by political demoagogues, first by the Liberals, then by the nationalists. That's another way of skirting the issue. In my opinion, the French-Canadian attitude can best be seen in the context of the phenomenon we now call "decolonization".

Before I begin this story, two preliminary remarks are in order. First, because so much of it is based on personal experience, the author must be pardoned if he frequently expresses himself in the first person. This is, I repeat, a memoir. Second, allowances must be made for the fact that in certain matters his ideas may have developed since. But for all that, he does not disown attitudes which he once held with conviction and often at the price of sharp inner strife.

CHAPTER 1

1937

In 1937 at the age of twenty-five I had just come back from two years' study abroad. My family were Bourassists* of long standing who had later come under the influence of Lionel Groulx.† I myself had been a militant nationalist in the ranks of the Jeune-Canada‡ movement. I had followed Abbé Groulx's history courses at the Université de Montréal and had been marked by his thought far more than by Bourassa's. In the name of ideas that passed for radical in those days, I had fought the aging Liberal regime of Alexandre Taschereau and had refused to put any trust in Maurice Duplessis's Union Nationale.

*Henri Bourassa (1868-1952). Founder, co-owner, and editor-in-chief of *Le Devoir* 1910-32. A nationalist in politics, he was an M.P. in Ottawa from 1896 to 1907 and again from 1925 to 1935, and an M.L.A. in Quebec from 1908 to 1912. He was a supporter of Le Bloc Populaire in later life.

†L'Abbé Lionel Groulx (1878-1967). The most influential nationalist historian of his generation. Professor of humanities at le Séminaire de Valleyfield 1901-15. Professor of History at the Université de Montréal 1915-48. Director of the review *L'Action Française* 1921-8. Founder of l'Institut d'Histoire de l'Amérique française in 1946 and of *La Revue d'Histoire de l'Amérique française* in 1947.

‡A group of young nationalist intellectuals, mainly students at the Université de Montréal, founded in 1932 and expressing its views in the student newspaper *Le Quartier Latin*, and in the review *L'Action Nationale*.

3

The two years I spent in Paris had been a prodigious adventure. I had thrown myself into it completely but, despite that, hadn't ever lost my sense of belonging wholly to French Canada. After explorations in several directions, I finally found myself in the Christian left, where I considered Jacques Maritain, Nicholas Berdyaev, and Emmanuel Mounier my spiritual masters. That didn't stop me from falling under the spell of Malraux, Bernanos, and Dostoevsky, too, but I still remained first and foremost a French-Canadian nationalist, though I should add that it took me years to clarify my own thinking and give it some kind of unity.

My beliefs led me to support the principle of collective security and to hold that countries that loved justice should unite against the aggressor. That didn't mean that I thought sanctions should go so far as participation in a war. When Fascist Italy pounced on Ethiopia (because, as a latecomer, this was the only colonial bone she could find to gnaw on), I shared the opinion of those Frenchmen who condemned the war as odious. But when those same Frenchmen approvingly held up the example of that England of clergymen and pacifists who wanted to see Mussolini's Italy ostracized by all civilized nations, the memory of the recent history of Ireland, and of London's harshness towards India, and, above all, of the history of my own people, came back to me too vividly for me to be taken in by such pious nonsense. Maybe there were also in Paris at that time young Moroccans or Tunisians who, at least privately, could have denounced the hypocrisy of such Frenchmen who were self-righteously indignant at Italian activities in Ethiopia, but I didn't meet them.

When the Spanish Civil War broke out my sympathies weren't pro-Franco. I had learnt from Jacques Maritain that the situation was less simple than we believed at home, and that in the modern world, while it was still possible to conceive of a just war, the days of the Crusades were over. These were two ideas I never forgot and, rightly or wrongly, I later applied them to the Second World War. But at the same time I was growing more and more opposed to Fascism, particularly to the Nazi brand, for I was discovering the challenges and grandeur of the idea of a democracy purged of its capitalist poisons. In those days my stand on the Spanish War estranged me somewhat from my fellow French Canadians; later it would help me rejoin them.

When I came back to Canada in the fall of 1937 to take over the editorship of the review *L'Action Nationale*, Duplessis had been in power for a year. The province was already disillusioned, and my friends saw him as chief agent in the miscarriage of the nationalist reform movement of 1935-6. They calculated that chances for the revolution we had all dreamt of had been set back a full generation.

We felt very much alone.

But problems of another kind were beginning to loom on the horizon. This time they came from Ottawa, where rumours of a European war were beginning to circulate.

In Ottawa the Liberals had come back to power in 1935. Since the First World War they had had a reputation in Quebec for being champions of Canadian autonomy. Their leader, William Lyon Mackenzie King, had recently declared in Geneva: "We will not necessarily become involved in any war into which other parts of the British Empire may enter, simply because we are part of the British Empire. . . . Any decision concerning our participation in a war must be taken by the Canadian parliament and the Canadian people." And Mr. King had assured the Commons that "questions relating to defence or foreign policy" would be decided "by reference to what is in Canada's interest".

Liberals and nationalists alike acclaimed such statements, but they sounded somewhat different to French-Canadian ears than they did to English-Canadian ears. For the former they meant a policy of almost total neutrality. For the latter they signified the freedom to stand outside any minor conflict that Great Britain might become involved in to protect her own interests, but at the same time the freedom to fly to the aid of the Mother Country if her life were threatened in a major war. King knew how to juggle such equivocal attitudes admirably, and his Quebec lieutenants gave his pronouncements—which were nearly always ambiguous—the interpretation that best suited their constituents.

But the day finally arrived when King's policies became more difficult to explain.

In those years our defence budget was ridiculously small. Suddenly, in the winter of 1937, it jumped from $20,000,000 to $34,000,000, an increase of 70 per cent. We were astonished. We were also alarmed, especially because the international situation was becoming blacker and imperialist propaganda was becoming louder. Between ourselves we said, "Old Man King has gone back to visit the Mother Country. His British blood is stirring. He isn't quite the same as he used to be."

A few Liberal M.P.s—and in the forefront Maxime Raymond, Member for Beauharnois—expressed their doubts, even on the floor of the Commons. The Prime Minister did his best to defend himself, but the nationalists just wouldn't buy declarations like this:

> As far as the estimates presented to parliament at this session are concerned, any increase in them has been only and solely because of what the government believe to be for the defence of Canada, *and for Canada alone. The estimates have not been framed with any thought of participation in European wars.**

King was trying to reassure the pacifist J. S. Woodsworth and the Province of Quebec. He only half succeeded. The resistance movement was afoot from then on.

*The italics are mine.

CHAPTER 2

Background

Before following up these developments we should stop a moment
to ask how they struck the average French Canadian in 1939.
He well remembered the conscription crisis of 1917. The experience had branded him. How, for that matter, could he have
forgotten it when he had been reminded of it at every election?
In the summer of 1930 I was living in Arthabaska county. I
was still at college and was not much interested in politics, but
some friends took me to a Liberal rally in a little country village.
It was in the middle of the Depression, war was still twelve
years away, and the political scene in Europe seemed relatively
calm. And what were the Liberal orators saying? "Don't trust
R.B. Bennett. He's political heir to that same Meighen and Borden
who drafted your sons and brothers in 1917...." The latest
news in *La Presse* was a story about some military escapade that
the Bennett government indubitably was going to drag us into.

Since 1917, and because of 1917, the Conservative party's fortunes had been at low ebb in Quebec. Even in provincial elections
they couldn't lay the ghost of conscription.

In spite of promises to the contrary, the Borden government
had brought in conscription during the First World War. It was
a coalition government; Laurier's English-speaking ministers were
part of it. But popular memory tends to simplify; it tended to
forget this Liberal collaboration and remember only Laurier and

7

his French-Canadian wing. And even here there was an element of imposture: Laurier had never formally opposed conscription; his stand had been to demand a plebiscite, and it is almost certain that a plebiscite would have come out in favour of general mobilization. In addition, it seems that Laurier had adopted a negative attitude on the conscription issue above all to prevent Quebec from falling into the hands of Bourassa.

To understand the situation fully we must go back even farther. Bourassa had been fighting "military imperialism" since 1899 when he broke with his old chief because Laurier had consented to participate in the English war in the Transvaal. Bourassa made his pitch to the whole of Canada. Invoking "the most basic of all axioms of English liberalism 'no taxation without representation'", he wrote: "and taxes paid in blood are the costliest of all public tribute." He went on to argue that the very fact of belonging to a parliamentary democracy should keep us from participating automatically in England's wars. We refuse, he said, to engage in wars caused by the failure or ambition of policies that we have had no part in shaping. We refuse to be mercenaries of the British metropolis. As citizens we will defend our country if it is attacked, but we will not let ourselves be dragged by force into every imperialist adventure undertaken in the name of Empire.

Bourassa spoke out like this to all Canadians. He used the same kind of attack on Laurier over navy estimates and in 1910 and 1911 succeeded in shaking the great Liberal leader's authority and prestige in Quebec. That was how Borden was able to gain seats and ministers in Quebec, that same Borden, who, when the time came . . .

But though Bourassa proclaimed his message from coast to coast, French Canadians were about the only ones to hear it. Blood is thicker than water. Anglo-Canadians were too near to their British origins, too tied to strong, fresh memories, too intimately involved in the Empire, too deeply convinced that to defend "Mother England" was to defend the most precious and noble part of themselves, to hear such a call for liberation.

French Canadians, on the contrary, were extremely sensitive to the least appeal to their desire for autonomy, to the point that some of them became deaf to all else. They have often been called cowards; the accusation is not only unjust, I think it is ridiculous. It required more courage to refuse to go along with the rest than to conform, even though conforming meant going against one's personal convictions. Individual cowardice is, of course, often masked by patriotic attitudes, and fear is an incentive common to all people. But fear wasn't the basic motive. The French Canadian of 1917 felt that he possessed only one country, the little bit of land that belonged to him. It was a poor man's reaction, if you will—the attitude of an agricultural people, somewhat closed in upon themselves, who know their own weaknesses and know that they must husband their strength, for there is no one else in the world to help them. Even though his religious and political leaders preached loyalty to him, he could see the cold hard facts of his situation; his sense of loyalty didn't stretch that far. He had no love for England; he didn't like the English. Can you imagine nineteenth-century Poles willingly allowing themselves to be conscripted by the Russians to fight in Russian wars? All that French Canadians asked was to quietly live out their own little history, hoping at the end of it to achieve a small measure of political liberty. They wanted to be left alone. Peaceable by nature, they could get angry on occasion. In 1917 they got angry, and they never forgot that they had been forced and humiliated. As I said, no one ever gave them a chance to forget it.

The Liberals, who had taken charge of their political education, trained them to mistrust the Conservatives; so it was the Conservatives who bore the sins of the Anglo-Canadian majority. This was accentuated by the fact that under Borden in 1917 and 1918 the federal government acted in a brutal and clumsy way. It's not easy to conscript people gracefully in the best of circumstances but it was far from necessary to give this conscription a blatantly English complexion at the very time when the provincial government of Ontario was banishing French from Ontario schools. There were riots, and conscripts took to the woods. The population helped the fugitives. In any other place there would have been guerilla warfare.

At the Collège de France in 1937 I heard André Siegfried describe the period of the first conscription crisis in these terms: Taking their cue from their Liberal leaders, "local politicians did not hesitate to say that French Canadians should at all costs avoid getting themselves killed in Europe so they could remain and flourish in Canada where it was their mission to preserve the future of the race. Never doubt for a minute the power of this argument. It corresponded to the instinctive conviction that the first duty of French Canadians is towards Canada —towards French Canada. . . . It was an instinct for local survival, a narrow but powerful instinct, which determined this attitude." Whereupon Siegfried raised the question of whether Canada was really one nation. . . .

Proofs to the contrary were once again to be provided by the events that followed.

CHAPTER 3

Skirmishes

But let's get back to 1937. The increase in the defence budget provoked opposition from several Liberal members in the Commons, especially from Maxime Raymond, who remained faithful to the electoral promises that had won him the seat of Beauharnois in 1925. At that time he had said, "If I am elected your representative for the county of Beauharnois I will go to Parliament to fight for Canadian autonomy, for Canadian policies drawn up in Ottawa and not in London, for policies made to keep Canada for Canadians." In 1925, a declaration like that was welcomed with open arms in Liberal circles. But was the same thing true in 1937?

Doubts were first raised in Parliament. Then in December 1937 they were put before the electorate at large in a by-election in Lotbinière. This contest paired off J.-N. Francoeur, the Liberal candidate, and Paul Bouchard, a nationalist, and editor of the separatist weekly *La Nation*. At the time it was the strength of M. Bouchard's arguments that impressed and fired up his nationalist followers. But later he was remembered mainly for the anti-participationist declarations he stirred up among the Liberals, and particularly the statements he provoked from Ernest Lapointe, the Minister of Justice. Lapointe was then uncontested chief of the Quebec Liberals—to the point where the federal government was often referred to as "the King-Lapointe ministry".

11

"If it's acts they want to defend the country, we're ready to act," said Bouchard. "But Ernest Lapointe wouldn't be minister a day longer if there was a cent more in that budget."*

Francoeur won the election. In the Commons he described the attitude that the Quebec Liberal ministers had adopted during the campaign: "In every public assembly my friends and I declared that we were all for defending the country but that we now considered the first line of defence to be Canada itself and that we weren't ready to contribute a red cent to arm or equip a soldier for any expeditionary corps, and that, in short, we had no intention of participating in foreign wars."

I do not want to misrepresent by quotation, though it is tempting to do so—and perhaps even necessary in order to enter truly into the spirit of the times—but it should at least be remembered that P.J.-A. Cardin, the French-Canadian minister most respected after Lapointe, also stated in words that afterwards were to take on an ironic ring: "Our adversaries have said, 'They have no mandate to plunge our country into war.' I, too, believe that we have no such mandate, *but we are not plunging the country into war.*"

No sooner had this battle ended than another developed in Saint-Henri riding. This time Camillien Houde, as an independent, was matched against an obscure Liberal candidate. Houde assumed a nationalist stance and defended it with customary brio.

He was defeated—by the promise of a tunnel at Saint-Henri. But he too forced the Quebec ministers to commit themselves to the hilt. For example, Cardin, according to *Le Canada* for January 17, 1938, went so far as to state:

> I've said it a dozen times before: Canada is not going to take part in any foreign war. Mr. Rinfret [Secretary of State] has told you the same thing a dozen times, too. Mr. King has said it a dozen times in Parliament. He said so the first time at Geneva before the whole world and before the British delegation: Canada will take no part in wars outside Canadian territory. What more do you want? . . . The military credits voted by the government are purely and simply for the defence of Canada.

*Reported in *Le Canada*, Dec. 20, 1937.

It will be noted that there was no question of conscription as yet. The question was, would Canada, following Great Britain, participate in the war which was now felt to be drawing closer? For his part Cardin expropriated and exaggerated his chief's promises, for King had not defended Canada's neutrality but her right to neutrality. However, political leaders felt obliged to use this language because French Canadians demanded it. The politicians did not create Quebec's will to neutrality, they were squarely confronted with it and felt themselves forced to reply. Perhaps they expressed their own personal convictions at the same time.

September 1938 was Munich. We had been on the brink of war and were beginning to realize that Mr. Chamberlain's umbrella could not protect us from Hitler's lightning. That didn't prevent Ernest Lapointe from repeating to a congress of the Confédération des Travailleurs Catholiques on January 21, 1939: "I notice this statement in your brief: 'The Confederation is opposed to Canada's participation in any foreign war.' I share that opinion."

And yet during the months that followed, a certain evolution in the political leaders' thought became apparent. King and Lapointe refused flatly to become locked into a neutralist position. They wanted, they said, to keep their freedom to manoeuvre, which was to say, as we observers saw it, freedom to follow Great Britain in her abstentions and commitments.

CHAPTER 4

In Search of English Allies

In 1938-9 some of us analysed the situation this way: The politicians are bluffing. They're playing to the gallery and in the long run they'll do just what they want anyway. Only an upsurge of public opinion can make them change. But French Canada alone isn't strong enough to move them. We desperately need English-Canadian allies. Where can we find them?

In France I was always humiliated whenever anybody asked me a question about English Canada because of my almost total ignorance of the subject. I had gleaned the better part of my meagre information at the Collège de France from a course given by André Siegfried. So here was a young French Canadian replying to questions about his own country with answers that had been slipped to him by a French intellectual. It was a pitiful situation. I resolved to seek some kind of dialogue with English Canada as soon as I got back. But on my return to Montreal I soon discovered that even in my own city, where there were several hundred thousand Anglo-Canadians, this was a difficult task, because the two groups lived so separated from one another. I solved the problem by signing up for some courses in sociology at McGill and in this way got into touch with a number of students and a few professors.

Occasionally we would talk together about international politics and raise the question of what attitude Canada should adopt in case of war. My "English" friends were not imperialists. Belonging to the political left for the most part—and some of them, as I learned later, to the extreme left—their opinions coincided quite closely with those of a nationalist fresh from Paris.

We decided then, in the fall of 1938, to form a study group. We would try, by making honest concessions on each side, to draw up a common program. Then it would be the job of each group working in its own milieu to actively publicize our common ideas. Necessity made us optimistic, for events were moving fast.

So we met regularly. Our progress was slow because we had to get to know each other and learn how to put the same meaning, and if possible the same emotion, behind certain key words. History, constitutional law, even our concepts of democracy and the state—everything seemed to divide us. Our terms of reference were barely the same. But on each side the effort was sincere. We didn't hide the truth from each other and gradually friendships sprang up and we were able to be gently ironic about our differences.

By spring 1939 our project was taking shape and we sincerely hoped to formulate a program that would be acceptable to both Anglo-Canadians and convinced French-Canadian nationalists. In the light of these hopes we even dared speak of a Canadian nation.

The French Canadians started off from a neutralist position. Little by little they discovered, ahead of the United States, the notion of a neutrality friendly to Great Britain (and to France too, for that matter). In case of war, Canada would give moral support to the allies; economic relations with Germany would break off immediately; those Canadians who wished to could sign on as volunteers in the British forces; more important, we would become suppliers of arms and products of all kinds to a militant Great Britain, but for payment received. In short, we said, since Canada is divided on this vital issue, let individual Canadians act according to their convictions, but let the country as a whole avoid taking "any action likely to spread the expense of a war across the nation".

Our Anglo-Canadian friends seemed pretty well satisfied.

There were just a few details left to iron out. Summer was almost here and the holidays would scatter us. We agreed to meet again in the fall to draw up the definitive text.

But the war beat us to it.

CHAPTER 5

The Second World War

It broke out on Friday, September 1, 1939.

I was in the country. Though it was the week-end I returned at once to Montreal.

One felt torn between conflicting feelings—horror at Hitler's invasion of Poland, fear that the fighting would spread, the wish to avoid, if possible, taking any part in it ourselves. As it nearly always is, action was a good antidote. During the first days we were less conscious of the threat to the world because we were trying to avert the danger that threatened our own country.

What could we do? One is always confined to the same futile acts: preparing manifestos, issuing communiqués to the press, holding meetings—and all that, in our case, without the least organization.

Paul Gouin had just reactivated the old Action Libérale Nationale movement. On Monday evening, September 4, he managed to draw a considerable crowd to the Maisonneuve Market. There René Chaloult, provincial Member for Kamouraska, asked French Canadians to abide by "conventional methods" of protest. But, he added, "once these means are exhausted, though I do not wish to see it, I am afraid that French Canadians would rather fight in the streets of Montreal than fight in Europe. (Thunderous applause.) We French Canadians in the Province of Quebec gave certain rights to Ottawa by the pact of 1867. But if 95 per cent of us refuse to accept something, then Ottawa cannot

17

bind the French-Canadian people. In that case, what should be done is this: the Quebec legislature should be called together to take the necessary constitutional measures to break the pact."

The crowd shouted

"We won't go."

"We don't want the war."

"The Jews and bankers—it's them that started it." (I'll come back to this later.)

"It's suicide for Canada."

"Down with Empire! Down with war!"

The next day we held our own meeting at the National Monument. Present were Gérard Picard, Secretary of the Confédération des Travailleurs Catholiques; Gérard Filion, Secretary of the Union Catholique des Cultivateurs; and many others. "They ask us," we said, "to come to the aid of a victimized Poland. But isn't the French-Canadian minority being victimized too when they impose on us a war that nobody wants?" We had chosen as our theme, "We Won't Go!", and this slogan came back every quarter of an hour. The crowd was angry and restless but in a sombre, tense mood, too. Once, just after I had repeated our slogan, a friendly voice called out: "Monsieur Laurendeau, you keep on saying, 'We Won't Go!' That's fine by me, but how are you going to stop them? In 1917 they shipped us off by force."

What "We Won't Go!" really meant was "We don't want to go". To make it stick we needed a wave of mass dissatisfaction. That and the support of the Anglo-Canadian population. But it so happened that we had just lost our own English-Canadian allies. We had called them to a meeting: One answered that in the present circumstances his views were uncertain; another referred with some embarrassment to principles of democracy and anti-Fascism; a third said, "I'd like to be with you but I can't, because if I turned up at your meeting I would become a traitor in the eyes of my own people and I'd lose my usefulness, even to you." That day I felt an indignation and a bitterness that was difficult to surmount. Despite all our patient efforts, the bridges we had tried to throw across from one nation to the other had been swept away like rubbish.

And what were the real feelings of the crowds we spoke to?

It seemed to me that what we were witnessing was a surface reaction, not a ground swell. To be sure, the public meetings continued: in Quebec City, Saint-Hyacinthe, Hull, and Jonquière (though not at Trois-Rivières, where the municipal council had banned it), then in Quebec again and again in Montreal and in Sorel. Then there were resolutions passed by various municipalities and associations, and a petition was circulated. . . . All that threw up a lot of smoke, but there wasn't much fire.

In the meantime the federal government had moved rapidly into action.

On the first of September it reinstated the War Measures Act and set up censorship. Prime Minister King issued a statement summoning Parliament and declared that "in the event of the United Kingdom becoming engaged in war", his government had decided "as soon as Parliament meets to seek its authority for effective co-operation by Canada at the side of Britain." In plain words this meant, if Great Britain enters the war, Canada enters it automatically. The British Prime Minister, Neville Chamberlain, seemed to have few doubts on this subject. He declared, in fact, that if war broke out, his country would enter it "with the support of the Dominions and the British Empire".

Sunday, September 3: Great Britain declared war. In Canada the National Defence Regulations came into effect. From this time on, "prejudicing recruiting" or "interfering with the success of His Majesty's forces" became a crime. Consequently, all the meetings that were held in the Province of Quebec during the next days and weeks were criminal acts; the orators were criminals, and it was a criminal offence to be part of the crowd listening to them. No one at the time drew attention to this. The government winked at it. But in Toronto, Holy War was preached from the pulpits, and soon the daily papers would be clamouring for conscription.

Monday, September 4: In Montreal the German consul protested against the arrest of German nationals and refused to leave Canada, which had not yet declared war. Fact and fiction jostled for the upper hand. It seemed as though we were already at war. The next day all commerce with "the enemy" was forbidden.

An "alien subject" was defined as "a person, wherever resident, who is a subject of a state or sovereign at war with His Majesty". But we hadn't declared war yet, and Parliament hadn't met. Who was the enemy?

We were not at war, and yet on Tuesday, September 5, in the *Montreal Star*, the Black Watch Regiment "calls for men for service overseas", repeating the identical advertisement of August 10, 1914, saying that the force would be imperial and would have the status of "British regular troops". Certain military minds seemed to have got their files confused. Which war was it exactly, 1914 or 1939?

Wednesday, September 6: Parliament met, at last! All that remained for them to do was to ratify decisions already taken by the government. Paul Sauriol, sent by *Le Devoir* to cover the opening of Parliament, described the attitude of the French-Canadian M.P.s in these terms: "Basically they form a bloc opposed to Canadian participation." But if they voted together against Canada's entry into the war, this undoubtedly would force Ernest Lapointe to resign, King would be handed over to the imperialists, and conscription would swiftly follow. "So they accept the principle of moderate participation as the lesser of two evils and as a concession by which conscription can be avoided." The throne speech referred to "the state of war which presently exists". If it is passed, Sauriol stated, the Prime Minister will make a formal declaration of war.

This avalanche of events and the series of decisions already taken before Parliament met prompted Mr. Frank Scott to remark: "The final declaration of war was an after-thought; looking over the events, it is clear that Mr. Chamberlain was the Canadian Prime Minister and his cabinet the instrument through which Canadians expressed their foreign policy."

Elsewhere criticism was even more categorical. The leader of the C.C.F., J. S. Woodsworth, took a pacifist line. His speech was the finest, the most human, the only truly prophetic statement of the whole session. But he didn't even speak for his own party. Maxime Raymond, a Liberal still, but growing more and more independent, wanted to submit a petition against participation signed by 100,000 Québécois. He was the logical and unflinching advocate of Canadian neutrality.

It was Ernest Lapointe's intervention, however, that was decisive. He had two choices: he could either resign, heading up the Quebec wing and turning the country over to the "imperialists" and thus risk an even grimmer repetition of the events of 1917, though in doing so he would provide scattered French-Canadian opinion with a firm sense of direction, or he could collaborate while imposing certain conditions. It goes without saying that he opted for the second solution.

Here is how he explained his reasoning in the Commons: First, addressing his French-Canadian colleagues, he told them that neutrality was impossible because it amounted to siding with the enemies of England and France. It was equally unthinkable to reject the idea of an expeditionary corps, for no government could retain power if it refused to comply with the wishes of the vast majority of Canadians. It was a sacrifice, he said, that French Canadians must accept in the name of Canadian unity. But this sacrifice accepted by the minority must be matched by a sacrifice from the majority: they must in turn abandon any idea of conscription for overseas service. On this point Lapointe remained adamant:

> The whole Province of Quebec—and I speak with all the responsibility and solemnity I can give to my words—will never accept compulsory service or conscription outside Canada. I will go further than that. When I say the whole Province of Quebec, I mean that I personally agree with them. I am authorized by my colleagues in the cabinet from the Province of Quebec [Dandurand, Cardin, and Power] . . . to say that we will never agree to conscription. . . .

In accepting participation Lapointe seemed to be contradicting twenty years of speeches and opinions, and in particular those which had got him re-elected in 1935 and which he had gone on repeating until a few months before. He took little part in the debate, for an adversary would have made short work of these contradictions. Had he been obliged to speak at length, he would undoubtedly have urged the fallibility of logic in matters of this kind. In any case, he was not cut out for ruptures and revolutions; he believed himself to be the only one capable of playing the role of mediator.

And yet under the lash of vigorous nationalist counter-arguments he became embittered. When certain Québécois claimed that we would have conscription anyway because it was just part of the logic of war, Lapointe charged that they were fomenters of disunion who were working for the enemy and were sapping the authority of the ministers who represented them. "I still enjoy the confidence of my province," he asserted, "because I have never deceived her."

These words, pronounced at the very time that he was performing his about-face, exasperated the nationalists. "Yesterday," they said, "Lapointe took just as formal a stand against participation. How can you believe a man when he turns his coat like that?" This stubborn stalemate was to go on for a long time.

But the Minister of Justice prevailed. The Quebec M.P.s let themselves be won over and accepted the idea of a compromise which, in electoral imagery, became "a pact" between English Canadians and French Canadians. We agreed to submit to participation; they agreed to limit participation to voluntary service.

Whom did this "pact"—as vague and dubious as the one of 1867—really bind? Mackenzie King presumably, which explains why, later on, he felt morally obligated to hold a plebiscite on the conscription issue. But what about the rest of English Canada? It silently ratified the agreement because the memory of 1917 remained strong, and Lapointe seemed to be the one man who could avert the danger of disunity; also because the war had scarcely begun and no one could foresee its length, its intensity, or the sacrifices that would be required. But English Canada didn't feel really committed. The Minister of Justice undoubtedly counted on his own personal prestige to see that his side of the pact was respected, but he entered into the compromise playing all his cards at the start. And when the time came for the other side to fulfil its part of the bargain, Lapointe was dead.

CHAPTER 6

Uncertainties

I have often wondered what exactly were the feelings of the French Canadians towards the advent of war. It is impossible to say for certain. My impression—that of a witness who was very actively engaged in events—was that they were in a state of great confusion. Yanked in different directions by contradictory propaganda from the two sides, it seemed to me that people felt bullied by events. The war had fallen on them like an act of God.

In September 1939, I was a militant anti-participationist, but there was little evidence that I was followed by the majority of my compatriots. The nationalists were active, were numerous enough to draw large crowds, and were passionate enough to soon reach extremist attitudes. But perhaps in this respect they out-distanced the French-Canadian nation and risked losing their countrymen altogether. The mass of the people held no clear ideology; they had no love for England and were leery of being dragged into English quarrels; they felt no sense of duty and remained reticent towards her. Above all, they were ready to detest any regime that would force their sons to enlist and go off to fight in a foreign land. So the government adopted a shrewd policy when it told the "minority" that they must accept Canada's participation in the war as an unavoidable destiny, but at the same time promised to leave their sons alone.

For that matter, what other party was there to turn to? The

C.C.F. — which had no roots in Quebec — accepted Commonwealth solidarity and modelled its action on that of the British Labour Party. The Conservatives, in Quebec eyes heirs to the political blunders of 1917, were natural double-dealers. In their ranks they numbered the most blatant imperialists. Their leader, Dr. R. J. Manion, a Catholic, had tried to woo Quebec with anti-conscription promises, but he was judged to be overshadowed by his lieutenants, and the Conservative leader in the Senate, Arthur Meighen, was feared and detested as a fanatic. As for the Quebec nationalists, they could never be more than a very small minority in Ottawa. Perhaps the most common feeling experienced by French Canadians was the familiar one of the isolation, solitude, and abandonment of a people who had been orphaned by history. Who was left for them if not the Liberals whom the people had trusted for so many years; if not Ernest Lapointe who knew how to speak to his own people with reassuring and familiar words, and whose views remained unchanging on the conscription issue?

The nationalist leaders remembered their history lessons better. The job cut out for them was, in the space of a week, to show, prove, and even more, make French Canadians feel in their bones, that in the modern world participation and compulsory military service go hand in hand, that one inevitably follows the other, and that Liberal backsliding was certainly a prediction of more to come, and of a more dangerous nature. Perhaps the nationalists missed the boat; who will ever know for sure? Political authorities and the press in general played up the idea of Anglo-French solidarity, a quasi-religious sense of duty, and the risks involved in any attempt to go it alone. The people remained closed in upon themselves, unmoved and unmoving.

The Anglo-Canadian majority on the contrary quickly sensed and got what it wanted.

CHAPTER 7

Why Was Canada at War?

So we were at war. It was a new situation to assimilate. Everyone was reduced to silence. In point of fact, the reign of censorship had begun.

I can remember the feeling of rage that possessed me when I was preparing the September number of the review I was editing, *L'Action Nationale*. It got me called onto the carpet twice—once by Georges Pelletier, editor of *Le Devoir*, and the other time by the official representative of the censorship board.

Le Devoir was our printer and as such was jointly responsible in law for what we wrote. Georges Pelletier had played the role of unofficial censor for the paper in 1914-18 and knew the risks of war-time publishing. The thing is, not to give in but to hang on, he told me. It would be stupid to let one rash act lead to the suppression of a journal that was necessary to the life of the French-Canadian nation. As a result, Pelletier required us to submit our texts to him before publication. This regime lasted several months. By that time we had little by little regained our liberty and tried not to abuse it.

The interview with the official censor was another matter. I knew him and thought highly of him (I still do), but the man I found myself sitting opposite was no friend. He took his job and the allied cause with tragic seriousness. He wanted to mobilize us all. He didn't let me speak for myself, he threatened me, and I left his office with the distinct impression of having been the victim of attempted intimidation. That kind of behaviour doesn't convince; it inspires either fear or obstinacy. I realized bitterly that the fight for liberty had begun for us with the death of our liberties. This was all the more noticeable for living next door to the United States.

In retrospect we think of the 1939-45 war as a world conflict. It became one. In 1939 it was a European war, exclusively European, except in so far as Great Britain and France had drawn on their empires.

Roosevelt had just declared his country's neutrality. It was months before the United States became well disposed towards Great Britain. Until Pearl Harbor we were the only American country to participate in the war. Even after 1941 only a few Latin American countries entered it, and none very whole-heartedly. We wondered why were were alone in the western hemisphere to take part in this crusade of democracy and why, among all American nations, we were the only one deprived of the liberty to pass judgement on the war.

We were told: It's because we belong to the Commonwealth. It is true that Australia and New Zealand had spontaneously taken sides with Great Britain. But in South Africa there had been considerable agitation; Ireland held jealously to its neutrality; and India—an imperial colony, therefore without liberty—was frequently to resist this forced collaboration, and Gandhi and Nehru were both to renew acquaintance with British prisons. In short, the dominions played their part in imperial solidarity to the extent that their populations were of British origin. At any rate, the only ones to hear and almost the only ones to respond to the rallying call of democracy were British people scattered over the globe.

Why was Canada at war? Because England was at war and solely because of that. To be sure, the participationists were at the same time defending a human cause by combating German ambitions and Nazi racism. But these motives were not the ones that had determined the Canadian stand. Maxime Raymond underlined this fact in several trenchant phrases in 1941. "In September 1938 the Canadian government was prepared to declare war if England declared it. England did not declare war. Therefore we did not. In September 1939 she did declare war, so we declared war. It's as simple as that."

Imagine a Franco-Russian or Franco-Polish war against this same Germany and this same Hitler. In this event it is certain that Canada would have remained neutral. We might even have remained neutral had the Americans joined the French. Furthermore there was no imperial legislative council. Great Britain dragged us automatically into decisions that we had no part in formulating.

I should add, for the benefit of younger generations, that in 1939 England still claimed to rule the seas; she possessed and exploited an immense empire; though she was far from being the most powerful military force in Europe, she remained the first financial power and perhaps the first political power in the world. She left us, like other members of the Commonwealth, a great measure of internal autonomy and even the right to diplomatic representation in foreign lands. In theory we had been free since the Statute of Westminster; in practice we ceased being so, thanks to the will of the Anglo-Canadian majority, every time there was a major crisis. We found this subjection heavy. Great Britain did nothing to relieve it. Hadn't she delegated her King and Queen—who were ours too—to pay us a royal visit in June, which tightened up the old bonds of British solidarity?

The thing that was hard to see at this time—while we were locked up in our own animosities—was how blind English Canadians were, in general, to being duped by British propaganda; how profound, on the contrary, was their conviction that they were freely following Great Britain, and, when following her, how little they felt that they were serving a foreign cause. They seemed to be acting under compulsion, but it was a compulsion bred of love. And so, often without wishing to, we were continually wounding them. And to English Canadians reading these words today, it may be that without wishing to I am opening the old wounds again. They have often enough twisted the knife in our own wounds without meaning to.

English Canadians are attached to parliamentary traditions. They were perhaps displeased with the off-hand way King had plunged us into war, but when it was a question of life or death for England such peccadilloes didn't count any more. The most liberal of them grumbled a little for the sake of form, the most fanatic had no inkling that they were being compromised. They pressed for greater and greater efforts, urging that any recalcitrant elements be reduced to silence and, if necessary, that the objections of the French-Canadian minority be swept aside along with the promises that Mackenzie King had felt obliged to make to them.

The religion of war sinks deep roots in the hearts of men. It is related to a powerful and complex network of feelings and interests. Democracy, civilization, Mother England, British supremacy, the struggle against racism, cultural solidarity—all these were mixed together and unanimously, though with varying degrees of intensity, loved, respected, and pinnacled as absolutes.

During the war similar sentiments were to be shared by a certain number of French Canadians, especially in the ranks of officialdom; the love of France egged them on. But they never were shared by the French-Canadian nation as a whole.

In September 1939 the war began. Canada became involved. Censorship forbade any discussion of the matter. Poland succumbed to the violent onslaughts, first of Hitler, later of Stalin, without any Allied intervention. The time of "the phony war" set in. In Canada the opponents of participation had been silenced. It looked as though they might be kept that way until the end of hostilities.

CHAPTER 8

The Provincial Election
of October 1939

Then suddenly a chance for freedom of expression appeared, thanks to Maurice Duplessis.

The Premier of Quebec had kept his peace since the beginning of the war. When some demonstrators insisted that he hold a special session of Parliament, he had refused, alleging that a provincial legislature was no place to discuss federal problems.

Abruptly; at the end of September 1939, he called a general election for October 25, that is, with the shortest delay possible. The motives for this announcement are not very clear, for the Duplessis government, which was elected in August 1936, still had a year and a half to run. But the Premier complained of a federal invasion of provincial rights under cover of the War Measures Act. This invasion, though it was undeniable, was predictable under the constitution. In addition, the province was in grave financial difficulty.

That much is certain. But the most plausible explanation must be sought elsewhere. Since his youth Duplessis had been a Conservative. He knew what discredit the war policies of Borden's government had brought to the Conservative party in Quebec, discredit so complete and lasting that Duplessis had only been able to take power eighteen years afterwards by changing the party's name. Now that the Liberals had been forced to commit the same error, Duplessis concluded that their prestige had been fatally compromised and judged circumstances ripe to renew his mandate. The war issue would help him make the electors forget certain contentious provincial matters where he felt himelf particularly weak. But in order to have his cake and eat it too (that is, placate the English voters as well as the French), and so that he would not be accused of acting outside his own sphere of influence, he opened his attack on the issue of provincial autonomy, a favourite Liberal stamping-ground.

Later it was said that the leader of the Union Nationale knew very well that he was risking a defeat, but in a game of "loser take all". According to this theory, Duplessis would have left to others the responsibility of governing and compromising themselves during difficult times and afterwards would reap the fruits of his tactical retreat. That is in fact what happened, but I doubt that in September 1939 the idea was ever very clear in anyone's mind.

When the election campaign opened, Duplessis's party seemed in good shape and a number of observers predicted a Union Nationale victory. I can remember writing myself that the election would be a kind of plebiscite on participation and that we knew in advance what Quebec's reply would be.

Quite soon, however, it became apparent that the Union Nationale lacked teeth. At Trois-Rivières the chief let slip a few words against participation. Unless I am mistaken, the *Gazette* was the only paper to pick up this capital sin against the rule of censorship. Thereupon two English M.L.A.s, one of them a minister, quit the party. As a follow-up, Union Nationale orators launched attacks on Liberal war policies, a strategy that soon became futile. Duplessis, who refused to submit the texts of his speeches to censorship, found himself banned from Radio-Canada. On provincial issues, too, the party defended itself rather poorly. The question of autonomy remained pretty nebulous. The chief—at least in Montreal where I heard him—lacked his habitual verve.

Very soon it became evident that the nationalists were divided. Those who gave their allegiance to the Union Nationale remained faithful to that party. Others followed Paul Gouin* in his Action

Libérale Nationale movement, which had taken a new lease on life but remained disorganized. Another group abstained altogether. Maxime Raymond, invoking the fact that this was a provincial election, took no part in it. Dr. Philippe Hamel* withdrew in disgust and then in a radio broadcast asked his supporters to vote for Gouin in counties where he made a show of strength and for Godbout elsewhere. René Chaloult* ran in Lotbinière supported by the Liberal leader.

Did this represent a rash of defections? The nationalists had been ridiculed by Duplessis in 1936 and had been subjected to his ragging in the legislature for three years. What they principally accused him of was sabotaging the reform movement they had fought for. How, in the circumstances, could they accept the alibi Duplessis provided, and how could they tolerate seeing a provincial election in which the guilty leader should have been soundly beaten turn into a plebiscite in which there was a good chance that he might be glorified?

The anti-participationists, then, were dispersed throughout every party. Camillien Houde even ran as an independent—with Liberal backing—in Sainte-Marie. Duplessis treated the issue as a politician. Paul Gouin proposed a coherent program but had no money and was without a political machine. Anything short of a tidal wave meant that he was condemned to defeat.

The Action Libérale Nationale was the only logical party. It attacked on two fronts, battling both Duplessis and the Liberals. Its leader, Paul Gouin, asserted from the very beginning of the campaign that he was not a separatist. However, he said, "We are ready to remain loyal to Confederation until the day, perhaps not too distant, but not here yet, when our own vital interests are no longer being served." On the radio he spoke out even more freely: "Once we are in power in Quebec, if Ottawa wishes

---

*Nationalist politicians, early leaders of Le Bloc Populaire who later split from the party. Paul Gouin, founder in 1934 of the political youth movement L'Action Libérale Nationale, director of the newspapers *L'Union* and *La Province*; Dr. Philippe Hamel, one of the directors of the review *L'Action Nationale*, a vigorous anti-trust crusader; René Chaloult, M.L.A., an outspoken anti-conscriptionist.

under the cloak of War Measures to surpass the reasonable limits of our resources, we will not resign, no, not us [an allusion to a threat made by Quebec's federal ministers], but we will block the path to federal power." And if Ottawa imposed conscription? "We will not resign, no, but strong in the unanimous will of our people, we would then cast off the insupportable yoke of Confederation." How exactly that would have been possible in wartime is hard to imagine. But what is remarkable is to see, throughout the war, this theme of "conditional separatism" recurring time and time again.

The provincial election of October 1939 was dominated by one man from Ottawa: Ernest Lapointe. For the provincial Liberals he was, as Paul Gouin cruelly remarked, the only strategist and the only real leader. Adélard Godbout was completely overshadowed by him. Lapointe charged his adversaries head on, but at the same time he enveloped and smothered them. I remember following his campaign, cursing him and secretly admiring him.

His first move was to announce that he accepted the challenge. Who was Duplessis really attacking? The federal ministers in Ottawa. "Since Monsieur Duplessis questions us, we are going to ask the Province of Quebec to demonstrate its confidence in us, a confidence which we esteem to be absolutely necessary." And he did not forget to ask the provincial Premier, Conservative heir to the Borden and Meighen of 1917, the telling question: "Just who do you propose to replace us?" Lapointe wanted the province to choose between himself and Duplessis. "I myself and my Quebec colleagues," he promised, "will submit respectfully to the decision of the people of my province." In other words, in the event of a Duplessis victory, the federal ministers from Quebec would resign, leaving French Canadians without defenders in Ottawa.

But that was not all. For the benefit of the public at large Lapointe took up the theory of the "pact". Here, for example, is what he said on the radio on October 9:

> We have told our fellow Canadians right across the country that we would accept with them the measures taken to come to the aid of Great Britain and France in the present conflict. But that we would never consent to conscription, and that we

would refuse to support any government that tries to enforce it. That is the stand we convinced Parliament to accept, and that is the way we preserved Canadian unity.

As Minister of Justice, as Mackenzie King's right-hand man, as his French-Canadian associate and, to all appearances, almost his equal, Ernest Lapointe spoke with undeniable authority. He repeated this theme in several public meetings, saying, for instance, in Sherbrooke:

> I told the English-speaking majority in my party and in the rest of the country, I told them frankly, honestly, brutally—we are going to co-operate, but you too, will have to co-operate to assure Canadian unity, the union of our two peoples, and the future of our country. And you will have to agree not to impose conscription. I salute .the generosity of spirit with which my English-speaking colleagues and the majority in Parliament accepted this offer. *And now the whole of Parliament is bound by the promise as made.*

A Parliament bound by a promise—that was what the French-Canadian people remembered; that, at any rate, was what was promised them by a debonair giant who was entering the lists for the last electoral battle of his life.* I heard Lapointe speak at the Forum in Montreal. The Liberals were uncertain of the metropolis; some three hundred policemen were mobilized, and the speakers entered the arena by a side door. They had miscalculated. The crowd went wild for Lapointe, who that night used the word "contract": " . . . this has been accepted by everyone, and the contract will be respected."

He pulled himself up to his full height. Who wouldn't have believed him when he declared in his rich accent from the lower St. Lawrence, "Between conscription and you, we are the barrier, we are the rampart"?

This image became the *leitmotif* of the election. They were, he was, the barrier, the fortress, the rampart. And Duplessis, the Tories' friend, could do nothing to protect French Canadians.

Camillien Houde announced his candidacy at the last moment.

---

*He was to participate in the election of 1940, but that was not a real battle, for the Liberals held all the trumps.

He supported the Liberals, who, eight months later, would send him off to an internment camp. We wondered how he would get people to forget that the year before he had been the man from Saint-Henri who had denounced the warmongering of the Liberals and had declared, with his native gift for the picturesque (it was just after Christmas), "Your armaments, cannons, rifles, bombs, and battleships, what kind of Christmas tree decorations are those?" We went over to hear him at Souard School on Sunday night, October 22, 1939. Would Camillien try to pass over what was fresh in everyone's memory? This is the way he began:

"You remember what I said last year at Saint-Henri: That cannons aren't Christmas tree ornaments? Today we're at war. Now I ask you, was I right or not?" "Yes!" shouted the crowd. Camillien was right, since we were at war. "But," Camillien continued (and I quote from memory), "now that we're at war, Camillien can't do anything about it. Duplessis can't do anything about it. So what's left for us to do? At least see that we get our fair share of wartime contracts. . . ."

My friend F.-A. Angers* and I listened dumbfounded. After this the crowd seemed to waver a little. Down in front of me I could see two little old men take their pipes out of their mouths, look at each other, and nod their heads, as if to say, "That's our Camillien! He's right, you know." I had the distinct impression that Lapointe had convinced the voters and that Duplessis, like the nationalists, was fighting a losing battle.

To wind up, there is nothing more to do than simply register the Liberal victory. Seventy seats for Godbout—which is to say Lapointe; sixteen for Duplessis; none for Gouin.

But we should also register a statement made by Adélard Godbout which was often quoted afterwards. At the beginning of the campaign the leader of the provincial Liberals had said on the radio:

> I undertake, on my honour, carefully weighing every one of
> my words, to quit my party and even turn against it, if between

*François-Albert Angers (1909-   ). Professor and director of L'Institut d'Economie appliquée at l'Ecole des Hautes Etudes Commerciales in Montreal. Sometime president of La Ligue d'Action Nationale and La Société Saint-Jean-Baptiste de Montréal.

now and the end of hostilities in Europe a single French Canadian is mobilized against his will under a Liberal government or even under a provisional government in which ministers presently in Mackenzie King's cabinet might be serving.

I write this text practically from memory from having quoted it so often from 1942 to 1945. One day it would put an end to the career of a politician and to a ministry that deserved better of destiny.

CHAPTER 9

An Expeditionary Corps

October 1939 was defeat right along the line. The Liberals, already in charge in Ottawa, had now become masters on the provincial level. The Godbout regime, in the most abject sense a creature of federal power, accepted every kind of collaboration. People who thought the way I did found themselves pinned to the ground.

Now began the long journey through the tunnel of war. We thought of ourselves as outcasts. We weren't sure of public opinion; and yet, life was grim everywhere. It really was "the phony war".

We believed that every one of our movements was monitored. Were our telephones tapped? Were there ears everywhere? What was safe to print or say? We often had the feeling of being suffocated. What could we do? At least we could record the passing moment and collect evidence for some later day.

King remained coy. He continued his game of cat and mouse, an uncomfortable one when you're the mouse. All you can do is recognize the fact and keep a close eye on the all-powerful adversary.

The cat's game consisted in classifying decisions and in moving softly from "least" to "most", but so imperceptibly that no one would notice, so invisibly that no one would dare notice, for it would be stupid for the opposition to suddenly rebel against such a slight increase in pressure.

How to prove it? One example comes to mind—that of the expeditionary corps. We were committed to the rule of voluntary service, so volunteers were needed. But what was to be done with them?

Before the war, the sending of an expeditionary corps of any size to Europe was stated to be anachronistic; King considered such a project "extremely doubtful" and Manion, the Conservative leader, termed it "improbable". As for Ernest Lapointe, he said: "The time has passed when expeditionary corps are sent abroad . . . and at any rate, it is Parliament that will decide such questions."

These politicians knew perfectly well that during the war of 1914-18 conscription grew out of voluntary service. Volunteers were sent, they were killed, wounded, or repatriated. One day the spring dried up. Conscription was the only solution.

But now the government had adopted a different attitude: participation without conscription. What then became of the expeditionary corps?

On September 8, King admitted to Parliament that the question "is particularly one of wide reaching significance which will require the fullest examination." It was necessary, he said, to consider "proposals for further participation in the war for submission to the people". As we have seen, on the eve of this declaration Canadian regiments were already recruiting volunteers.

Lapointe was more honest. He asserted on September 9 that thousands of English Canadians would want to volunteer and that no government "could resist the pressure coming from all parts of Canada that favoured the formation of an expeditionary corps."

The "fullest examination" lasted eleven days. On September 19 Ottawa announced that Canada was going to "organize and train one division as an expeditionary corps *if and when required.*" It goes without saying that Parliament had disappeared from the scene.

Had the government gone a little too far? It backed up a bit. The new Minister of Defence, Mr. Rogers, assured the country that the two divisions being raised would, in the first instance, serve in Canada. "However, the mobilization plan is conceived so that at the same time a unit for overseas service can be furnished if, in the light of circumstances, such a decision becomes necessary."

The light showed fast. Undoubtedly government intentions

38

were already fixed, but time was needed to prepare French-Canadian opinion. In this respect I can quote the following note which appeared in *L'Action Nationale:*

> From mid-October until December, Radio-Canada, which serves as official spokesman for the government, has been getting the public used to the idea of an expeditionary corps. First it was announced that such a unit would not be leaving for overseas before spring. Contrary to procedures followed in 1914, Canadian soldiers, it is specified, will be trained in Canada. Then, instead of spring, they begin talking about February. Finally, as if it had suddenly occurred to them that there are winters in Canada, the state radio explains that because of the cold weather it will be impossible to continue the training of the Expeditionary Corps at home. These calculated gradations permit the transformation of a mortal sin against public opinion into a series of venial sins that are intended to pass unnoticed. . . .*

On November 16 a group of officers landed in England. This was the vanguard of the first contingent that arrived a month later. By December 31, troops abroad already numbered 16,000. They were followed by airmen, artillery, and technicians.

From then on the habit was fixed. From then on there was no need to fear any violent reaction from Quebec.

But how were volunteers recruited? I won't say anything about techniques universally used to raise a mercenary army. It should not be forgotten, however, that the effects of the Depression had not yet been eliminated. Many were unemployed. If they were young, it was suggested discreetly in many Canadian centres that the army was waiting for them, a social pressure that was hard to resist. The leader of the C.C.F., J. S. Woodsworth, referred at a later date to certain odious practices.

> It is true, because of opposition from the Province of Quebec, that we do not have conscription. But it is also true that in many parts of this country men who have been unemployed for years have been pressured into enlisting under the threat

*"Calendrier de guerre", April 1949, pp. 301-2.

that their welfare payments would be stopped. This is the most despicable form of conscription that I can imagine.

Could such accusations be proved?

Mackenzie King was a past master in the art of political manoeuvre. But the powerful always get more credit than they deserve; perhaps his adversaries saw Machiavellian tactics in what were often nothing more than hesitations, contradictions, and false moves. We were convinced that we were being handsomely deceived, and we always felt that the official explanations masked the true ones, and we judged those who swallowed them without question as very naïve indeed.

Censorship drove us to perform veritable mental gymnastics. The problem was how to get around it. As for those of our opinions that were totally unpublishable, we chewed them over amongst ourselves.

This "we" is an ambiguous reference. I am speaking here of the little group at *L'Action Nationale*, of some colleagues on *Le Devoir*, and of intimate friends. It was impossible to know what our compatriots thought. Among them were sincere converts, opportunists, and many whom fear kept so silent that it was impossible to know what feelings they were keeping to themselves. The press and the radio carried only opinions that expressed the official line. We kept getting into hot water without having a chance to reply. When we complained, the officials and their flunkeys answered, "We have to put up with censorship too." It was a brand of irony we didn't relish.

And the war stretched on.

CHAPTER 10

The Fall of France and the First Conscription

In June 1940 fate struck: Dunkirk; France fell; Churchill rallied England; and King imposed national registration on all Canadians and conscription for service in Canada. For my family and myself, Paris meant more than the Eiffel Tower and the Folies-Bergère. My father had lived there. My wife and I had lived for two years in the Latin Quarter, and our first child had been born there. France wasn't just a prestigious but distant intellectual symbol; I had French friends and memories. As if to make these feelings all the more acute, chance brought a young French couple, whom we had known in Paris and who were now on a technical mission to the United States, to spend the summer holidays with us. Together we listened feverishly to news of the war which rapidly degenerated into news of defeat. Belgium was over-run—where were my friends Jean Delfosse and Canon Leclerc? Then it was France's turn—what had happened to Emmanuel Mounier and Father Paul Doncoeur, our concierge, our classmates, and the vegetable woman in la rue Mouffetard? Where would the Daniel-Rops, André Siegfried, and Emile Baas go now, and all those young families who had welcomed us when we felt alone in Paris, and those lay sisters from la rue Tournefort who had shared their potato soup with us during my wife's long illness? The invasion swept on at the speed of the attacking tanks. The French army withdrew and dispersed, and fleeing civilians were machine-gunned on the roads—on those narrow roads of France I loved so much. It was the blitzkrieg.

What exactly was going on? Where was the glorious French army, the only one in Europe that could stand up to Hitler? What had become of the famous "*Système D*", which was supposed to allow the French to make a quick comeback and face up to any eventuality? On the banks of what Marne would a new Joffre or a new Galliéni put an end to this nightmare advance? These were vain questions to which each day brought ever more disastrous replies. Prime Minister Reynaud made a pathetic and futile cry for help to the United States, but Roosevelt was powerless to act—his country still had no air force.

One night we learned that Pétain had replaced the civilian leaders. There were forty of us in the house organizing a shipment of clothes and food to France. For everyone, Pétain meant Verdun. My French friends thought the tide had turned. "With Pétain and Weygand everything is going to change." Angers and I looked at each other and the same thought crossed our minds: "France is beaten: they've chosen the best negotiator for the surrender."

The thing that most surprised me in those days was the dull pain you could read in the faces of the Montreal crowds. I didn't think France represented that kind of reality for them. But for several days, for several weeks even, it was as if the city was in mourning. People were wounded personally; they felt pained, deceived, perhaps a little ashamed, for their pride in the name "*français*" which they bore and loved had been roughly shaken. Later they would hear talk of the weaknesses and faults of France, but what dominated them in June was the sense of her distress.

This feeling overwhelmed us. We hadn't been expecting it. It was accompanied by a feeling that the end of the war might be near. Everything was lost, Hitler had won. For if France had been vanquished what could Great Britain do?

From this point on, reactions were less unanimous. It seems to me that at the time people wished this *was* the end, that de Gaulle was scarcely listened to, and above all, that the resistance of the English was judged to be foolhardy. But little by little it stirred up admiration. This was due particularly to the regular broadcasts of Louis Francoeur, a journalist whose influence on public opinion became enormous. He had the knack of finding the exact tone for translating the war into our language. For a time, propaganda ceased to be official; Francoeur took us with him into the bombed streets, made us share the nightly anguish

of the Londoners and admire Churchill's stubborn stand. And
he took us back to France, back to occupied Paris. I remember
an American tune that was popular in the autumn of 1940. It
was trite, but it was impossible to listen to it without getting
choked up. *The last time I saw Paris...*

Other feelings prevailed among a group of French Canadians
whose numbers can never be exactly known.

The fall of France had political and military consequences in
Canada. Prime Minister King had general mobilization voted
through Parliament. In a message to French Canadians on Saint-
Jean-Baptiste day he declared: "The tragic fate of France delegates
to French Canada the duty to carry high the traditions of French
culture and civilization and a burning love of liberty." But he
also told French Canadians: "The mobilization of our manpower
is uniquely and exclusively for the defence of Canada on our
own soil. . . . the solemn engagements that I have many times
made in Parliament, I repeated again publicly in the same place
just the other day. The government that I represent will not
put forward any measures for conscripting Canadians for overseas
service."

Ernest Lapointe specified that his "nevers" had always applied
exclusively to conscription for overseas service; our expeditionary
corps would continue to be made up of volunteers.

In the confusion of June 1940, public opinion was numbed
to the point of accepting anything. This, in fact, was a new
complaint that some nationalists directed against King. He is
taking advantage of the general disarray, we thought. He's exploiting our emotions. True enough, but on our side we didn't reckon
on the irresistible will of Anglo-Canadians to fly to the aid of
Great Britain, which now stood alone.

Maxime Raymond announced that he would support the motion
for general mobilization. In this he remained logical, for he had
always adhered to a policy of Canadian defence. But this stand
threw me completely. The Liberals had gradually dragged us
from neutrality to participation, then from participation that was
mainly economic to war policies that were much more intense.
General mobilization was yet another stage that neither King
nor Lapointe had let us anticipate. From now on, all they would

have to do was strike out three little words from the text of the law—"for overseas service"—and all the promises would be violated, and we would be back starting 1917 all over again. This was what René Chaloult thought when he tabled a motion in the provincial legislature, seconded by Camillien Houde, against the general mobilization of Canadian resources. The motion was defeated 56 to 13, which means that Duplessis and the Union Nationale supported it. Liguori Lacombe* and Wilfrid Lacroix[†] spoke against the measure in Ottawa.

The worst thing was that a dangerous mechanism had been set in motion. There was now to be an army of conscripts. How long would they be allowed to remain useless and idle in Canada when Great Britain requested reinforcements? Then, too, a conscript is subject to military law. If he receives an embarkation order he is not likely to go and discuss it democratically with his colonel. So by now I had completely and utterly lost confidence in government promises and above all in those made by French-Canadian ministers. My friends and I saw them as simply the emissaries of majority decisions. They had ceased to represent us.

On the other hand, how could one flatly oppose the law when its avowed intent was the defence of Canada? How many Canadians would have followed us into a battle that really was far more against the intentions of the government than against the text of the law?

Once the law was voted, every citizen would be obliged to register; we would be forced to give it tacit support.

At this point Camillien Houde started up a revolt. My faith in him had dwindled considerably—he had changed tack too fast, too often. From being anti-participationist in Saint-Henri in 1938, he had become an ally of Lapointe and Godbout the next year. Now, ten months later, here he was back with his first love. Of course he had clever explanations for his erratic course, but his cleverness was beginning to pall.

---

* Liguori Lacombe (1895-1957). Liberal M.P. for Laval-Deux-Montagnes from 1925 to 1936 and from 1935 to 1940; Independent Liberal 1940; Independent 1945.
†Wilfrid Lacroix (1891-   ). Liberal M.P. for Quebec-Montmorency from 1935 to 1958.

On August 2, Houde preached open disobedience to the law in a declaration that only the *Gazette* published, a breach of the War Measures Act in itself, but a fault that was easily pardoned. The Mayor of Montreal denounced conscription as hypocrisy, and national registration as a prelude to something worse; it was a manoeuvre to which he refused to submit, and he asked his fellow citizens to refuse likewise. The R.C.M.P. picked him up and whisked him off to an internment camp, where he spent four years with exemplary courage.

Some nationalists—though I was not among them—considered following him. I am told they even composed a collective letter which would have sent them all immediately to the concentration camp. There they could have rejoined Houde as well as Adrien Arcand, who had been interned since May but for quite different reasons. (Arcand was a Hitlerian. He was also a pan-Canadian, whatever has been said to the contrary.) Then the dissenters hesitated and backed down. There was considerable bickering. Almost all the press blamed Houde for superficiality and disloyalty. As far as I was concerned, I thought he was the only one among us to be perfectly logical. But he had miscalculated; his was only an empty gesture. Cardinal Villeneuve, in contrast, preached obedience to the law and explained his position from the pulpit. It was, he said, a strict duty to submit to civil authority. His judgement swayed my own but not enough to win it over, for there are unjust laws which it is a duty to disobey.

What finally influenced me was, I think, the feeling of impotence. What could a single citizen do alone against the state? Not even serve as an example, for the papers would hush the thing up or report the act without being able to explain it. If a resistance movement had existed, I think I would have joined it. It would have been passive resistance in my case, for I believed in Gandhi, and terrorism repelled me. But I had lost faith in the value of an isolated act.

Perhaps there were other motives that made me and others like me act as we did, motives that never became totally clear. To choose the moment of France's greatest distress to refuse to collaborate in policies that were intended to avenge her had, it seemed to me, something repugnant about it.

So I went and registered like everyone else. For me it took

place in the country. I can still see the little office where I answered my questions and signed my signature before the representative of the State. I came out of there feeling that I had just contradicted and perhaps betrayed myself.

CHAPTER 11

A Long Tunnel

So that was how we entered the darkest months of the war.

I was still with *L'Action Nationale*. We continued to run our own little monthly war against the powerful government and its policies. We had skirmishes with various moralists trying to involve us in their own particular crusades. Our readers began to subscribe again but correspondence was practically nil and we were left wondering whether they really shared our ideas. How had the fall of France, Churchill's call to arms, Louis Francoeur's broadcasts, and the government's endless one-way propaganda affected them? At times we felt like an isolated platoon, a tiny group of perfectly useless Don Quixotes. The French-Canadian bourgeoisie, whose representatives I met from time to time, accepted the war effort and the idea of collaboration. At least they seemed to. The rest were silent.

Under a dictatorship one cautiously feels one's way, and it takes time to find it. And war fosters dictatorship, as we learned to our cost. There were rumours everywhere, talk of arrests and disciplinary action. The conscripts, it was said, underwent a real brainwashing. Many were persuaded to enlist in the expeditionary corps "voluntarily", for they were told that this way they could choose their branch of the armed forces; whereas when conscription for overseas service came in, as it was sure to, they would serve where they were put. But all this remained unverifiable.

At this point we were able to make contact again with some young Anglo-Canadians from the Christian Student Assembly.

Their intentions and motivations didn't always seem clear to us. However, together we organized a "plebiscite" on overseas conscription, a poll whose chief value was propagandist. Students from the Jeunesse Etudiante Catholique, both boys and girls, helped us compile the results. Our plebiscite consisted of ten questions. What a time we spent reading off and totting up the answers! I have only to close my eyes to hear that rhythm again.

"No yes no—yes no yes—no no yes no."

I have forgotten the exact sense of those noes and yeses, but in their way they echoed the "nevers" of Ernest Lapointe. I still can see us at the Union Catholique des Cultivateurs with those college students, running our improvised census and pondering the vanity of such enterprises. No, yes, no—that didn't prevent a single conscript from being packed off to military camp or a single volunteer from getting himself killed. . . . By now we were beginning to be a little more sceptical about our Anglo-Canadian colleagues and even to suspect them of Communism. Later one of them published a pamphlet in French extolling with exaggerated praise the great patriots Raymond, Lacombe, Chaloult, and Laurendeau. The government banned it. This was in the spring of 1941. Then Hitler attacked Russia and Communists the whole world over did a spectacular about-face. Our Communists published a new French pamphlet—not banned this time—furiously denouncing the traitors Raymond, Lacombe, Chaloult, and Laurendeau. In five weeks it was a pretty change of tactics. At least we were rid of these sticky and dubious allies for the duration.

I remembered the stir caused by an article I wrote in November 1940, entitled "An Alert to French Canadians". It asserted that under cover of war French Canadians were victims of incessant attacks. The way things were going, it was as though Ottawa, with the Godbout government as accomplice, was using circumstances in an attempt to denationalize us. I drew up a table of suspect coincidences and tried to stir up public opinion.

This time readers began to write. Enthusiastically they registered their agreement. They dared to speak out again as though, having assimilated a series of defeats, they were ready to take up the fight once more. It was the first sign in our immediate circle of a resurgence of public spirit.

When the U.S.S.R. became our ally in June 1941, Russians

suddenly became popular in Canada and one felt that the war had taken a new turning. Propaganda outlets spoke of Napoleon's defeat at the hands of a Russian winter. Communism itself even became almost respectable, and there was much talk of the "democratic" camp. The bourgeoisie and, if I am not mistaken, some high-ranking members of the clergy, joined the "Friends of Russia". But at this point credibility began to crack.

The Godbout government, which had been elected thanks to federal intervention, remained federalist in inspiration. One explanation advanced for this subordination was economic. Under Taschereau, it was said, the electoral coffers belonged to the provincial Liberals, and Ernest Lapointe, who had no love for the provincial leader, was obliged to pay court to him. When the Liberals were beaten in 1936, however, the provincial party became poor while the federal organization, nourished on war contracts, became rich.

But another explanation goes even further: Elected with the help of Ernest Lapointe and dragged along in the wake of the King administration, Godbout's team was never able to regain its independence. Instead of keeping its distance, it collaborated for all it was worth. This led to a break with traditions which were still firmly implanted, and in particular the tradition of provincial autonomy. Godbout contracted fiscal arrangements with Ottawa which weighed heavily on the province right through the post-war period. Some time before this, by a simple exchange of letters and without giving the legislature a chance to intervene, he had accepted an amendment to the constitution. He embarked on a campaign in favour of the English language which, even without the war, would have raised the wrath of the nationalists. Later, as we were to see, his anti-conscription stand weakened and he cut his roots in the province. This was too bad, for in many areas Godbout initiated vigorous reforms and tried to renovate some sectors of Quebec life. He was concerned about education and gave women the vote. His administration had none of the disorganized character of the first Union Nationale government. He dared to nationalize Montreal Light, Heat and Power and create Hydro-Québec. These were all steps that counted.

Right after his triumphal election Godbout was powerful and popular. He was monolithic, but he was respected. No one missed

Duplessis except the Duplessists. But almost immediately the Premier began to give the impression that he was attached to the King government and that it was his job to carry out federal orders and transmit them to the province. The result was a growing malaise, even within the Liberal party as we were to learn later.

Cardinal Villeneuve, Archbishop of Quebec, also sided with the war policies of the King government. As time passed, his exhortations were listened to less and less. His directives exasperated parts of the public, but of course he spoke in high and grandiose terms. Bourassa, during the by-election in Outremont, was so bold as to remind his audience that "prudence is a Cardinal virtue". They caught on immediately and the witticism enjoyed a wide success. In private it was allowed that the Cardinal was following the traditional pro-British attitudes of the hierarchy. But several of his bishops, as was well known, did not see eye to eye with him, and on the whole the lower clergy sided with the people. The Cardinal chose to separate himself from them, which was all the more painful because, as simple Father Villeneuve, he had formerly defended the cause of French Canada and even now acted in full sincerity. This was recognized, but the day came when his advice was no longer welcome in a domain that was essentially political, and therefore free.

CHAPTER 12

The Moment of Truth

Three warnings. The first two were local, and the third one was next door and shook the world: Meighen succeeded Manion as leader of the Conservative party; Ernest Lapointe died; the Japanese attacked Pearl Harbor and the United States entered the war.

These three blows followed in quick succession at the end of 1941. No more games; no more sitting around in silence; the crisis was on. These three warnings were the signal that the moment of truth had come.

Until then, the Conservative opposition to the King government had been quite innocuous. But now the style of Dr. Manion, who had been defeated in the 1940 election, ceased to satisfy. The Conservatives wanted to force the Prime Minister's hand and loosed on him that old veteran, Arthur Meighen. They wrote Quebec off their books, for Meighen was the love of Empire incarnate and stood for an all-out war effort. His very name evoked the conscription crisis of 1917 and he had been denounced by Liberal propaganda, along with Borden, for twenty years. A just man, a real crusader, but absolute in his opinions, he's exactly what we need to clip King's wings, the Conservatives thought. Rumour had it that there were Meighen partisans even among King's ministers, who, if attracted neither to his person nor to what he represented, at least found his ideas simple and strong.

At almost exactly the same time Lapointe died of sudden illness.

His death struck the popular imagination, which conjured up stories of plots and assassinations. Wasn't it a sign that the rampart was beginning to crumble? He had been chief spokesman for Quebec in the cabinet and before the bar of Anglo-Canadian opinion. It was thanks to him that the French-Canadian delegation had accepted participation. He had overthrown Duplessis in October 1939. He was also the man of the pact, the guarantor of the compromise—"participation without conscription". I doubt that at this stage he could himself have quelled the crisis, either by persuading Anglo-Canadians to moderate their demands or by once again drawing French Canadians into the wake of the King government, but this remains pure conjecture. What is certain is that his disappearance from the political scene weakened the cause of national unity.

Then, two weeks later, the United States was catapulted into the war. American isolationism disappeared overnight. Until then we had been the only American country at war. Now the most powerful democracy in the world had entered and was to throw all its energies into the war effort and mobilize all its human and natural resources. At the same time its entry on the scene was marked by disaster. Immediately the war took on a more tragic complexion. A feeling of duty and urgency swept over English Canada.

At home we had already gone through some difficult times. Canada's two nations were not functioning at the same rhythm. But appearances had been saved, for neither group followed its own ideas, traditions, or will to their ultimate consequences. English Canada accepted a minimum of discipline. French Canada didn't seriously think of rebelling. Under these conditions a group of politicians who were relatively moderate had succeeded in maintaining a semblance of unity.

Brooke Claxton, who at that time was a federal M.P. but not yet a minister and who belonged to this middle-of-the-road school, stated in January 1942 that he didn't like the word conscription because it had become a symbol, "or rather two symbols, and symbols are powerful emotional forces. For some Canadians conscription is the symbol of an all-out war effort; for other Canadians who have just as deep a love for their country as the others, the word conscription is the symbol of racial domination."

This formula sums up the period we were now entering. The

time was coming when Canadians would realize that they no longer understood one another, that they despised and hated each other, that they formed two nations that had suddenly become mutually intolerable. This realization was to be all the more traumatic for French Canadians because they had to organize their resistance with the meagre means at their disposal and had to feel their way almost by touch, for the official representatives of the nation, in Ottawa, in Quebec, and in the highest echelons of the Church in Canada, all preached submission to the inevitable. Popular feelings that were to defy loyalty, political organization, financial power, and the authority of a Cardinal, and develop to a high pitch in less than two months, had to be passionate, universal, and desperate.

In January 1942 the Conservative party opened fire. Its press began to harass King. Hanson, the Conservatives' parliamentary leader (for Meighen didn't have a seat yet), called for immediate conscription. Colonel Drew, leader of the Conservative opposition in Ontario, did likewise, and Hepburn, the Ontario Premier who, though a Liberal, was a fierce adversary of King, expressed a similar opinion.

Meighen himself demanded the formation of a coalition government. We need more soldiers overseas, he declared. For that matter, voluntary service is a ridiculous arrangement. And why does King reject conscription?

> The reason for it, according to the present head of government, is that if we oblige Canadians to fight where they should be fighting for the defence of Canada, we will destroy national unity. Can any normal person accept such backward reasoning? Can we not then preserve a united Canada except by letting her turn deserter at the moment of danger? Can we not protect our unity by equality of military service? Must we protect this unity by inequality of service, or by failure to serve?

Meighen also stated as a fact that many Liberals thought as he did, and he offered to be their "national" leader. Hadn't the United States and Great Britain adopted obligatory military service? It was said that an intense propaganda campaign in favour of conscription was being waged among the Liberals in Ottawa.

At the other end of the line, Quebec's Premier, Adélard God-bout, was also talking about conscription. "If I were under the impression that conscription was the last way to win the war," he said, "I would be for conscription."

By-elections were announced for February 10 in Toronto and Quebec. Both were of capital importance. In York South the Conservative candidate was Arthur Meighen, and in Quebec East the Liberal was Louis Saint-Laurent. A strange phenomenon, there was no confrontation between either of the major parties. In Toronto, the Liberals let the C.C.F. candidate, Joseph Nose-worthy, carry most of the attack against the Conservative leader, while in Quebec, the Conservatives abstained. Mr. Saint-Laurent's adversary was the nationalist Paul Bouchard, supported indirectly by the Union Nationale.

The battle was savage in both ridings. A group of powerful businessmen and clergymen was formed to support Arthur Meighen. They called themselves "Total War Now", but in Quebec they were called "The Toronto Two Hundred"* and they became a favourite nationalist target. Meighen asserted that conscription in 1917 had been effective. He appealed to "British" sentiments and called for "equality of sacrifice". Saint-Laurent declared himself for the time being to be opposed to obligatory military service.

King had played his cards well. On the evening of February 10, Meighen was beaten in Toronto and Saint-Laurent was elected in Quebec. Total War Now suffered a severe set-back; Meighen's political career came to an end; the Liberal Prime Minister could breathe easily again, for English Canada had rejected imperialism and French Canadians had refused to opt for integral nationalism. And Louis Saint-Laurent, still relatively unknown, entered Parliament.

But in the meantime forces had locked in a decisive battle.

---

*The name, perhaps unconsciously, had as its inspiration the "Two Hundred Families" who had been denounced in France by the Front Populaire. Our Toronto Two Hundred also had the reputation of controlling the greatest fortunes in the country.

CHAPTER 13

A Plebiscite

On January 22 the speech from the throne announced that a plebiscite would soon be held on conscription.

"Treason!" cried Meighen, who was then in the midst of his election campaign and wanted immediate conscription.

"Cowardice," accused Premier Hepburn.

"I am opposed to conscription, which would be a crime in the present circumstances," declared Premier Godbout at a stormy meeting of Young Liberals.

What was it all about?

King continued to finesse. He had bound himself never to impose conscription, but he now wished his government to regain its liberty. He intended, he said, to ask the Canadian people to free him from his promises. But this would not mean conscription, at least not necessarily. According to the happy formula he discovered later: "Conscription if necessary, but not necessarily conscription." The military situation remained favourable; there were more than enough volunteers and for the moment there was no question of change. All his government wanted, he repeated, was to be given a free hand. He wasn't holding a referendum in which the people would make the decision, he was organizing a plebiscite to learn the views of the electorate. After that, it would be for Parliament to decide. For that matter, the text of the question Canadians would be asked in the plebiscite was not made public until mid-March. Here it is in all its elegance and limpidity:

Are you in favour of releasing the government from any obligation arising out of any past commitments restricting the methods
of raising men for military service?

But these commitments were made with the consent of the
French-Canadian people, and King himself recalled this when
he explained to the pro-conscriptionists the reasons that had determined his acceptance of these commitments in the first place:

Every honorable member of this house knows that, except for
the assurance that, in the event of a European war, there would
be no conscription for service overseas, this parliament would
never have decided, in the immediate and unanimous manner
in which it did, to stand at the side of Britain. . . .

Honourable members are also aware that if, at the time when
Canada's participation in the war was challenged in an election
in the Province of Quebec by a government professing a different
political faith, a like assurance with respect to service overseas
had not been given in the name of the present government
. . . the verdict of the people of that province might have
been wholly different.

In short, the anti-conscription promise had had its little hour
of utility; it had facilitated Canada's entry into the war and the
conduct of the country's war effort, since it had preserved Canadian unity. The government had committed itself to French Canadians, that is, to the minority. Why now was it asking the
country as a whole to "free" it from its obligations?

This was the question that the nationalists were to repeat time
and time again. Maxime Raymond formulated it first in the Commons on February 5, and stated it with particular clarity. He
referred to Ernest Lapointe's explanation of the compromise
accepted at the beginning of the war. This compromise had
become a "contract" between the two nations, a pact of honour
ratified by the general election of March 1940. French Canadians
had accepted participation in the war; English Canadians had
consented never to resort to conscription.

"Now with this plebiscite," the nationalist M.P. told the Commons, "what is being sought is not the complete setting aside
of the pact of September 1939, ratified by the people in March
1940 — this being impossible, since one of the parties thereto has

already fulfilled its obligation and the parties can no longer be replaced in their previous state—but the setting aside of the obligation of one of the parties, the sole condition which the abstentionists set to their participation, namely, that there should be no conscription for service overseas."

Raymond pressed his case with apparent coolness, using legal terminology, but you can sense the undercurrent of revolt that runs through his words. "Now," he continued, hammering his point home, "now, as I say, that one party has fulfilled its pledge, the other party to the contract, the conscriptionist group, would like to repudiate their sole obligation, which was to abstain from demanding conscription for overseas service."

Directly addressing "all sincere advocates of conscription in this house," the Member for Beauharnois repeated to them: "On September 9, 1939, a compromise was made whereby you agreed not to demand conscription for overseas service, provided those who opposed participation in the war, especially in the Province of Quebec, consented to participate in that war. On the strength of that agreement, the important part of our population which opposes war has consented to participate in it. Were you sincere at that time? I dare not question your sincerity. Did you wish to obtain that consent through false representations? I dare not believe it. Now that those who opposed war have liberally and generously fulfilled their pledge—and God knows how much fervour and devotion M. Lapointe brought into the fulfilment of his pledge—will you refuse to fulfil yours?"

Raymond had a weak voice. He was no crowd-mover, but he was logical and tenacious and was stirred by indignation to the depths of his being. He kept pressing his adversary with questions: "Since when is a debtor left free to decide himself whether he will pay his debt or not?" Since when do democracies at war with Hitler accept the principle that the stronger party can tear up a contract if it doesn't suit them any more?

The Member for Beauharnois was a confirmed Bourassist. He believed in Confederation, in the union of races, and in the independence of a bi-ethnic Canada. So how could he conclude a speech like this? "We are not advocating separatism," this moderate-minded man was led to say, "but we should not be driven to it. We are willing to live in the same house as long as it is comfortable for all. We are advocates of national unity on certain fair terms and once our conditions, laid down in advance, are accepted, we demand that they be adhered to.

"I greatly fear that the Toronto Committee of Two Hundred who are leading the struggle in favour of conscription for overseas service, in direct violation of the agreement of September 1939, are forging the weapons that will slay national unity and possibly Confederation as well."

In short, the French-Canadian nationalists were opposed to the very principle of the plebiscite. They refused to let the government ask the majority to wipe out a promise made to the minority. In advance, they denied the validity of the response Canadians would make.

The contract involved was a moral one. Judicially, Parliament could impose conscription. What the French-Canadian minority demanded of the majority was that it should refuse to act on a thing that it had the political power to enact.

Is this not an absurd position in a democracy? No. Public life in a complex state must be based on fundamental postulates of this sort or else the state becomes an open persecutor. For if strength of numbers alone regulates relationships between an ethnic majority and the minority, then life in common becomes impossible, and all that remains is to separate. The minority must quit the house that has become uninhabitable.*

To demand the execution of a moral pact when one hasn't the strength to enforce it is to put a great deal of faith in mankind. The men whom Raymond was addressing were carried away by quite different preoccupations: they had the war to win, the Empire to save, and what, in their eyes, in such circumstances, could be the worth of a promise made by a few crafty politicians to several million French Canadians?

Here, for example is the response of the *Winnipeg Free Press*

---

*In 1917 in the Quebec legislature, Liberal Member J.-N. Francoeur had proposed a motion in favour of separation. Five years later, Abbé Groulx's *Action française* proceeded to make its inquiry into *Our Political Future* and concluded that in certain circumstances separation was the solution.

58

to the nationalist attitude. The *Free Press* was Liberal and enjoyed great prestige on the Prairies.

> Those who, in 1942, continue to insist on the maintenance of any kind of limit [on the war effort] will do themselves and their fellow citizens of the same race and religion the most grievous and lasting damage.

The supreme law once laid down, ". . . the majority must prevail . . . "; then came the threat:

> Is Quebec going to share in the terrible corruption which besmirched the name of France herself and covered it with shame? We do not think so. But time is running out when virtue could speak effectively.

The *Globe and Mail*, the Conservative paper in Toronto, shared the views of the *Free Press* and the tone soon became injurious. A little later the *Ottawa Citizen* denounced "the aggressive drive to make Quebec the leader of this country"; which is to say that, in demanding that a promise be respected, the minority was taking itself for the majority.

Take this line of thought, push it to the limit, stir in the idea of the congenital cowardice of French Canadians, and you have this pregnant little piece taken from Toronto's *Saturday Night*: "The desire to influence the population ratio by incurring less than the proportional risks in active service against the enemies of Canada will be deeply resented."

In the same journal, the Reverend M. Silcox explained us to his compatriots. He did so with a great effort of good will, since our medieval shortcomings, as he saw them, as well as our poverty, were attributable to the Church, and not to the fact that we were simply French. However, French Canadians, he opined, "have reached the critical point in the history of their survival." On April 27 (the date of the plebiscite) they themselves would provide the answer to the problem of their continued existence. Let them beware, he said, "of destroying the faith we have in them. . . . For if they do so they will find themselves a despised and helpless minority of some 3 million people on a continent of 140 million English-speaking people." The seventy-

fifth anniversary of Confederation might well be the last, he concluded, for its dissolution might be the only wise step, "with
whatever transfer of minority elements of the population may
be necessary". Ship them all off to the reservations! This time
the separatist thesis came from Toronto.

T. S. Ewart, son of the famous jurist, tried in vain to defend
the principle of the contract on Radio CFCF in Montreal. In
vain, too, other voices were raised in attempts at appease-
ment—for example that of J. T. Thorson, Minister of National Selective Service. According to him it was unjust to
assert that opposition to conscription was restricted to Quebec.
"I myself could name twenty-five Ontario ridings," he declared
in April, "and some of them exclusively of British extraction,
where opposition to conscription runs strong. And I could do
the same for other regions in Canada."

Who had the ready answer for Thorson? Another of King's
cabinet ministers, Colin Gibson, Minister of National Revenue,
who had it printed in a government advertisement.

> As I see it—Hitler would vote "No", Quisling would not vote,
> and Canadians will vote "YES."

It was only the enemy or the traitor then, a Quisling, a turncoat,
or a filthy collaborator, only types who in the eyes of official
propaganda deserved to be cast into outer darkness, who would
dare vote anything but Yes.

It would be easy to cite many more examples of statements
of this kind, all drawn from respectable newspapers or made
by men in positions of authority. For incomprehension had
reached gargantuan proportions and on both sides people indulged
the worst elements of themselves. And yet I find the most basic
explanation of one type of Anglo-Canadian reaction elsewhere — in the words of a political figure who didn't really have
the soul of a politician and who spoke for widespread popular
feeling. Not that everyone shared his thought to the same degree,
but it coloured, I think, the most diverse attitudes, and those
who did not accept it in its most absolute form still felt its reality
in their hearts.

It was the same day or the day after Maxime Raymond's speech.

The Finance Minister, J. L. Ilsley, one of King's principal aides, rose in the Commons and said:

> I represent people whose ancestors for the most part left the British Isles centuries ago, people whose loyalty to the British empire, whose belief in the British empire and its institutions, are deep-seated, and for that matter taken for granted. They call it the British empire and not the British commonwealth of nations. They do not think too much about home defence. . . . The distinction between serving in Canada and serving overseas is a distinction which for them has no meaning whatever. They would consider it their duty to defend what they call the British empire, and what I call the British empire, in any part of the world in which the continued existence of the empire was in peril.

Compared with the sharp squeals I quoted earlier, can't one decipher here the booming tones of the great organ? A religious note is struck and the weighty words and resonant phrases bespeak total deep-seated conviction. Ilsley is one of the true believers anchored in a faith, in a rite even, for he does not deign to speak of the Commonwealth, a mere desecrated version of the old British cult. He prefers the good old word "Empire". In the circumstances he was the incarnation of English Canada, just as Maxime Raymond was the symbol of French Canada—that is to say, beyond the norm, though in direct line with it, well out in front of the pack, though not cut off from it, having the courage to indulge to the full feelings which were everywhere dominant but which most people were afraid to admit to themselves. Certainly Frank Scott didn't belong in this company; but can one be sure that Ilsley's credo didn't awaken a sympathetic echo in King or even in Coldwell?

If we had been a little more cool-headed we simply should have said: "Here is the adversary, the honest and implacable adversary who must be defied and who deserves our respect. For he knows the name of the thing he is fighting for and even if his ideals seem old-fashioned to us, they do have a human dimension, they are based on a system of values and they represent a certain mode of existence."

And he had warned us himself: we weren't to mistake him for some recent British immigrant. His ancestors had left the

Isles centuries ago. In his own way he was a Canadian. Perhaps he was a descendant of those Loyalists who, in Scott Symons' definition, had accepted "the great upheaval" of coming north in order to be able to live a life in conformity with the truth symbolized by the British Crown.

Ilsley had old English-Canadian roots, roots that are often denied nowadays. He represented in every detail the English Canada that we could not tolerate, for it stood for our own disappearance, our downfall, our servitude. Naturally, he had drawn certain advantages from his situation, which he clung to, but having a sense of responsibility he was ready, in the present crisis, to accept some sacrifices along with the advantages.

What were we to him? A thorn in his side. He went on: "These are the people . . . whose view-point, which is my view-point, I reflect in the cabinet. . . . These people believe and I believe that this government, without too much regard for remotely distant consequences, should adopt the most efficient and effective methods now of carrying on the war."

Needless to say, the anti-conscription promises were a tether he could no longer abide. He told Canadians to vote Yes. "I need hardly say that I will do my utmost to obtain this result. And when we have full liberty to act, we will act in the best interests of this country and of its war effort."

So the landscape was coming into focus. In one solid block English Canada leant towards Yes. Of course there was debate. Conservatives and socialists denounced the Machiavellian ways of Mackenzie King. But the Prime Minister had set up the problem in such a way that, like it or not, everyone had to pull with him. The federal parties—Conservatives, Liberals, C.C.F., and Social Credit—asked their members to vote Yes. They pulled Quebec officialdom in after them. Cardinal Villeneuve did not take a stand on a question that was so patently political, but he was known to favour the central government and the war effort. The ministers in Ottawa kept rank with their colleagues. The Godbout government leant the same way.

CHAPTER 14

The League for the Defence of Canada

The League for the Defence of Canada was born from the divorce between official opinion and popular feeling in Canada.

Several of us had reached the same conclusion. We knew that part of Quebec opinion would rebel but that it was leaderless and unstructured. There was danger of anarchy, and if this was the case the revolt would be more violent and less effective. These forces had to be channelled. How were we to go about it? By drawing on different structures already in existence. We would group together in a new movement the representatives of rank from the most important organizations, or at least from those who would consent to delegate us one of their members. In this way the movement would have great freedom of action and at the same time would be in contact with influential bodies. These were:

—L'Union Catholique des Cultivateurs, who delegated Gérard Filion, their secretary general.

—Les Syndicats Catholiques, represented by Philippe Gérard, president of the Montreal Council of the Confédération des Travailleurs Catholiques.

—La Société Saint-Jean-Baptiste of Montreal, represented by its president, L.-Athanase Fréchette.

—Les Voyageurs de Commerce, represented by J. Alfred Bernier, who, if I am not mistaken, was their president.

—Various youth movements represented by Jean Drapeau and Roger Varin.

—La Ligue d'Action Nationale, represented by André Laurendeau, editor of the revue published by the League.

The presidency of the League for the Defence of Canada was conferred on Dr. J. B. Prince, a veteran Bourassist. I became its principal executive officer. Everyone contributed very actively.

The League had two real leaders. The first was Maxime Raymond, who was still a Liberal M.P. but who was becoming daily more openly independent. His clearness of vision, his parliamentary experience, his tenacity and prestige placed him in the very front rank. The other was Georges Pelletier. He was more withdrawn but was intellectually vigorous and a real fighter. He had been on *Le Devoir* during the first war and his knowledge of contemporary history and of English-Canadian society, as well as his journalistic skills, earned him our esteem and respect. Raymond spent the week in parliamentary session in Ottawa, so we only met him on week-ends. He brought back something of the atmosphere of the capital with stories of the sharp and nervous reactions to the reigning imperialism there, and of the weak-kneed resistance of the average French-Canadian M.P. Pelletier was more closely in touch with the militants, though he never attended our meetings. But how many times when the day was over did I go and hunt him out in his office on Notre Dame Street. At such times this blunt but timid man opened up a little. I admired his serenity, which grew deeper and deeper, which found its roots in more and more profound reaches of himself as the battle closed in around us and the risks multiplied.

We had nothing to begin with, no money, no aides, no organization. We were a headquarters without troops.

But thanks to Pelletier one paper supported us to the hilt: *Le Devoir* was the only French-Canadian daily to take up a position frankly and systematically on the side of the Noes. Thanks to Gérard Filion we could count on the support of a large weekly, *La Terre de chez nous*, which gave us a voice in the agricultural community and in which Dominique Beaudin showed himself to be a master of caustic allusion. As soon as our finances permitted, we made use of the radio—stations CKAC in Montreal and CHRC in Quebec. Such were our arms, but they were likely to prove ridiculous compared to the enemy's artillery.

We were mortgaging our future but we were never short of money. Contributions remained modest. I don't think, for example, that the Saint-Jean-Baptiste Society and the Union Catholique des Cultivateurs contributed a thousand dollars between them. You could become a member of the League for a dollar, and we received tens of thousands. In terms of individual subscriptions, ten dollars was a substantial contribution. I have never in my life seen this form of financing flourish to such an extent, and this view is shared by other witnesses.

Soon branches of the League were formed in nearly every centre in the province. First in Quebec City, where the principal supporters were Philippe Hamel, René Chaloult, the lawyer Marie-Louis Beaulieu, and the student representative Jean Boucher—then in Sherbrooke, Granby, Trois-Rivières, Saint-Hyacinthe, Chicoutimi, Shawinigan, Rouyn, Hull, everywhere — everywhere. The memberships were spontaneous. The Union Nationale was at first suspicious, and then became sympathetic, but never played a dominant role. Local committees were set up in imitation of the Central Committee and drew their executives from professional associations and patriotic groups. All this happened little by little. A few scattered sparks became in the end a raging fire.

Nor have I ever encountered such a spirit of co-operation. Personal ambition was almost non-existent; everyone seemed to throw themselves into the immediacy of selfless, urgent work practically unmarred by personality clashes. Later in the Bloc Populaire we experienced grave divisions. In the League there was perfect unity. It was not a party. It did not aspire to power. It did not attempt to de-Liberalize the province. It only wanted French Canadians not to change their opinion, but to vote No. To this end it made good use of the Liberals because they were the most effective target. Indeed the job was to contradict King's cabinet, not to replace it.

The League set down its aims in a manifesto. It invoked the right of every free citizen "to reply to the plebiscite according to the dictates of his own judgement and conscience without the slightest sense of acting in an unpatriotic way or of being party to dangerous agitation." It established its own legitimacy and necessity: "... In a time rife with threats, no province and no ethnic group has the right to abstain or remain silent either through opportunism or fear. To do so is to fail in a solemn duty and to accept the equivalent of political abdication."

Why reply No to the plebiscite? "Because no one asks to be relieved of an obligation unless he has already experienced the temptation to violate it, and because of all the promises made to the people of Canada, there is only one that King wishes he was not obliged to keep: the promise not to conscript men for overseas service."

So we continued our opposition to conscription. It should be remembered that this was wartime and that we were living under the rule of the War Measures Act. There was never any question of being anti-participationist; in 1942 such a stand would have been senseless.

What arguments were available?

First this one, tactical in nature: "According to our political and military leaders, Canada is increasingly threatened by the enemy." (We didn't believe a word of it, but they kept saying so.) "Therefore our first and supreme duty is to defend our own country."

Another argument *ad hominem* was aimed at Mackenzie King. "According to statistics furnished by recruiting officers and the government itself, volunteers still provide, in February 1942, twice as many men as can be absorbed into our various services."

And in this one the underlying application was not hard to guess: "A small country of 11,000,000 inhabitants cannot be, as it is claimed, the arsenal of the democracies and the allied nations, and at the same time an inexhaustible reservoir of fighting men. *Because* Canada has already achieved and even surpassed the limit of its military effort, and because we do not wish to find ourselves in a situation where we will be worse off than defeated nations; because *relatively speaking we have already done at least as much as any of the major belligerents* —Canada has no right, let alone obligation, to sabotage itself."

The League adopted a consciously Bourassist point of view. As a Canadian movement it spoke to all Canadians. "We ask them to put their country above any racial considerations [this for the English-speaking Canadians] and above any partisan feeling [this for everyone, but particularly for French Canadians]. *We ask them to vote as free men.*"

As in the best days of Bourassa, of course only French Canadians heard the call.

CHAPTER 15

The Campaign Gets Under Way

On February 11, 1942, the League held its first public meeting in the Saint-Jacques Market at the corner of Ontario and Amherst streets. The crowd, estimated at 10,000, filled the building and the street outside.

The principal speakers were the League President, J. B. Prince, Maxime Raymond, Gérard Filion, and Jean Drapeau. Henri Bourassa was present, and thinking that he had heard Drapeau assert that "We are the only real Canadians", he spent part of his speech refuting this view and severely criticizing the late Armand Lavergne, formerly one of his chief lieutenants. Near the end, he declared in his most strident voice, "Young men, hear me. Whatever the result of the plebiscite, if the war goes on two more years, you'll have your conscription anyway." He was right. We were to have it anyway in December 1944. But it was a strange way to launch the anti-conscription campaign. Inside the market, the close of the meeting was a rather mournful affair. Luckily the students and the police outside saved the day.

I was in the hall. From the street came a mounting murmur which soon became a regular uproar. In no time, the hall was half empty. The main action was taking place outside.

Here is how we reconstructed what took place, and there was no shortage of witnesses. The loudspeakers in the street weren't working properly; you could scarcely hear, especially when the streetcars went by. Some of the younger demonstrators began to get impatient. They protested that the streetcar route should be changed. Naturally, the trams kept on coming. Pieces of ice began to fly; then bricks greeted each new arrival. Windows were smashed.

At this point, a little group of English soldiers hove into view. They listened to a few of the speakers' remarks, and then were heard to say: "This is an English country. These French Canadians should be speaking English."

Unfortunate sentiments to express at the corner of Amherst and Ontario that night. Still, the real trouble was yet to come. The activists left in a gang, student style, to turn out the occupants of a well-known whorehouse near by. The police, on motorcycles now, charged them.

The atmosphere got really tense. The young men re-formed ranks, came back to the meeting, and began worrying the poor streetcars again, shouting insults at the Montreal Tramways Commission and chanting: "Down with the *Gazette!*" Then: "Down with the Jews!"

A squadron of mounted police appeared. It charged the demonstrators. This time it was a first-class free-for-all, and the police lost their heads. The result was eight arrests, eight policemen hurt, and, on the civilian side, an impressive number of injuries.

Bourassa's speech was much discussed. All the French papers in the city, *Le Devoir* included, praised his measure and reserve, but the *Star* spoke snappishly of his "misguided impulses", Premier Godbout denounced him, from Quebec, as a "traitor to his country" and begged French Canadians to think twice before replying to the question the government was asking. *La Presse*, a paper that was generally sluggish and toed the official line, signalled the excessive zeal of some of the police. Others suggested that hereafter the League be refused the use of municipal halls, a proposal which was turned down by Montreal's Executive Chairman, J. O. Asselin.

As the secretary of the League, I was summoned to appear the next day before the Chief of Police. I wondered why. I did not like, had never liked, and would never like violence. Did they suspect the League of having planned to start the brawl? Drawing himself up to full height, Chief Dufresne raked me over at the top of his voice and, hardly letting me speak for myself, did his best to intimidate me. To tell the truth, this man, who remembered the riots of 1917, was afraid of the times that were on us.

"It's my job," he proclaimed in his thundering voice, "to assure order, and I'm gonna assure it, and I'm gonna take measures, and I'm gonna fix you and your little troublemakers."

Each "I'm gonna" was driven home by a terrific thump of his fist on the table. Everything shook. I was jerked out of my books, my lectures, my editorship. This time I felt I had been well and truly precipitated into a life of action. I tried to reply; I would have needed a bull-horn. At last the Chief thought he had made his point and shut up long enough for me to reply: "We too want order in the streets. We didn't incite anyone to violence. Just the opposite. But you—you'd better stop Montreal Tramways from sending empty streetcars around to sabotage our meetings. And try to discipline your men."

These words, uttered in a strained voice, provoked another uproar. I was able to observe once again that a certain way of preaching order stirs the pulse of anarchy in even the most moderate hearts.

During the following days *Le Devoir* spoke of *agents provocateurs*. I didn't believe them. The manifestation resembled more those student pranks and horseplay that were common in university circles. One point however remained inexplicable: those insistent shouts of "Down with the Jews!" which were totally out of place. Who had yelled them? We were to have an explanation of that a little later on.

The second mass meeting in Montreal took place towards the end of February. It, too, nearly became explosive. This was the meeting where some wag began to sing the *leitmotif* of the plebiscite (at least as far as Montreal was concerned) to the tune of "God Save the King":

> *Down with con-scrip-tion*
> *Down with con-scrip-tion*
>   *Con-scrip-tion*
> *Down with con-scrip-tion*
> *Down with con-scrip-tion*
> *Dow-ow-ow-ow-ow-ow-ow-own with conscription.*

The words were easy to remember. Sung in this way the anthem took on a funereal quality. Sometimes it would be seasoned with a pinch of mockery, and it always ended with a huge burst of laughter as a finale, for everyone knew a sacrilege was being committed—and committed with general approval. Sometimes, on the other hand, it came out as the solemn expression of a sinister resistance.

While Jean Drapeau was speaking, a Miss Preston began to interrupt him (she excused herself later in the papers) at the precise moment when a group of pilots in uniform were taking their seats in the front row. The crowd growled; Drapeau had to calm them. The thing that aggravated this incident, minor enough in itself, was that hundreds of soldiers were massed in the Maisonneuve Baths close by, and when journalists asked them what they were doing there, they replied, "Military secret."

My friends were convinced that "they" (but who were "they"?) wanted to start a riot which would have ended with the troops being called in. Rumours of this kind circulated easily in wartime.

Public meetings in those days were quite different from what they are today. They were heavily attended. There was electricity in the air. The crowd was partisan, participant, and full of life, often to excess. As a general rule, it was well disposed and good-humoured. There were few outbursts of hostility. And yet, with the exception of René Chaloult, Philippe Gérard, and Edouard Lacroix who held their rural audiences, and picturesque speakers like Dr. J. B. Prince, or plausible ones like Gérard Filion, the level of eloquence was mediocre. It was the situation and the theme that excited the masses. And the masses came, jostled, laughed, booed, and applauded. Since 1945 I have never again heard the same sort of lively reaction, except perhaps in some of Camillien Houde's meetings.

I am speaking, of course, of the anti-conscription reunions. In the other camp they scarcely dared hold any meetings, except for one or two, like the one Louis Saint-Laurent and Chubby Power held in Quebec, or the one at the Saint-Jacques Market to promote Claude Jodoin as a candidate in a provincial by-election. You had to have a printed invitation to get in, and outside the crowd booed Adélard Godbout, accusing him of saying neither "yes", nor "no", but "nyes".

I don't intend to tell about every one of the League's manifestations. I should, however, mention the Youth Rally held at Jean-Talon Market on March 24. The speakers were Gérard Filion, Jean Drapeau, the Liberal M.P. Jean-François Pouliot, and an Anglo-Canadian, Landon Ladd. We knew nothing about this last speaker twenty-four hours before he came. He announced his arrival by telegram from Toronto. He was a labour leader and proved to have remarkable oratorical charm. He stepped up to the platform and spoke in English—thunderous applause. He was certainly the only Anglo-Canadian to express anti-conscriptionist ideas at any of the League's meetings.

Despite, or perhaps because of, the obstacle of language, he whipped up the crowd, who began to shout:

"Down with the Tories!"
"Down with the Gazette!*"*
"Down with the Toronto Two Hundred!"

Ladd was with them. He continued his speech. Suddenly other voices broke out:

"Down with international Jewish finance!"
"Down with the Jews!"

Ladd reacted. He stopped. He eyed the heckler. Then he attacked. No newspaper recorded his words, but they still ring in my ears because of the force he gave to them; because of the risk he knew he was running; because of the silence that first greeted them, and then the roar of applause that shook the hall when he had finished.

> No, my brothers, no. Don't say "Down with Jewish finance."
> Don't say "Down with the Jews." The Jews are our brothers,
> too, and they have been slandered often enough. The question
> we are asked today has nothing to do with Jews or Christians.
> Some people in here are trying to use us. You don't like the
> Toronto Two Hundred, eh? You don't care for them? [The
> crowd roared.] Well, take a look at who they are. Look at
> their names one after another. They're all Christians, my
> brothers, all Christians. . . . My enemy is not the Jew or the
> Christian but anyone, whatever his race or creed, who wants
> to conscript our youth but doesn't want his own wealth conscripted. . . .

I have rarely seen a more immediate contact between a speaker and the crowd. Ladd had a rich voice, a little throaty like an Irish tenor. He was generous and sensitive, but I don't know anything more about him beyond this brief appearance. It was as if he had dropped out of the sky on us, and as he came he went; we never heard a word about him again.

When the meeting was over, part of the crowd remained grouped around the Market. I came out just then and went to my car. It was impossible to drive through the crowd. Getting impatient—we were working eighteen hours a day—I made the mistake of honking once or twice. In no time a bunch of boys jumped on the running-boards, covered the car with League stickers, and started ragging me. If I had told them who I was, they would have carried me off in triumph, but I didn't want that kind of treatment. And it was just as well I missed it, as I was to learn the next day. At last they let me through.

Fifty or so of the young men had already closed ranks and I saw others drawn in with them. They seemed extremely well disciplined and knew how to marshal curious bystanders. They started to march down St. Laurent and I went my own way. They had a bugler leading them and one of them pushed a baby buggy, obviously empty, to symbolize, it seems, the feeble British birth rate. The group branched off down rue Saint-Denis to serenade Liberal M.P. Paul Gauthier and the provincial party secretary, Hector Périer. Then it turned back onto St. Laurent, where it met another group. A car drove straight for them; they scattered briefly but in revenge broke a store window. They stopped people in the street and asked them: "All right you, are you for conscription?"

A young Jew answered back, then went to get reinforcements from a restaurant. A little gang armed with sticks came out on the street yelling: "Kill them! Kill them!"

The procession now turned their attention to smashing windows in Jewish shops. Their enthusiasm grew by leaps and bounds until the police arrived. Then it became a real brawl — blood spilt, many arrests, and the next day general indignation — that's why I was glad to have passed incognito among them.

Who were they? I hadn't recognized a single one. Their discipline surprised me. Where had they learnt it? Certainly not in any nationalist group. . . . I always thought that these young anti-Semites were some of Adrien Arcand's former blackshirts. Their leaders had been interned since 1940. Now, two years later, where should they demonstrate if not among the ranks of opponents to the government and the war? They were dangerous allies, but how could we be rid of them? They played no role in the League, but they seemed on several occasions to have tried to work on the crowds that the League drew.

Our audiences had perhaps inherited the vague anti-Semitism of the Depression years. It was a feeling that came naturally to shopkeepers going broke who were furious against merchants who were smarter than they were and reputedly less scrupulous. It was a kind of astonishment and revulsion directed against foreigners whose habits were disconcerting, and who had the reputation of getting rich quick. It was a kind of pseudo-religious emotion working against the people who had crucified the Saviour, against the race who had shouted, "May his blood fall on the heads of our children and our children's children." In short, it was the whole apparatus of anti-Semitism which was popular in the western world.

For that matter French Canadians had no monopoly on this prejudice, but they expressed it more noisily than others. I must admit its existence among some of us. It was older than Nazism and had no connection with dogmatic racism. More often than not it was a skin-deep sentiment, unpleasant enough, but luckily quite harmless.

In the end Canadian Jews, through their national organization, declared themselves officially in favour of Yes in the plebiscite. That was certainly no surprise! Nor were we much surprised to see this stand cause a mild stir in the anti-conscriptionist camp.

That at least is how I explained to myself those cries of "Down with the Jews!" which broke out on several occasions and particularly at the end of that meeting where Landon Ladd had won applause with his plea for Jewish-Christian friendship, but which had ended in the smashed windows of the little Jewish shopkeepers on the Main.

CHAPTER 16

The Chaloult Motion

The battle was also developing on other fronts.

In Parliament in Ottawa a dozen Liberal M.P.s and a few independent Conservatives declared themselves against the plebiscite. They recalled their old promises and, without attacking the government, showed up its self-contradictory posture on this point. These M.P.s came back to hold meetings in their own ridings with or without the support of the League. But the majority remained faithful to King, Cardin, and Saint-Laurent.

In Quebec, at the beginning of March, René Chaloult gave a notice of motion. He wanted to ask the provincial legislature to advise the Quebec electorate to turn in a negative vote. Time went by. The motion remained on the legislature's order sheet. Nationalist opinion began to grow restless. We urged the government to face the problem. At last the debate got under way. Paul Beaulieu seconded the Chaloult motion. Long speeches were made, then the issue was shelved. Another long wait. Onésime Gagnon insisted that it be taken up again. The provincial Liberals were embarrassed by this problem. Which should prevail, solidarity with the federal government or electoral self-interest? Adélard Godbout and some of his ministers believed in the necessity of the war effort. They had tried since 1939 to draw the province after them. For some, this conviction was as sincere as it was for Cardinal Villeneuve. Up to this point they had seemed to succeed. Even in the middle of the plebiscite issue, they had won the by-election in Montreal Saint-Jacques against Omer Côté. But now the task had become more difficult. Part of Godbout's party was beginning to rebel, and Godbout himself was on the point of committing political suicide without realizing it.

One of his ministers, Oscar Drouin, had asked French Canadians to vote No. Drouin was well known for his flair. Formerly a Liberal, he had taken part in the battles of the Action Libérale Nationale, was a minister under Duplessis, had resigned and become a militant for Dr. Philippe Hamel's Parti National, then had re-entered the Liberal fold, got himself re-elected M.P., and became one of Godbout's ministers. All that in less than four years. He was a good sort and his rapid changes of heart weren't held against him, they were laughed at. But at the same time he was known to be very close to the grass roots and to have very good sense of which way the wind was blowing. When he came out in favour of No, he was party organizer for Louis Saint-Laurent in the by-election in Quebec East, for the same Louis Saint-Laurent who in a short time, through solidarity with the cabinet—but by personal conviction as well—was to fight on the side of Yes. All this became very complicated and Liberal journalists began to lose sight of the ball. A case in point was that of Eustache Letellier de Saint-Just, editor-in-chief of *Le Canada*. He was a good common-sense journalist and when he heard Oscar Drouin recommend the No vote, he thought that the provincial Liberals had decided to give up walking on the ceiling and had got their feet under them again. In an editorial he too recommended a negative vote. The reaction was not slow coming: Letellier de Saint-Just was neatly suppressed and the editorial direction of *Le Canada* was put into more orthodox hands.

So how were the Liberals to handle René Chaloult's motion? After three meetings of the party caucus, the ministers resigned themselves to fight the motion. By virtue of an amendment proposed by M.L.A. Caron, the Chaloult motion finally proclaimed that everyone was free to reply to the plebiscite as he saw fit. Chaloult broke away from the Liberals more and more decisively. On CKAC I spoke of Pontius Pilate, meaning Godbout and company. The Premier himself had never ceased wavering in his public pronouncements. Now he clearly implied that he favoured Yes.

The Union Nationale remained prudent. Certain of its members—such as Paul Beaulieu and Antonio Barrette—committed
themselves early on in the game. The party continued its own
little wars. As the campaign developed, it appeared to opt for
the No camp. But it never made a formal declaration. It hadn't
yet got over its 1939 defeat, and its leader, Maurice Duplessis,
was gravely ill and did not take his seat again in the Legislative
Assembly until April 22, five days before the plebiscite.

CHAPTER 17

The Colour of the Times

How can one recreate, for one who did not live through them, an accurate impression of those times? Feelings that had long been suppressed at last found an outlet. They burned to the point of incandescence. Things that the League could not express directly—because of the War Measures Act, which never ceased to hang like a threat over the adversaries of official policies—were expressed as well as could be in "The Tract". You can sense the indignation smouldering in this League circular where those attitudes of the King government which stirred up most resentment are ticked off one by one.

> The Government wishes, by means of a plebiscite, to be released from promises made to the Canadian electorate, promises to which it owes its present power.
>
> Why?
>
> Is it to decree national registration? — No, that's already been done.
>
> Is it to oblige young Canadians to do a month's military service? — No, that's already been done.
>
> Is it to prolong military training to four months? — No, that's already been done.
>
> Is it to keep conscripts indefinitely in the service? — No, that's already been done. [A thing that should not be forgotten. Conscripts were already in military camps and a great many

had already finished their training. Those who are referred
to here could be sent overseas in no time flat.]

Is it to send to England those who freely accept overseas
service? — No, that's already been done.

Is it to send poorly equipped regiments to Hong Kong? — [An
allusion to a badly organized expedition that had been a failure.]
No, that's already been done.

Is it to raise new troops for the defence of Canada *which official
propaganda continues to describe as being in danger?* No — to do
that the government already has all the power necessary.

Is it to spend two, three or four billions a year on the war? — No,
that's already been done.

Is it to make a gift of a billion dollars to England, in other
words to oblige each Canadian to give $100 of his income to
the Empire? — No, that's already been done.

Then what's left that the government hasn't already done? *In
other words, what is the single promise left to violate?* It has not
yet voted conscription for overseas service or the obligation
for young Canadians to serve on the battlefields of the Empire
in Africa, Asia and the Far East. *What's at stake then is conscription.
The same conscription as in 1917.*

In that case the answer is: NO.

Tell your M.P. — with all the respect he deserves! — Honorable
Mr. So-and-So, you promised for a quarter of a century — from
year to year, and from election to election — that there would
be no conscription. You promised that, and you seemed really
courageous, really firm and sincere, when you did so back
there in the days when we were at peace and there was no
danger on the horizon. You promised it "with all your might"
and didn't hesitate to call heaven as your witness. What you
promised for 25 years, — NOW IS THE TIME TO KEEP
THAT PROMISE.

And if they weren't ready to keep it, we called them cowards,
turncoats, sheep. (An anecdote will serve to describe the sheep:
A Liberal M.P. comes home to his riding. He has voted in favour
of the plebiscite. His electors express their surprise. "Yes," he
says, "I voted for it. I couldn't abandon Mr. King. I voted for
it; but from the way I did it, they could easily see I was against.")

The two camps detested each other with equal sincerity, and
their scorn and hatred were openly expressed. The Anglo-Cana-

dians thought we were traitors who hadn't the courage to fight. We saw in them the horrible embodiment of "might makes right". We were rebels against a government which in our hearts we had ceased to recognize, a government that listened to the Toronto Two Hundred rather than to the people it had used as a stepping-stone to power.

These feelings were nourished by even the most minor details.

The League had rented office space on the top floor of a building that belonged to the Royal Bank of Canada at 354 St. Catherine Street. The quarters were roomy and sparsely furnished, which suited us. We had only taken them for a month, for the League was poor and at the time no one knew when the plebiscite would be held. Then we wanted to renew the lease. Not on your life! In the meantime the Royal Bank had discovered what kind of traitors it was harbouring in its attic. They told us politely that they had to take the floor over for other uses. It wasn't true; we checked on it later; the space remained unoccupied. We had to move out, right in the middle of the campaign. It was the last straw. Others, too, refused to lodge us. At last we took our belongings to *La Prévoyance*, where Maxime Raymond was installed. It was very cramped, but there at least we were sure that the roof wouldn't cave in.

A menace of another kind, much more serious, was the War Measures Act.

Camillien Houde had been in an internment camp for two years. Which of us would follow him there?

Of course we tried to be prudent. But a law like that has a lot of arbitrariness in it. It was easy to forget oneself momentarily in a heated meeting, and we knew we were under surveillance.

In April, Father Paul-Emile Robert, president of Les Jeunes Laurentiens, had spoken of "big, blond babies, six-foot-two, who strut around free as air while our boys go off to fight". Canada had taken in many English children at the time of the bombing raids on British cities. Popular rumour had it that British draft-dodgers had used this opportunity to hide out among us. On the strength of erroneous information, young Robert believed that a disembarkation of this kind had taken place a few days before. He mentioned it in rash terms during a public meeting.

In Quebec M. Saint-Laurent, Minister of Justice, denounced such sowers of false rumours and stated that the person who had spoken of "six-foot-two blond babies" would be prosecuted. In reality the men in question were some soldiers who had escaped from a sinking and had been landed in Montreal while waiting to be posted elsewhere.

I was working at the office one day the following week when I had a desperate call from Father P.-E. Robert. The R.C.M.P. had just arrested him; undoubtedly he would be sent to concentration camp. I have rarely had such a strong feeling of responsibility and revolt.

Picked up at his home on April 21 — less than a week before the plebiscite — the young man was released after providing $2,000 bail. He went on trial. The error was evident. He was found guilty and sentenced to pay a token fine. But it was a time when we were about to engage in a public trial that had far greater repercussions.

We remained convinced that the young Robert had been ill-informed, but that he had denounced a real practice. The "Blokes" behaved poorly in Canada and often stirred up the anger of the natives. In our own ranks we suffered easily from xenophobia. Nothing very good ever came to us from the outside world.

However, our main difficulty came from another quarter, from an institution that was dependent on Ottawa and served as a dispensary of government propaganda.

CHAPTER 18

Strict Partiality

It's Radio-Canada I'm talking about.

Would the Yes camp be the only ones welcome there? Would the state network only broadcast official opinion?

We were convinced this would be the case, but the game was worth the candle. As Canadian citizens we insisted we had as much right to express ourselves on the C.B.C. as anyone else. It was my job to challenge them to battle.

On February 13, as Secretary of the League, I wrote to Augustin Frigon, associate chairman of the Corporation, beginning a correspondence that was to last more than two months and was soon to become public.

Then, as now, Radio-Canada only accepted speakers from recognized political parties, which is normal during an election campaign. But we were involved in a popular consultation of another kind, and I wrote:

> Since it is a plebiscite that is being held, and not a general election, and since, in all likelihood, the four political parties will be unanimous in recommending an affirmative response to the question asked, *the problem as we see it should be stated in the following terms:* "Is it Radio-Canada's intention to give an equal chance, that is, an equal number of hours to citizens who hold that the response to the plebiscite should be NO and who wish to influence public opinion in this sense?"

Frigon served up to us the expected answer: "Most likely, our regulations which apply to general elections will be enforced during the campaign."

Therefore, only political parties recognized as such could have free use of the corporation's stations and network. Besides this, "... our general regulations do not permit us to rent our facilities to individuals who wish to treat on the air subjects that are either political or open to controversy."

What possible outlet could there be for us then?

> Your League may use private stations separately (not linked into network), if it so desires, and if the stations concerned agree. But it may not use our corporation which, because of its national character, must remain neutral in all political matters. (Letter of February 16.)

Naturally we did not agree and we let him know why two days later.

It would be abusive, we replied, to apply to a plebiscite rules which govern a general election. First, because the question of which party will take power is not at issue. *What is necessary is to inform the people of the reasons for voting Yes and of the reasons for voting No.* Therefore, an equal number of hours should be allotted to the two opinions. In addition, your second principle becomes unjust in the present circumstances. It so happens that all the official parties (the only ones according to your regulations who are empowered to use the state radio) are going to plead in favour of Yes. If they are the only ones accepted, *a strong moral pressure, as strong as that used in totalitarian countries, will be exerted on the Canadian people.*

For since the government is asking a question to which the answer can be either Yes or No, then No is considered to be a legitimate reply. It seems reasonable to expect that this will be the choice of millions of Canadians. Is Radio-Canada going to exclude them systematically? They have the same rights as the others, their taxes are just as good, and *therefore your decision to exclude them from your stations and networks is purely and entirely arbitrary—and what you call your "strict neutrality" becomes strict partiality.*

In his reply of February 24, M. Frigon stuck to his guns, and yet you could tell he had been shaken, for he wrote: "In view of the importance of the plebiscite and the peculiar conditions of the campaign which will be waged on this issue, it is quite possible that our board of governors will place a special interpretation on our regulations."

He would let us know "in due course".

No, we replied, that wasn't soon enough. The plebiscite law would be voted any day now, and *it was impossible to delay putting the question before the public any longer.*

For several days the Corporation didn't budge. Frigon telephoned to ask us to wait until the vote on the law. It was voted. Four days later, on March 9, we wrote to ask what was *the definitive decision* of Radio-Canada.

They replied on March 11: "Nothing has been decided yet." We went on waiting.

At the beginning of April, the newspapers announced that several M.P.s — Hanson (Conservative), Coldwell (C.C.F.), Blackmore (Social Credit) — as well as the Prime Minister and some of his colleagues, were going to broadcast speeches in favour of Yes on Radio-Canada. On April 6, we wrote again to Augustin Frigon. The campaign was in full swing. We reminded him of the immense power of the radio and of how fascist and communist dictators had used it to *subjugate the masses and drown all opposition.* They had transformed it into *a weapon of oppression.* And *was this immense power now to be handed over almost entirely to the partisans of the Yes vote? Was the upcoming plebiscite to be a Hitlerian one?* Would the official radio be used to "educate", in totalitarian style, all Canadians who believed that the government should keep its promises? Was the opposition, which in the present case numbered perhaps more than the "single party Yes vote", to be banished from Radio-Canada?

To be sure the League could use the private stations, if it had the means. But the financial strength of the League was restricted. The rich could use the official radio for nothing; the poor had to pay. Moreover, in paying we obtained restricted service, for we were forbidden to use the network. For each speech we had to:

1. Obtain the censor's approval.

2. Reserve air time according to varying schedules.

3. Cut records—tapes didn't exist yet—and send a copy to each private station where, when finances permitted, we had reserved time.

Each of these operations took time and money. It was a constant handicap. We could not fight in our own province with equal arms. We were treated like second-class citizens.

Our reply came to us through the press. Radio-Canada had allotted eight half-hour periods of network time to English speakers and eight to French. (My God! Equality for once!) They would be given over to party leaders and a few ministers. As M. Frigon informed the League on April 8, the government had taken Radio-Canada in hand. "In conformity with instructions received from the federal government..."

We actually received the news from the Ministry of Public Works, that is, from the office of P. J. A. Cardin. M. Adrien Pouliot, chairman of the board of Radio-Canada, declared on April 15, that the *decision had been taken directly by the government*, whose prerogative it was, and not by the board of governors, who had nothing to say in the matter.

Our final question, addressed to the Honourable Mr. Thorson, who was the minister responsible before Parliament for Radio-Canada, remained unanswered. We asked him if it was the government's intention to prostitute Radio-Canada.

So that was the way the advocates of Yes, who held the reins of power, banished the advocates of No from the state radio. During the war Radio-Canada became, quite willingly it appears, the creature of the government—with the complicity of English Canadians who found such an arrangement natural—we were at war, weren't we? Thus, according to the *Globe and Mail*, "since the government is master of the airwaves," it should use this means to favour the Yes vote. Thus the *Gazette* congratulated Prime Minister King for giving the radio to partisans of the affirmative alone. On that side of the fence there was almost perfect unanimity.

CHAPTER 19

An Avalanche

But after a certain point obstacles serve a useful purpose. Everything was difficult for us as far as English Canada and the world of officialdom were concerned, but everything became easy for us on the French-Canadian side.

The movement now picked up momentum and became an avalanche. The police and employees of Montreal Tramways tore down the posters we stuck up on telephone poles; but we always had sympathizers to inform us when to put up new ones. We had written to all the town councils and county councils in the province, to all branches of the Union Catholique des Cultivateurs, and to various unions, to suggest that they take an anti-conscription stand. Replies arrived in hundreds. Local committees sprang up everywhere, sometimes clandestinely as in Sorel — Cardin's county and the fief of the Simards — where, for fear of reprisals, the organization remained secret.

It was sufficient to advise French Canadians that the plebiscite dealt with conscription to win the support of the majority. It was sufficient to bring them together and show them that others thought as they did to get them to express themselves. From these meetings, broadcasts on the private stations, newspapers, and circulars, expanding waves seemed to radiate out which reached distant corners of the province where we were never able to go. The Liberals had worked twenty-five years for us; so had Bourassa and a whole tradition of political resistance that was far from dead. One doesn't eradicate in three months the work of several lifetimes.

And yet we remained uneasy. What last-minute offensive was reserved for us by an enemy whose cunning and inexhaustible resources we knew all too well?

As it turned out it was feeble enough.

On the French network of the C.B.C. on April 7, Mackenzie King, without ever naming names, tried to explain to English Canadians why he had made certain anti-conscription promises, and to French Canadians why it was now necessary to break them. The argument used in either case was "national unity". On the one hand, "without this assurance," he said, "I do not believe that the Parliament would have given, as it did, prompt and wholehearted approval to Canada's entry into the war."

On the other hand, the limitation of the power of the state "in the past few months has... become a matter of controversy and a threat to unity," as well as "a source of misunderstanding" with our allies. It was necessary to proceed with the plebiscite, for if not "it would have been asserted that we were no better than the Nazis; that we had ceased to have regard for the will of the people and were now relying upon force to give effect to policies which were the direct opposite of those on which we had been returned to power." Why was it necessary to "free" the government when "our army today is just as large as it would have been if conscription for overseas service had been adopted"? Because "conscription has been made the symbol of a total [war] effort."

And yet, "the issue at present is not conscription.... The Government is not asking you to say whether or not conscription should be adopted. That responsibility the Government is asking you to leave to itself and to Parliament, with entire freedom to decide the question on its merits."

For conscription is a military problem, King explained, and one that must be discussed in Parliament in the light of information in the government's possession. In short, Canadians were being asked to show confidence in one another. "In the greatest of all emergencies, I ask you, are you not prepared to trust the Government and your own Parliament to see that only those things are done which are wholly in the interest of the country? If not, who or what are you prepared to trust?"

For the existence of "the nation" was at stake. The military situation in the world was critical. We were fighting to defend Canada: "Let no one tell you that Canada is in this war to uphold some selfish cause of empire. It is not true. We are fighting to preserve our freedom and our national existence, to defend our homes and families from an enemy drawing ever nearer."

This speech had little effect. And one that Minister Cardin made on April 9, also on the French network of the C.B.C., came no closer to reaching the population of Quebec.

For a quarter of a century Cardin had been first tenor of the Liberal party. He was intelligent and extremely skilful in the art of talking without saying anything. This time he should have tried to give an impression of total commitment. Did he lack inner conviction? At any rate, he didn't bring it off.

His *leitmotif* was, "Put your trust in Mr. King's government," though he added for the benefit of Conservatives that they could "vote in the affirmative on the plebiscite question without feeling bound by that to express a vote of confidence in the government." Yet confidence was a must, even after the promise had been annulled. To refuse to vote Yes, wouldn't that be "a strange way to show our confidence in Mr. King and in his government? Indeed, that would mean that your confidence is founded entirely on the link of the promise, that you would be afraid to leave him free to act. . . . "

As for the interpretation of the vote:

> The plebiscite does not ask you to approve or disapprove conscription. You will not be voting for or against conscription. You will be voting whether to give or to refuse Mr. King and his ministers, in the tragic times we are going through, an authority and a freedom of action similar to that which other chiefs of state already possess for the methodical, logical and free organization of our common war effort. If later circumstances warrant that the question of obligatory overseas service be considered, Mr. King wishes to be free to study it before submitting it to Parliament.

It was a noble effort to disguise the poison. In short, all King was gently asking us for was permission to study a difficult subject.

As for Cardin, personally, he didn't overly commit himself. "I reserve my own freedom of choice," he affirmed.

"To my fellow citizens in Quebec," he continued, "I would simply like to say, without weakness and without shame, that it is better not to run the risk of isolating ourselves.

"A No-vote will get you nowhere and will assure you nothing," he continued. "We should vote Yes because it is in your own interest to do so, first as citizens, and second as members of a minority which not only has need of its laws and treaties to be able to develop according to its own ideals, but one which must also count on the good will of all and feel in its soul the respect and comfort of the friendship of the great majority of the citizens in this country."

To which the League replied: "M. Cardin is inciting us to cowardice."

It should be well understood that as far as we were concerned Mackenzie King had known since the start of the war where he was leading us. We were convinced of his bad faith vis-à-vis French Canadians, but we feared his shrewdness, for he knew how to scramble a problem and manipulate the right psychological levers. Thus, you could never believe the first sense of what he said; you had to look for the hidden meaning that he would ingeniously find there later on. Maybe his skill was admirable, but in the long run it inspired something closer to disgust. With him a problem was always devious. It was impossible to tackle it straightforwardly. The idea that the plebiscite had nothing to do with conscription, but was merely concerned with giving the government its freedom, for all its ingenuity, was treated as a joke; its malice was too transparent; it cut no ice.

As for the French-Canadian ministers in Ottawa, we considered them as spokesmen for King and English Canada; their role seemed contemptible. Moreover, as a group they lacked prestige. Only Saint-Laurent seemed honest, for since he was a latecomer to politics, he hadn't been obliged to swallow, one by one, all of the Liberal promises. But he had only been a minister for three months, he was little known to the general public, and he lacked authority. His speech of April 10 on Radio-Canada consisted in returning to the basic issue, which was the war itself. After a long denunciation of Nazi ideology he concluded: "If it is true that we are engaged in a total war, then it is evident that to win it we must reply with total war." Therefore by conscription if that had to be. The Minister of Justice referred to Cardinal Villeneuve's stand and ended on these words of Mackenzie King's which were quoted earlier: "In the greatest of all emergencies, I ask you, are you not prepared to trust the Government and your own Parliament to see that only those things are done which are wholly in the interest of the country? If not, who or what are you prepared to trust?"

There, precisely, was the crucial point; that confidence we did not have. What were we to do? Put ourselves into the hands of the imperialists of the Conservative or Liberal parties, or into those of the C.C.F., which came under British influence through the agency of the Labour party? How, on such a vital question, could we turn ourselves over to the opportunism of King and the Yes-men? We had hit rock bottom in the breakdown of confidence. There was no real communication between the source of power and ourselves. The games that had been played to neutralize our vote and to silence our voices seemed to us to be contemptible and inspired by contempt.

The effect of German and Vichy propaganda is sometimes forwarded as an explanation of our attitude. Nonsense. It is true that Pétain was admired in French Canada, perhaps because he had done what we were forbidden to do: he had withdrawn his country from the war. We knew nothing then about the conditions he governed under, or what was happening to Frenchmen and Jews in France. The only news we got came with the stamp of British propaganda on it, and we didn't believe it. That's the unfortunate thing about systematic propaganda — it either carries, and is blindly accepted, or it inspires mistrust and is rejected even when it tells the truth. Among my friends and colleagues of the time I knew two who listened to broadcasts from Paris or Vichy. The rest couldn't have cared less, but that didn't stop them from thinking the way they did. Does anyone believe that Bourassa got his news from France? And yet he spoke once of "Pétain, greater at Vichy than at Verdun", which seems singular today. This moral adhesion soon became an error in judgment, but it was an effect and not a cause. Thinking the way we did, we tried to latch on to something. The truth was that we felt terribly isolated—we were intoxicated with solitude.

Not being free to reopen the debate on the war, we dug our heels in on the conscription issue. In that domain we were wilfully deaf. Georges Pelletier had written in our name: "Either Mr. King is against conscription, in which case we should protect him against every external pressure and not abandon him; or Mr. King is, after all, for conscription, and if so, why should we free him from his promises? So he can send our young men to war? Never."

But now we began to feel a ground swell that shook the earth. Ernest Lapointe's "Never" was taken up by the masses. The handful of rebel Liberal M.P.s who were fighting in favour of No won the confidence of a public who until then had been traditionally Liberal in politics.

Liguori Lacombe, a Liberal M.P., quit his party and, prematurely, founded a Canadian Party. He held a meeting at Brébeuf College in Sarto Fournier's riding. He invited Fournier to the meeting, and Fournier had the nerve to come and declare: "As to the question at issue, it's No to conscription and Yes to the plebiscite." He was booed.

The League invited the rebel Liberals to a mass meeting that was to take place in the Forum. I rented the arena myself, and the manager formally promised, before two witnesses, that we would have it. Then the management withdrew the reservation. We had to go down to the Atwater Market. The crowd was estimated at more than 20,000. It wasn't what was said that was so important; people came in a spirit of public holiday.

That was the evening of April 22, five days before the plebiscite. We were authorized to use the radio for two more days. We had planned one last appeal to be made on the 24th by Maxime Raymond and the League secretary, and to be broadcast over a dozen private stations across the country. Because we didn't have the right to use a network hook-up, these speeches had to be recorded on twelve separate records which then had to be sent to the different stations. On Wednesday the 22nd, bad news came by telegraph. In every case our records had arrived smashed to pieces. Was it sabotage? I think myself it was careless packaging. But what were we going to do now? Let the Yes-men have the airwaves all to themselves on the last night?

We got hold of a technician, and had him wait at home for us after the Atwater meeting. Raymond, though worn out, came over and re-read his radio speech. The broadcasts went on as scheduled.

On April 24, Maurice Duplessis rose in the legislature on a question of privilege and announced that he was going to vote No on the plebiscite.

The same evening, at 11.45 on CKAC, I made the last speech for the Noes. In this way we were the last ones to use the radio. It was a point of pride with us. At that time Louis-René Beaudoin was announcer at CKAC. After my talk was finished, he read a news bulletin. Prime Minister King had just declared: "It is in the interest of the Canadian people to give me their confidence." Beaudouin read the statement with the deepest conviction. I felt that I had been betrayed. . . .

The next day *Le Canada* printed King's declaration eight columns wide. We thought it was a crushing blow, a last-minute manoeuvre, a kind of blackmail using the threat of resignation, for if to vote Yes was to vote confidence in King, wasn't to vote No to ask him to leave? And wouldn't the will of the French-Canadian people buckle under this threat?

As it turned out, King's statement displeased the Conservatives, too. Their acting leader, Hanson, was willing to accept the appeal for an affirmative vote, but not the idea of solidarity with his adversary's government. Trapped, King was forced to repeat what he had said in February: "You are not invited to vote for or against the government." This withdrawal firmed up the Yes vote in English Canada and the No in French Canada. As a result, the English network of the C.B.C. repeated it as a special bulletin on every occasion, while the French network mentioned it only once, in passing.

This new manoeuvre exasperated us. I telephoned Radio-Canada, got hold of some subordinate, and turned the place upside down until I finally got through to a department head. I have a reputation for not losing my temper, but perhaps that department head remembers the conversation we had that day. Finally the network agreed to treat its listeners a little more like the English network treated theirs. The statement was broadcast twice again.

But we were wrong to get so worked up; the cards were down.

CHAPTER 20

A Vote by Race

On Monday night, April 27, 1942, results of the plebiscite were announced.

"Do you consent to release the government from its anti-conscription promises?"

"Yes," replied English Canada, to whom these promises had not been made. "No," replied French Canadians, who were the only ones who had an interest in them.

The over-all response was: Yes 63.7%, No 36.3%.

The provinces (and the Yukon) had replied No in the following proportions:

Quebec	71.2%
Yukon	31.7
New Brunswick	29.1
Alberta	27.1
Saskatchewan	26.6
Nova Scotia	21.3
British Columbia	19.6
Manitoba	19.5
Prince Edward Island	16.6
Ontario	16.1

It had been—the phrase is Français-Albert Angers—"a vote by race".*

By an immense majority, English Canada — by which I mean

*"Un vote de race", *L'Action Nationale*, May 1942.

91

Canadians of British origin — had voted Yes. By an immense majority, French Canada had voted No. New Canadians, particularly those of German origin, were divided, but the negative vote was significant.

In Quebec, fifty-six ridings out of sixty-five had given the No-vote a majority that was nearly always enormous. The only ridings to vote as King and the four federal parties had asked were those in Montreal.*

For certain French-Canadian ridings it is almost embarrassing to record the proportion of the Noes: Beauce (97%), Bellechasse, Berthier-Maskinongé, and Montmagny-L'Islet (Godbout's riding) (93%), Chicoutimi (91%), Quebec-Montmorency (90%), the city of Quebec (80%), the most French-Canadian ridings of Montreal (Sainte-Marie, 80%, Saint-Jacques, 76%, Hochelaga, 75%, Saint-Denis and Mercier, 74%), etc. . . .

How should one summarize these statistics? According to M. Angers, "The French-Canadian vote is 85% No in Quebec, and 80% No for the whole of Canada including Quebec."

Here was the most surprising phenomenon: though we had hardly reached them at all with the League's propaganda, the French-Canadian minorities of Canada wherever they formed an important group voted in majority No. It seemed to be a natural reflex.

So we had, after all, despite provincial and sociological frontiers, lived together an experience of unanimity which we had rarely known in our history. And this experience, thanks to the plebiscite, was recorded in official statistics. On the other side, English Canada had also manifested its unity with, as its rallying-point, a total war effort. But French Canada had refused to be pushed around.

What strikes one first of all is the ample margin of the majorities. It is rare for a people to freely reach such universal cohesion. It existed, none the less, on every level:

—Geographically: In the farthest corners of Quebec, but also, to a lesser degree, in the Acadian maritimes, in Ontario, and among the French minorities in the prairies.

*And in the ridings with an anglophone majority the results were: Mount Royal (82% Yes), St. Lawrence-St. George (81%), Cartier (71%), Verdun (63%), Outremont (61%), Sainte-Anne (59%), St-Antoine-Westmount (59%), Laurier (57%), Jacques-Cartier (55%). From these percentages you can guess the proportion of French Canadians living in these ridings.

—Socially: A majority vote was registered in every milieu. Above all in country districts, but also in the towns; among farmers, among the middle class, among workers, and, as far as can be established, among the bourgeois (for example, in Outremont).

—Politically: Here Liberals, Conservatives, nationalists, and independents were all united. The thing that accounted for a certain fluctuation among majorities was not so much environment or belonging to a certain social class, but the fact of living together with our own people or else living in or beside an English-speaking milieu. This explains why Quebec was more unanimous than Montreal in its refusal; and, of course, why the Province of Quebec voted more massively against conscription than the minorities in Saskatchewan or Alberta.

French Canadians not only reacted in the same way but also dared to voice their reaction no matter what the risks involved in exercising their franchise. During the last days of the campaign the feelings of French Canadians seemed unmistakable. But we never ceased to wonder if they wouldn't run scared. Wouldn't they, when they had been told so often that they were a minority, consider it safer not to cut themselves off from the rest of the country? Liberal propaganda was aimed at this fear. It failed because emotions were running too high.

It should not be forgotten that in voting as they did, they were rejecting the counsel of their own authorities—of their ministers in both federal and provincial governments, and of the hierarchy of the Church. As for the latter, the priests and lower clergy sided with the people, not in their function as priests but as French Canadians. Perhaps it was just that collectively we were only too happy to shake off that two-centuries-old yoke. I repeat that, on the whole, as long as they were not provoked, plebiscite crowds were joyous ones.

Yet most French Canadians had a relative or a friend who was serving as a volunteer. And many young militants from the League signed up later in the army. But that didn't change the common will to refuse to act under constraint.*

*I knew many conscripts and volunteers both during and after the war but I never knew the military establishment as such. So I don't pretend to be able to judge the general French-Canadian feeling in the services—if there was a general feeling—much less to relate their experiences.

For that matter, from about this time on we began to collect insults. In Montreal, canvassers for the Federation of French-Canadian Charities had doors slammed in their faces with: "We're not going to give one cent for French Charities." In Quebec a journalist was hailed by a soldier with: "I speak no foreign language." But the most common formula was, "Speak White," speak a civilized language, not nigger-talk—which coupled two kinds of racism. Such insults were widespread. They helped to cement the unity of the nation.

All the same, the majority of the country had voted Yes. Consequently, the Anglo-Canadian press with one voice proclaimed that an affirmative vote meant the country had opted for conscription, and several papers urged the government to impose the measure. The leaders of the parliamentary opposition informed the government that the vote was "a green light".

According to the *Toronto Star*, "The divergent views of one province cannot counterbalance the strongly expressed opinion of the eight others." The *Ottawa Citizen* and the *Globe and Mail* claimed that the majority Yes was a mandate for obligatory military service. The *Ottawa Journal* held that minority feelings could be discounted. In Montreal, the *Star* deplored the fact that French Canadians had not seen the light soon enough. The only result of the plebiscite, concluded the *Gazette*, was that "the country is divided into two irreconcilable camps." The *Winnipeg Free Press*, which took a distant view of the whole proceedings, was surprised at the half-hearted campaign that pro-government forces had waged in Quebec. "It never equalled, in vigour or efficiency the audacious and unscrupulous tactics employed by The League for The Defence of Canada, that ridiculously named and richly endowed League which so successfully organized the No vote." A fine tribute, especially to the League's treasury.

Maxime Raymond made this statement: "The Province of Quebec consented to participate in this war on the express condition that there would never be any question of obligatory service for overseas; it has carried out its part, and it refuses to free the other party from its obligation."

As for the League, it stated: "Neither the government nor the Parliament are relieved of their present engagements. . . . A pact remains a pact."*

*The texts I use are quoted, and where necessary translated, from *Le Devoir* of April 28 and the days following. Once again I must state that I am quoting the Anglo-Canadian opinion that reached us at the time.

CHAPTER 21

Parliament Votes Conscription

In calling for the plebiscite, Mackenzie King had officially divorced himself from this point of view. He had put the question to the country as a whole and now he must abide by the over-all response. So on May 8 he announced that by Bill 80 the government proposed to revoke Article 3 of the Mobilization Act. This Article read as follows:

> *Article 3 —*
> The powers conferred by the next preceding section may not be exercised for the purpose of requiring persons to serve in the military, naval or air forces outside of Canada and the territorial waters thereof.

This article corresponded to Ernest Lapointe's "Never". King now proposed to suppress it. So we were passing under the rule of conscription for overseas service.

Now Cardin felt obliged to say that the "study" of the "subject" —which is what he called the plebiscite—hadn't really lasted long enough. For that matter, like all the other French-Canadian ministers, he had found his own stand rejected by his constituents:

Richelieu-Verchères (Cardin)	13,185 No—3,992 Yes
Quebec East (Saint-Laurent)	22,846 No—3,277 Yes
Restigouche-Madawaska (Michaud, Acadian)	
	12,258 No—8,484 Yes

He found himself in an awkward position. Nothing, he now said, justified a quick vote on conscription. On May 9 he resigned, approved by *Le Soleil*. A Liberal caucus gave a vote of confidence to their leader. A few French-Canadian M.P.s gave theirs to Cardin. Others, among whom Maxime Raymond was one of the most prominent, renounced their Liberal label and crossed the floor to sit with the Opposition. At home, the French-Canadian majority wavered. In the Quebec legislature a Liberal motion was tabled against conscription. That was a sign of evolution: Godbout was deciding to catch up with the people.

The League ironically congratulated Cardin and his colleagues for having "finally seen, after 1,600,000 Canadian voters, where an affirmative response to the April 27th plebiscite was leading us." It held a meeting at the Saint-Jacques Market which I will speak about in due course.

But the time of complications wasn't over yet. Bill 80, King stated, didn't have to mean conscription for overseas service. His speech of June 10 is really quite an extraordinary performance. At the time we took it for a long piece of doctrinaire deception. But reading it today it leaves a very different impression. He spoke briefly of the opposition between French Canadians and English Canadians to point up the success of the "new nation", asserted that the future of Canada was far more important than the question of conscription, and borrowed a quotation from the *Montreal Standard* as a call to unity. As for the rest, his line of thought could be summarized something like this:

We have in fact been living since 1940 under the regime of conscription. The law for the mobilization of national resources just set a limit to the judicial powers of the government, excluding the use of conscripts for overseas service. This restriction was written in for the sake of national unity and because the government believed—as it continues to believe—in the superiority of voluntary service. It came to be felt that this was a limitation to our war effort. Therefore it was necessary to suppress this clause from the text of the law; hence the necessity of the plebiscite to cancel the previous promises. Now the government is free to ask Parliament to restore its freedom of action. But just as the plebiscite was not primarily concerned with conscription, and therefore its results cannot be interpreted as "a mandate for conscription", in the same way Bill 80 does not mean that the government is declaring itself in favour of conscription. For the Mobilization Act is only a measure to enable the government to act, and the government will use the powers the Act grants only if and when it needs to. In fact "the government believes that conscription for overseas service is not necessary at the present time and will perhaps never be necessary." Consequently M. Cardin was wrong to resign. We will only have conscription if voluntary service becomes insufficient. Conscription if necessary, but not necessarily conscription.

These policies, King reminded us, have two sorts of adversaries: the total conscriptionist and the absolute anti-conscriptionists. Both opinions are extremist, and both are wrong.

King's thoughts unfolded slowly. He spoke and wrote without fire and without colour. But behind it what an effort of imagination! What an energy there was! Despite the sinuosities of the argument, the apparent disorder, the ebb and flow of his thought, what a simple, clear, and vigorous system.

It was only possible to take exception to it if one lacked confidence in the speaker. That, of course, was the case with the "extremists". One group held that conscription was a must, here and now. The other, for very complex reasons that have been analysed throughout this essay, were opposed to the principle of conscription. The two groups attributed contrary intentions to the government, but both accused it of opportunism.

The debate on King's speech was doomed to sterility. What could Maxime Raymond reply to a political statement of this kind? All he could oppose to it was a moral attitude, a moral judgment. "In the name of the rights of the majority we see the most solemn promises violated and at the same time we are asked to go and fight for the rights of the world's minorities." Later on he would say to King: "In the Province of Quebec a man of honour is one who keeps his word and his promises and fulfils his obligations."

He also claimed that "for a long time already a kind of covert, hypocritical conscription has been in practice." This accusation threw a strange, sinister light on Mr. King's voluntary service. In this speech—made on February 10, 1943, a few days before that serious illness that immobilized him for months and was perhaps the death blow to the Bloc Populaire Canadien— Raymond asserted;

By an Order in Council dated June 27, 1941, no person of masculine sex aged from 18 to 45 can obtain employment in the civil service without presenting a medical certificate issued by the Military Authorities stating that he is unfit for military service. In September 1941, the Minister of National Defence. [Mr. Ralston] asked employers to "free" employees of military age in order to encourage them to enlist, thus leaving them the choice of enlisting or dying of hunger. That was conscription of the poor. By virtue of the Mobilization Act of 1940 young men were drafted and then, once installed in military camps, various means were used — intimidation, blackmail — to incite them to sign up for overseas service. There is your disguised conscription that has been in effect for a long time now.

Under the cloak of the legal system, volunteer-making machinery had been functioning for years. We heard hundreds of formal testimonies to this, nearly all of the same kind. The most "legitimate" of the methods used has already been described. It consisted in telling conscripts for service in Canada: "Compulsory overseas service is going to be voted or decreed. When that happens they'll put you wherever the authorities decide. Today you can still choose your service. Hurry up before it's too late."

The conscripts had been under the care of their sergeants and wardens since February 1941, so there had been plenty of time for applying systematic pressure, and many N.C.O.s didn't spare themselves. It needed a lot of inertia or unusual strength of character to resist the needling or persecutions that a subordinate officer can always inflict on his men.

In our eyes, then, the discussion of Bill 80 was the last phase of the conscription debate.* Once the amendment was voted, the system was watertight, even if the government chose not to proceed to the brute exercise of its powers. From then on, the question was closed. The vote took place on July 23. The government obtained its "freedom of action" by a final vote of 141 to 45. As expected, the majority of French-Canadian M.P.s were opposed.

*As is well known, the final episode took place in Parliament in November and December 1944. Following a cabinet crisis, King found himself obliged to send 16,000 conscripts to Europe. A detailed and fascinating account of this is given in *The Conscription Crisis of 1944* by R. MacGregor Dawson, University of Toronto Press, Toronto, 1961. In English Canada these events seem to have left a more vivid impression than the crisis of 1942.

CHAPTER 22

The Chaloult Trial

About this time we were involved in an affair that had far-reaching consequences, the Chaloult trial.

On May 19 the League had held a meeting at the Saint-Jacques Market to mark its opposition to Bill 80. The speakers were Dr. Prince, Philippe Gérard, federal M.P.s Jean-François Pouliot and Maxime Raymond, and René Chaloult, M.L.A. for Lotbinière. The latter was very spirited and much applauded. The newspapers reported a little skirmishing and the intervention of the police after the rally.

But soon the *Star* and the *Gazette* began to clamour for Chaloult's arrest, claiming that he had, among other things, praised Pétain, said "Never" to conscription, spoken ironically about "our excellent friends the Communists", scorned national unity, and made remarks about the small number of British soldiers in Hong Kong and Singapore.

A few days later, the First Deputy-Attorney General of the Province of Quebec, Maître Gérald Fauteux, admitted that he had received instructions from the federal Minister of Justice to open proceedings against Chaloult. At the beginning of June, Chaloult was summoned to appear in criminal court and soon found himself in Police Court before Judge Edouard Archambault. His lawyers were a Liberal, Fernard Choquette, and a Conservative, Philippe Monette. He was not obliged to appear in the dock.

The trial was set for July 6.

At the same time the Ministry of Justice commenced proceedings against Colonel George Drew, leader of the opposition in the Ontario Parliament, because of the rash statements he had made on the Hong Kong affair. At Chaloult's trial the Crown wished to establish that certain remarks actually had been made by the speaker. No official text existed, so newspaper accounts had to be consulted. The *Gazette* had slammed Chaloult; was it trustworthy? *Le Devoir* had furnished the basic coverage; was it complete?

The form a speech takes is generally improvised. The speaker may stumble, get carried away, outrun his own thought. In wartime an error of this kind may lead its author straight to internment camp. As a result, *Le Devoir*'s policy was extremely precise and conscientious. Georges Pelletier was determined to save nationalist speakers from their own passions. He reported the speeches accurately but left out any excessive language. At the same time he was protecting the paper itself, for a newspaper has a certain legal responsibility for the texts it publishes. Consequently the Member for Lotbinière might well have expressed opinions that *Le Devoir* did not record.

As for the *Gazette* reporter, he was obeying other imperatives. In regard to Chaloult he felt himself to be a witness for the prosecution. After the meeting he had checked out with the speaker certain statements that he thought had been made and that he intended to use. True enough, but it was done in the hubbub and excitement at the end of the meeting. In addition, the reporter's maternal language was English; had he really heard all he reported? On this point Monette, for the defence, put him to the test, much to the amusement of those present—except the reporter, who simply turned a shade paler. He didn't much relish the role that circumstances had cast him in, and Chaloult and his ilk remained a kind of curse, an affront to his most profound convictions, a multiplication of sacrileges. He had to testify against them.

The cross-examination continued. Had René Chaloult shouted: "I believe that this war will break clean the ties that presently bind us to England"?

Did the statement begin with "I believe", or with "I hope"?

If he had said "I believe", he had confined himself to a simple prediction; but if he had said "I hope", he had sown seeds of disaffection towards an ally, and what an ally!

Had he, or had he not, said with reference to the plebiscite, "we have perhaps wrecked Canadian unity but we have re-established the unity of French Canadians." Was he registering a fact or celebrating a victory?

He had spoken of "our allies, the Russians, our excellent friends, the Communists, our cousins, the Chinese . . . (laughter from the audience) Don't laugh, the Communists are our friends and allies." Had the speaker been serious? or sarcastic?

And so on.

They stopped at every sentence and dissected it, giving it ten times more importance than it had had at the Saint-Jacques Market. The papers were allowed to report the court proceedings. The province was amused or indignant, but at all events sided with Chaloult. Other witnesses were called, among them Gérard Filion, whose assurance and wit added to the fun. . . .

As for Chaloult, he disowned none of his remarks. What he had said, he had said, and he maintained it all: his irony on the collaboration between the democracies and Stalin, his hopes to see the end of the British Empire, his joy at French-Canadian unity, even if at the expense of the unity of Canada as a whole.

He was acquitted on August 3 in a subtle fashion. The judge exonerated the speaker as a man accustomed by his profession as a politician to enjoy great liberty of expression, but he condemned the speech.

How, in those times, could we publicly express our solidarity with one of the accused? Already in the June number of *L'Action Nationale* we had written:

> It is with great pride that we remind our readers that M. René Chaloult is a director of *L'Action Nationale*.
> Monsieur Chaloult was one of the architects of the April 27th victory. Everyone remembers how much his bold motion upset the Liberal sheep in Quebec. He took part with as much courage as eloquence in the whole of the plebiscite campaign. In short, he has shown himself to be one of the nationalist leaders of French Canada, a fact which the fanatical Anglo-Canadian press was not slow to see when, from Vancouver

to Halifax, it set up the hue and cry for his arrest. But this degrading hostility only sharpens our esteem and admiration for René Chaloult.

That wasn't enough, though; we wanted to get the public at large in on this tribute. So we decided to launch a subscription campaign in favour of the accused, for we felt it unjust that he should have to pay for the costs of his trial. Little people from all over took care of that, and Le Devoir each day published a list of their tiny donations.

When the news of his acquittal came, the League announced a banquet at the Saint-Jacques Market. The speakers were Maxime Raymond, Philippe Hamel, Paul Gouin, and René Chaloult—the stars of the future Bloc Populaire. It soon appeared that the hall would be too small, so Atwater Market had to be rented instead. What a headache, what a lousy meal—but what a new day seemed to be breaking.

Were these manifestations isolated events? L'Action Catholique for August 22 published this paragraph from a Gallup poll taken on the opinion of French Canadians in Quebec.

> . . . As this poll indicates, one cannot assert that opinions expressed by men like René Chaloult are only those of a noisy minority. The fact that *84 percent of the people questioned had heard of René Chaloult*, might be attributed to the publicity which surrounded his recent speech and the trial to which he was submitted under the Defence of Canada Act. But publicity alone does not explain the fact that among those who had heard of the Member for Lotbinière, *74 percent approved of his stand*, 17 percent disapproved and 5 percent remained neutral. The other 4 percent expressed no opinion.

I have italicized the two revealing passages. They show to what extent we were dealing with a popular movement.

That August evening in 1942 at Atwater Market we all had felt in our bones that a new party was about to be born.

CHAPTER 23

The Conscripts' Candidate

I could stop here. The essentials of the conscription crisis have been told. For I do not intend to follow the history of the Bloc Populaire Canadien, which was founded by Maxime Raymond in September 1942 and whose secretary I became in January 1943. This party, born of the war, tried to enlarge its field of action but did not succeed, first because of internal strife, then because public opinion identified it with the crisis which had given it birth. Once the war was over, the Bloc was unable to survive.

Besides this, it suffered two pieces of terribly bad luck. The first was the grave illness of Maxime Raymond which struck him down in February 1943 — just five months after the party's founding — and permitted internal dissensions to develop. Raymond returned in the autumn of 1943 but he was much less active. It was too late and his heart condition didn't allow him to devote himself entirely to the leadership of the party.

The second piece of bad luck was the fact that in Quebec a provincial election preceded the federal one. The Bloc was engaged on both fronts. It faced its first test of strength on the one where it was the least well-armed and the most divided. For in the provincial contest it was running against two parties, Adélard Godbout's Liberals and Maurice Duplessis's Union Nationale. In other words, it forced the anti-Liberal opposition into a split vote at the very time when the Bloc's most respected leaders (Hamel, Gouin, Chaloult) were vehemently denouncing any tendency to division.

In the circumstances, it's perhaps a wonder that in 1944 the party got 16 per cent of the popular vote. But when it tackled the federal election in 1945, it had burnt out the best of its resources, was low in manpower, and had lost its zip. Its brief alliance with Camillien Houde caused a lot of talk but didn't help much. It was a lost cause.

These remarks raise more problems than they solve. I would have to devote another book to my memories of the party. For the time being, I will restrict myself to recalling certain events which occurred as a direct aftermath to the conscription crisis.

The Bloc was founded in September 1942. At the time I remained with the League, which continued to have an independent existence.

Though scarcely afoot in October, the Bloc had to decide whether it would participate in two by-elections that King had announced, one in Charlevoix, the other in Montreal-Outremont. We hesitated to risk its fate prematurely. In Charlevoix the Liberal party did not dare to field an official candidate. Madame Thérèse Casgrain, an independent Liberal, was to be defeated in this riding by an independent anti-conscriptionist, Frédéric Dorion (a Conservative by origin like his brother Noël Dorion), who was supported by the Union Nationale.

In Outremont, the defeat of a nationalist candidate was made certain by the presence of an Anglo-Jewish majority. In the plebiscite this riding had voted 60 per cent Yes. The Liberal candidate was the new Minister of Armed Services, Major-General Laflèche. A priest of my acquaintance claimed to have been commissioned by Cardinal Villeneuve to try to get the Liberal elected by acclamation.

It was at this point that Jean Drapeau decided to run. He was still a student. He would run as "the conscripts' candidate". He got together a very young team: at thirty I was the oldest of them.

Drapeau knew that he would be beaten, but even saving his deposit would be a moral victory. How were we to go about it in this Outremont dormitory where no one ever attended meetings? But the federal riding was curiously laid out and included Saint-Jean-de-la-Croix, a poor neighbourhood north of the C.P.R. tracks, and it was here that the nationalists concentrated their efforts.

The fight was on. It was November. The crowds were young and lively, and the speakers young and fired-up. Michel Chartrand launched an attack on the army chaplain Abbé Sabourin, who had just become famous for a long tirade he had made to the glory of Great Britain. "I love England because..." had been l'Abbé Sabourin's formula. "I love England..." repeated Chartrand, but his "becauses" hardly echoed the chaplain's. In his virulent style and with a caustic violence that left us all breathless, he mustered every historical grievance that we had ever held against Mother England. The R.C.M.P. had men planted in the crowd. Chartrand recognized them, singled them out, and repeated certain of his charges, word by word, to give them time to write them down. We were sure he would be arrested. However, the person the Mounted Police picked up the next day was Marc Carrière, our very young campaign organizer. He had made the mistake of saying that he would not answer his military call-up, and he spent several months in Bordeaux prison despite the efforts of his lawyers to get him out and the support of public opinion.

We closed ranks. Michel Chartrand replaced Carrière as organizer. But could one really speak of an organization? Jean Drapeau had extraordinary energy, a sense of propaganda, and the ability to lead his troops at the double. Did he ever sleep? He ate only one meal a day, at Glaby's on rue Laurier where we met every evening. My own home became one of our committee rooms, much to the astonishment of my young children.

The speakers who appeared most frequently at our public meetings—Marcel Poulin, Michel Chartrand, Drapeau, and myself—by some kind of state-controlled chance either got draft-calls or were required to provide certain information about themselves. In my case, for instance, I was summoned to declare whether I had my "national registration card". I had it. In return I wrote to ask just what recruitment procedures the services were following and what curious coincidence was prompting functionaries of the central state to meddle with the political adversaries of Major-General Laflèche. At our evening meetings these incidents were made public, discussed, and thrown out to the crowd, who tried their teeth on federal politicians, the services, Liberal sheep, and the English press in Montreal. One night Jean Drapeau, who had been taking the *Gazette* to task, had to personally protect one of its reporters whom the crowd had turned against.

Near the end of the campaign, we learnt that Henri Bourassa would be glad to come and support Drapeau if we took the trouble to invite him. We hadn't dared. Perhaps, too, remembering February, we were suspicious of the old orator's quirks of temperament. He came. The welcome he received moved him. He probably felt that he was back in his own true family again. This wasn't the man who had set French Canada on fire years ago. His high-pitched, crabbed voice surprised some of his listeners. But he was supremely at ease, his tone was firm, his memory good, and he had the gift of the happy formula: "For prudence, too, is a cardinal virtue," he said with a sudden burst of insolence (everyone caught the allusion) which Cardinal Villeneuve never forgave him, and then continued his speech. . . . The main part of what he said was recorded, and you can still hear Bourassa at Saint-Jean-de-la-Croix on records put out by *L'Action Nationale* introduced by Canon Lionel Groulx. A fine ruin, one of his contemporaries said in front of us. That may be, but we would have gladly used that ruin to make a brand new edifice.

Drapeau won his moral victory. Saint-Jean-de-la-Croix supported him to the full, and he saved his deposit. To celebrate it, we met one last time in the parish hall. But how many of those young men who had come to cheer the candidate and his team would, in the months to come, be called to the colours?

The theme of the "conscript" continued to be a popular one for our propaganda, like the theme of the billion-dollar gift to England. . . . I can't go into detail, but I find an echo of the former theme in the newspaper *Le Bloc* fourteen months later. Dominique Beaudin wrote the conscript's chronicle under the title "The Firing Line". Perhaps these paragraphs will help give the atmosphere of the times:

> . . . what's this conscript doing going to Hong Kong? That's a stupid question! He's going to defend his own village on an island that belongs to England.

... I knew a poor devil who signed up active because he was out of work and his parents needed the money. He got himself killed at Dieppe. Since he made the mistake of not coming back, the British Empire neglected to give him a medal. It's to the glory of the Liberal party that at least he wasn't a victim of conscription.

... All our Liberal speechmakers keep telling us that Mr. King "loves us". That must be a great consolation to our soldiers in Italy. Mr. King loves them to death.

... The Liberals have got at least one man who's remained true to himself. Before he was elected Member for Saint-Jean, Martial Rhéaume was a butcher. He's a butcher still.

Bitter humour... but when a nation stands unanimous, and when it expresses this solidarity on a subject which everyone takes deeply to heart, and when all that is to no avail, why then, unless you are completely "gutless", you experience a feeling of revolt that you can never get used to.

CHAPTER 24

Stanstead and Cartier

In the summer of 1943 the federal government announced two new by-elections, a chance to test public opinion once again.

The choice of ridings was scarcely favourable to the Bloc, which this time was directly involved. Stanstead, a constituency with a strong anglophone minority, had turned in a No vote but in the relatively feeble proportion of 63 per cent. Montreal-Cartier, a very cosmopolitan riding, had voted 70 per cent Yes. In neither of these ridings did we have the slightest electoral organization.

Maxime Raymond had only just left the hospital. He couldn't even take part in the contest. Philippe Hamel and Paul Gouin, who mistrusted Edouard Lacroix, refused to participate unless Raymond offered them impossible guarantees, and René Chaloult decided to stick by these two friends. We went personally to Quebec, to Kamouraska, and to l'Assomption but couldn't shake them. We were discouraged (by "we" I mean Philippe Gérard, Jean Drapeau, and myself), and we advised Raymond to pull out or he'd sink the ship. He refused. We admired his determination. "Let's fight," he said. "If the people don't want us, we'll resign, but not before."

So the fight began, and we held some trumps.

Stanstead had an urban centre at Magog, whose population lived principally off the textile mill. It so happened that Raymond had often defended the textile workers as an M.P., and Philippe Gérard, our organizer, had already supported a strike there. The

Bloc's candidate was J.-Armand Choquette, president of the diocesan Union Catholique des Cultivateurs, a fine man who knew the numerous rural communities well.

It might have been stupid to do battle in Montreal-Cartier if it had not been for the fact that our candidate, Paul Massé, was multilingual and had friends among several of the ethnic minorities represented in this constituency. Also, there was a large slate of candidates; the vote would be split between a Labour Progressive candidate (the communist, Fred Rose), a Liberal, a C.C.F. aspirant, and others whom I forget.

In two weeks, with his magnificent tact, vitality, and spirit of adventure, Philippe Gérard built up an organization in Stanstead with his own hands. Paul Massé plunged into Cartier and started knocking on every door. From the central office in Montreal I directed our propaganda and the deployment of our militants. I mention this because if we only gained one victory instead of two, it was perhaps due to my pessimism. We could, we should, win Stanstead, but I doubted our chances in Cartier. So I pampered Stanstead.

An anecdote will illustrate the state of mind that little by little took over that riding. Our candidate, J.-Armand Choquette, was a farmer, a French Canadian, and a Catholic. His opponent was a gentleman farmer, an anglophone, and a Protestant. One Sunday, in a rural parish, the priest stepped into the pulpit and said: "Dearly beloved, I am your pastor and it is not up to me to tell you how to vote. But it is my right, perhaps my duty even, to call to mind certain general principles.

"You are farmers. It would be normal for you to be represented by a farmer.

"You are French Canadians. It seems to me you should favour a French-Canadian candidate.

"You are Catholics. It will not surprise anyone if, as your pastor, I advise you to vote for a Catholic.

"I haven't the right to say more without betraying my particular role. Go out and vote. Follow your conscience. Amen."

No one raised a complaint against this rather unsubtle predication. And why? Because everyone, or nearly everyone, seemed to be of one mind. The curé was only telling his parishioners what they already thought themselves.

Bourassa came to Magog and he spoke in Cartier.

J.-Armand Choquette was elected by a solid majority in spite of the anglophone element, which voted in a bloc against him. Fred Rose won by 150 votes over Paul Massé, the Liberal candidate running fourth. The federal Conservatives had not even dared present a candidate. Sixteen months after the plebiscite, French-Canadian unanimity was still as strong as ever.

CHAPTER 25

The Assassination of a Conscript

But such was not the case for unanimity within the Bloc Populaire. If I were telling its history, this is where I would begin the chapter of public quarrels.

With Hamel, Gouin, and Chaloult gone, and Lacroix powerful but unacceptable, they had to fall back on me. In February 1944, Maxime Raymond named me provincial leader, a decision that was ratified later at a party congress. But the following months were painful ones. It was a weird group that claimed to unite French Canadians and couldn't remain united itself, a cracked block, inexplicably divided. . . .

The Liberals nationalized the Montreal Light, Heat and Power Company to create Hydro-Québec, hoping thereby to divert the voters' attention. The Union Nationale profited from our mistakes, and we slipped into the shadows. People talked less about conscription. Wartime prosperity settled in. Young soldiers overseas seemed to be the price that had to be paid for this domestic well-being.

One night three of us, L.-Athanase Fréchette (who was still president of the Montreal Saint-Jean-Baptiste Society), Victor Trépanier, editor-in-chief of the weekly *Le Bloc*, and myself were on our way home from the office and Fréchette suggested we stop off for a glass of beer.

112

I don't suppose I'd been in a tavern more than a dozen times, but I remember that one well.

We were talking when Trépanier broke out with: "I've got news for you from Quebec. Roger Vézina [one of our colleagues] has a story about a murder committed by the R.C.M.P." He told us about it. We sometimes heard of incidents of this kind, but the witnesses always vanished into thin air. This time there were people on hand to describe what they had seen: The police had shot down a draft-dodger.

When millions of men were dying in Europe and Asia do I have to invent excuses for having been so violently disturbed by the death of this poor devil?

Le Bloc for May 27, 1944, printed the article which is reproduced in large part below. It echoes in somewhat cooler terms a speech that I gave at ten public meetings. This text, too, should help to give the colour of those times.

> In St-Lambert two weeks ago Sunday, the federal police shot down Georges Guénette, a young conscript 24 years old who was guilty of having taken King's and Godbout's anti-conscription promises seriously.
>
> Georges Guénette, wanted by the RCMP, had seen his father's house searched by the police on Saturday, May 6. But the hunters hadn't found the accused and they were on their way back, empty-handed, when several of them decided to return for a second look. This group arrived that night at Georges Guénette's home. While the search was going on, one of the officers heard a noise upstairs. He ran up and saw the fugitive jump out of the window. The police rushed after him. One of them shouted, "Stop, or I'll shoot," But Guénette went on running. The police fired seven shots, one of which entered his heart. They saw him fall, get up, and then fall again.
>
> The perpetrators of this pretty exploit brought Guénette's body back to the house but the broken-hearted father told them: "You killed him. Now do what you wanted to do with him!"
>
> ... On hearing these facts, one of the jurymen, M. Gosselin, asked: "Do you have the right to fire in a case like this?" and Constable Victor Massicotte was obliged to answer no.
>
> One of the witnesses, a man of sixty, M. Georges Larochelle, asserted that if the police "had not been such cowards, they could have caught Guénette without firing a shot."

... What was the nature of the crime that he deserved to be shot down point blank in the middle of the night like an assassin?

Guénette was one of those conscripts whom King had called to arms to serve for a period of four months. One fine day, these young four-month conscripts found themselves locked into the army for the duration of the war. It was just one more promise that King had violated. Georges Guénette, who one day joined the army, deserted it on another, and they hadn't caught him yet. *That was his only crime.*

There followed a little more information on Guénette's family, on the reign of terror that the R.C.M.P. had imposed on Saint-Lambert, and the gruesome details of the assassination.

Of course we demanded an immediate investigation and the rigorous punishment of the guilty parties.

For the parents of conscripts, who are already obliged to inform on their children, have the right to know whether, through some escapade or other, their sons risk being shot at close range.

In the past we have seen the province terrorized to the point of being reduced to silence. Those were the days when, right out on the street, as though he were a common malefactor, they arrested the Mayor of the City of Montreal. Those were times when certain newspapers were specialized as informers and got the Minister of Justice and his Gestapo to do the dirty work dreamt up by the hatred, spite, or envy of their scribes. Those days are over. And those who are responsible for them have got to pay.

And who was responsible? The Liberal politicians, and first among them the Premier of Quebec.

In October 1939, the Honourable Adélard Godbout, leader of the Liberal party, stated on the radio, repeated at a public meeting, and printed over his own signature: "*I undertake, on my honour,* carefully weighing every one of my words, to quit my party and even turn against it if between now and the end of hostilities in Europe *a single French Canadian is mobilized AGAINST HIS WILL* under a Liberal government or even under a provisional government in which ministers presently in Mackenzie King's cabinet might be serving." Was the young man from St-Lambert a French Canadian, M. Godbout? Had this young man been mobilized, M. Godbout? Had he been mobilized AGAINST HIS WILL, M. Godbout? What do you think about it? Was his biggest mistake to have taken your word for it? To have trusted your honour, while he was running away, scared to death, under fire from Mr. King's and Mr. Saint-Laurent's policemen? It's too bad one of the witnesses couldn't have remembered and repeated your oath: *"I undertake on my honour . . . a single French Canadian . . . mobilized against his will under a Liberal government . . ."* Can you think about that chase and that fear coolly and calmly? After what has just happened can you, without blushing from shame, reread those words on which you staked your honour?

. . . One can't use the blood of others for electioneering. You had brought up the youth of this nation in the fear and horror of conscription. . . . Every one of our little towns, every one of our villages, every country sideroad had heard your violent denunciations against participation in the wars of Empire. Your oath, M. Godbout, was the crowning deceit to twenty-five years of lies.

For suddenly you completely changed course . . .

When the League for the Defence of Canada or the Bloc Populaire take up your old arguments, you go hunting through the vocabulary Borden and Meighen and Sévigny used to find insults for us. You bring René Chaloult to trial, you imprison Camillien Houde and Paul-Emile Robert, Dr. Pierre Gauthier and Marc Carrière.

And when our people cease to follow you, when they continue to think in terms of the lessons you so liberally preached for a quarter of a century, why you turn the police on them. And when a young man behaves so abominably as to turn and run, your police fire on him.

The time had come for a settling of accounts. The Bloc presented itself as the arm of justice, as "the instrument of the legitimate revenge of Canadians against their corrupt masters".

From the people of this country we ask for a generous collaboration. With their help we will put an end to the nightmare of the old party system and at last inaugurate a social and national regime that will treat men like men and cease to hunt them down like beasts.

The crowds we met in public meetings, which had once more become lively affairs, shared these sentiments, sentiments that our opponents classified as criminal demagoguery. I have no wish to disown these feelings; they are a part of my life that I threw myself into body and soul.

Sometimes in those days I would shut my eyes and think of the misfortunes of men on the battlefields and in the bombed cities of Europe. I felt as incapable of helping them as we feel today of helping people in the satellite countries behind the iron curtain. The comfort of our life sickened me, just as it makes us ashamed in the West now. But I detested physical violence; I felt a premonitory horror at certain types of "liberation", and I didn't believe in crusades. If I had had the makings of a hero, I would have been attracted, not to the kind of holy war that was trumpeted all around us, but to the passive resistance of a Gandhi and his civil disobedience marches. I had already spoken about this philosophy to my compatriots some time before, but without stirring up the slightest interest, of course, for it was an ideal that we were not prepared for, and I had barely touched on it. What impressed us more in those days was the anti-imperialism of Gandhi and Nehru.

About the time of the plebiscite, Sir Stafford Cripps had been sent as a special envoy from Great Britain to hold talks with the Indian leaders. His task was to discover what conditions the Congress Party would impose in return for their support in the fight against the Germans and Japanese. We followed these discussions with passionate interest. They were due to fail and Gandhi and Nehru would renew their acquaintance with British prisons. But we adopted as our own Gandhi's declaration that "the greatest crime ever committed against India" was British imperialism. He also said, "England's greatest sin in India is imperialism. . . . Let her confess it and make reparation."

In a similar fashion Latin American countries, when not neutral, participated sluggishly in the war and only in proportion as they were in tow to the United States. We asked ourselves why we — a small American nation that had suffered from the crime of imperialism, though to a lesser extent — why we should have inflicted on us the vocation of becoming soldiers of Empire and civilization?

For we felt ourselves forced by a foreign power. And when a people feels itself enslaved, how can it be expected to go off freely to defend the freedom of others?

CHAPTER 26

Epilogue

The French-Canadian people rejected the Godbout government. In August 1944, they gave 39 per cent of the popular vote and a parliamentary majority to the Union Nationale. The Bloc Populaire won 16 per cent of the vote, and 40 per cent went to the Liberals. That may seem a lot, but while Anglo-Canadians voted massively for Godbout—except in some rural ridings—it must be owned that in the French-Canadian circles he suffered a major defeat.

In 1939, Lapointe, the rampart against conscription, had given the province to Godbout. In 1944, after the plebiscite, King, whom Godbout had supported, took it away from him; Duplessis picked it up, and we know how long he kept it.

But Godbout had paid instead of King. In June 1945, just after the end of the war in Europe, a federal election took place. King swept the Province of Quebec and the Liberals held it for thirteen more years.

In one sense French Canadians had reversed their stand. Here is how I explain this strange phenomenon.

The affluence of the war years somewhat weakened our aggressiveness. King paid frantic court to Quebec with his family allowances. Most of the Liberal anti-conscriptionists remained faithful to him.

His only cross-Canada rival, the only one who could have taken over power from him, was the Conservative party, the same party that, with Liberals like Ralston (who had resigned by now), had constantly increased the pressure and forced the Prime Minister to impose conscription for overseas service. But the Province of Quebec as a whole never believed in the theory of "balance of power" that the Bloc advanced; it had never, to my knowledge, coldly determined to move over to the side of the opposition. The Bloc's thirty candidates—as well as the independents who were supported indirectly by Duplessis—were doomed to fail. Association with Camillien Houde didn't help things. A party divided, weak, and impoverished, the Bloc had a hard time getting two candidates elected — its leader, Maxime Raymond, and René Hamel in Saint-Maurice-Laflèche.

We had felt defeat coming. I remember an enthusiastic rally held for Roger Duhamel in the Saint-Jacques Market. Jean Drapeau had gone down to inspect the crowd, both inside the hall and out. He wanted to study their reactions. Coming back to the platform he gave them a dirty look and, turning to me, said: "You see those people out there? It's really going to break their hearts to vote against us."

Unless I am mistaken that meant: They think the way we do, we're telling them what they want to hear, but what they want doesn't seem possible any more. They don't believe we stand a chance, they think we're licked. Sum it up this way: With Quebec you can do what you like; with Ottawa you do what you can.

But what if their anger had been at the same pitch as in the days of the plebiscite?

I think that in the long run French Canadians held much more of a grudge against Godbout, one of their own people, than against l'Anglais, Mackenzie King. He at least, with his British origins and the job he had keeping all the anglophone provinces satisfied, deserved our sympathy.

It was something like the hanging of Louis Riel which, at the end of the nineteenth century, had caused the downfall of the Conservative party in Quebec, whereas in Ottawa, despite his refusal to grant an amnesty, Sir John A. Macdonald succeeded in getting re-elected—and was supported even by French Canadians.

In the same way, at the end of the war, they were to support two enemy governments—on one side King and his successor Louis Saint-Laurent, and on the other Maurice Duplessis. War and conscription stimulated their will to autonomy, and provincial autonomy means escaping from the control of Ottawa, hence from the majority, on vital issues. But they had never envisaged a break with Ottawa. In this regard French Canadians continued to be conformists. They have always chosen to be on the side where the power lies.

Is this a sign of timidity or of political wisdom? Or were French Canadians after all demonstrating a feeling of solidarity with the rest of the country? Twenty years after the plebiscite it remains an open question.

Post-Face

In the full and formal sense of the term, conscription never occurred. Was this whole long story then nothing but a sinister farce? We have seen extremists of both breeds going out of their way to create difficulties for the King government: on the one hand never ceasing to clamour for conscription even though the policy of voluntary service efficiently filled the need; on the other, accusing the Prime Minister of intentions which he never acted upon until the end of 1944, and which perhaps he never had in the first place.

At least it might seem so.

During the war King demonstrated his genius for manipulating men. He knew the trick of holding a vast, divided country together. Like a diligent tailor, each night he mended the wear and tear of every day; he sewed and darned and redarned so much and so well that the cloth more or less held together.

He was the still centre; his qualities were wisdom and practicality, at least in appearance. In fact, he pursued a ceaselessly shifting centre with a quick and penetrating intuition of what was possible at any given moment. That was his secret, and it made him irreplaceable. If he had disappeared, a reign of violence would have followed. His gift was to guess the point of balance and to stick with it as long as necessary.

Without the plebiscite, the centre would have shifted elsewhere.

In fact, the majority never ceased to dominate. Imagine a Canada that was almost entirely French. This hypothetical country would have acted as Ireland did at first. Then, after Pearl

Harbor, like several Latin American states, with cold politeness it would have let itself be drawn into the war. So King and English Canada led us where we did not wish to go. We never took the initiative. All we could do was to delay the outcome; but that we did.

It was the matching of two unequal forces, and we gave in. By his artfulness King succeeded in partially masking the element of constraint; but constraint there was.

During the war, many French Canadians in Quebec had the feeling that they were living in an occupied country. The English were the occupiers, they were the ones who dictated our conduct and prevented the national will from freely asserting itself. Our own politicians were *collaborateurs*. In comparison with Hitlerized Europe, it was a benign occupation. Thanks to King's moderation the yoke remained bearable. All we risked were our liberties, and here again the threat seldom became reality. But its very existence is enough to poison one's life.

This feeling of having been occupied reveals the extent to which a large number of French Canadians escaped in heart and in spirit from the powerful influence of the central state; the greater the physical constraint, the weaker their moral adhesion and their feelings of loyalty. Certainly we respected French-Canadian volunteers because they were risking their lives, but when, on the strength of their courage on the battlefield, we were asked to give our support to King's policies, our reaction was one of violent rejection. Our heroes were the conscript, the nay-sayer, the rebel. And yet the spirit of revolt practically never went to the limit. The internment of Camillien Houde caused, on the whole, few repercussions. After his return he did not play an important role politically. This was because the exercise of constraint, too, seldom went to the limit, and because, though we possessed so little, we still preserved the morale of possessors.

Is it any wonder then that we see ourselves so clearly in plays like *Ti-Coq* and *Le Simple Soldat*?

We were a flock that was readily led; but though we were led we were not possessed. Russia and the United States might each in turn gear themselves for war. But we remained stubborn in our refusal. Perhaps to refuse so doggedly one had to blind and deafen oneself. I sometimes have felt to the point of suffocation the bitter solitude of my own people in the world.

In the end it was all a question of feeling. But one of man's feelings is his sense of self-respect. For that matter, the whole world is a complex of feelings, and I wonder why we should be expected to play down the feeling that man directs immediately towards himself, the one that is called the sense of human dignity.

FROM

Le Devoir

Independence

The political and intellectual career of Henri Bourassa was so rich and influential that it cannot be summarized in a few words without committing an injustice.

Nor is it easy to isolate its dominant themes. Should one choose his Christian concept of politics which was always vigorous and demanding and uppermost in his mind? Or the battles he waged for his Canadian *patrie* against the ever-present pressures of imperialism? Or should one cite his crusading for justice on behalf of religious and ethnic minorities? Or his struggles to prevent the pillaging of our natural resources? . . . All these areas of interest and many others bore the unmistakable stamp of his concern.

But there is something deeper and more intimate which is irrevocably his own and which inspires all the rest. I mean his independence of spirit.

M. Bourassa gave himself generously to diverse causes — to the point of becoming identified with several of them. Yet none could claim to have dominated him. He fought side by side with the traditional parties with the zeal of a conqueror, but none could ever begin to pride themselves on having corralled him. He remained a free man and an independent spirit all his life long.

And yet he spent the whole of his life championing ideas. He was the French Canadian whose work has had the greatest impact since Papineau and Lafontaine, an infinitely greater impact than that of any respectable politician occupying an official position in government.

124

His success was due to his exceptional oratorical powers, to his intellectual rigour, and to a gift of foresight which he sometimes possessed to an incredible degree. But he also owed it to that intransigence of character which always made him shun doubtful compromise and follow the path that led straight ahead, though it sometimes meant going on almost alone.

So he stayed free. But he did not consider freedom a licence to remain neutral. Though independent, his independence was pugnacious, high-strung, "committed".

Parties, cliques, groups of all kinds appeared to him in their true colours, as expressions of realities that were all too human, to be used as means, never as ends.

That is the way he appeared in history, entering into brief associations with the most various kinds of men. With Laurier or against him as Laurier himself fluctuated; with the Conservatives or against them according to their vicissitudes; with Mackenzie King or against him as he doubled back on his tracks.

And who would seriously deny today that he stood out above those parties? But when he was waging one of his campaigns and was swinging hard and free, what yelps came from those he laid the whip to, what slanders, what sly and self-interested justifications. Don't think for a minute the Liberals believed in his independence when he was putting the screws to them. Or that the Conservatives recognized his liberty when he was unmasking them.

I cannot, for a very good reason, remember Arthabaska and the crisis of 1911, although I have heard about those embattled days so often that I can almost believe I lived through them. I do, however, remember the wrath of the Conservatives in 1926 over the Byng of Vimy incident when Bourassa denounced the intervention of a British Governor General in Canadian affairs, and I have still fresh in memory the insults the Liberals heaped on him during the war.

Political parties never really want to believe in independence. It upsets them. It destroys the system. It disturbs the gentle alternation of power. They can bring themselves to accept a temporary ally who will support them for reasons that are foreign to their own causes. But basically that bothers them. In their eyes, the worst villain is the non-conformist who refuses to play by the rules of the game. Against him they are ready to muster all their forces, first to encircle him, then to starve, and finally to crush him.

Bourassa experienced all these tactics. And triumphed over them. When he founded his newspaper he made it in his own image, that is, vigorous and free. That is the tradition of *Le Devoir* and it is one that we intend to carry on, without the same brio perhaps, but in the same good faith.

Never has this mission of independence and commitment been more urgent than today. The old party lines re-form continually and the pattern we observe on a very small scale here is repeated in the vaster world beyond us. Two ideologies, two power blocs, two imperialisms are setting out to divide the world between them. Since our geography places us next door to one of the giants, everything tends to draw us into its system, to rid us of our own identity, and to erase personal thought. And atomic war is at the end of the road.

To give in is impossible. Man can never give up, he must never resign himself to that fate. We no longer believe in the corrupt "crusades" we are invited to join. Neither imperialist nor autonomist propaganda can win us; they are elaborate smoke screens to mask sordid realities.

Whatever a particular regime offers that is true and good we must recognize for what it is worth. Whatever it proposes that is close to our own thought we must agree to defend together. Beyond that we are bound neither by vested interest nor by any automatic sense of duty.

Of course, independence is no guarantee of infallibility. One can still make a wrong choice while remaining free, but to remain free is a good choice. The problem simply is to think as justly as one is able. As for the rest, let the dogs howl at the moon. . . .

November 29, 1947

Isolationism and the Anglo-Canadian Press

The Anglo-Canadian press has a convenient way of pushing aside questions that Quebec raises about Canada's foreign policies.

It charges "isolationism" and that seems to settle the issue.

It bases this judgement on a facile prejudice which has been carefully cultivated over the past thirty years, and which claims that French Canadians are not interested in world affairs, that they live within their own Great Wall of China, and that they are opposed to everything that occurs outside their own little society.

For thirty years, for fifty even—ever since that unfortunate misadventure in Transvaal—the English-Canadian press has assiduously told its readers that Quebec's sustained anti-imperialism is really anti-internationalism, and that our will to independence is just a stubborn desire to stay in our own back yard.

Only a few days ago, the *Winnipeg Free Press* was investigating the attitudes of various political parties towards the North Atlantic Alliance. Liberals, Socialists, and Conservatives all seemed pretty much in favour, the *Free Press* stated. Then, taking a crack at Mr. Drew,* Duplessis's friend, the editorialist asked whether "the nationalism and isolationism of Quebec were acceptable to him and to the party he led?"

This allusion to Quebec nationalism and isolationism is the one solitary reference made in the *Winnipeg Free Press* to French-Canadian opinion on foreign policy. Nationalism and isolationism seem to cover the subject. The reader will "understand", he may spare a shrug at the thought of the half-century history of such blindness, or may perhaps regret the fact that one whole province should be so patently backward, and then he will pass on to more serious matters.

One question comes to mind, however. Beyond a few rare

*George Drew (1894-1973) had become leader of the Progressive Conservative party in October 1948.

exceptions, do our English counterparts read the French-Canadian press? Language, obviously, constitutes a barrier, and the "news services" as a rule seem governed by a clear intent to distort and slant the facts.

We wonder whether English-speaking journalists ever read our newspapers and magazines because they seem to be extraordinarily ignorant of their contents. One would think that we lived in two foreign countries separated by thousands of miles and oceans of prejudice.

The Anglo-Canadian press does not seem aware, for example, that French-Canadian papers have been devoting more and more space and interest to international questions. That is an undeniable fact. A quick glance through any paper is enough to prove it.

As to the problem of the North Atlantic Alliance, our journalists have been asking a great many questions about it for over a month. They have seized this occasion to raise the possibility of neutrality as a course of action. They have done so, no matter what their political affiliation, in an almost identical spirit, whether it was *L'Action Catholique*, or *Le Soleil*, *Montréal-Matin* or *Notre Temps*, *La Frontière*, *La Voix de l'Est*, *L'Action Nationale*, *Le Bien Public*, or *Le Progrès du Saguenay*, nearly always the same questions were formulated—questions that were in no sense isolationist and had little connection with nationalism.

French-Canadian journalists had all welcomed the idea of Canadian participation in the United Nations as a duty and a necessity, realizing that in today's world every state must contribute to international order for moral reasons as well as for material ones. Some of them even wished that the United Nations should not assume the image of a group of conquering states determined to lord it over the defeated nations and muzzle unsympathetic neutrals.

Then the U.N. became the arena for struggles between two imperialisms. Those who guide world opinion were expected to collaborate in splitting the world into two entrenched camps. At that point some commentators here, as well as leaders of opinion elsewhere, began to seek a third solution from which peace would not necessarily be excluded *a priori*. They often drew inspiration from principles set down by a power which has nothing either isolationist or nationalist about it: the Vatican.

When people began to speak openly of war again as a way to settle accounts, certain voices were raised to suggest that neither World War I nor World War II had solved international problems and that the way to crush Communism was not by a conflict that would be "a world suicide".

The reaction became even more vigorous and widespread when Mr. Saint-Laurent began to vaunt the fatal and automatic participation of Canada in World War III. The concepts that inspire our new-style warmongers are, in our opinion, neither Christian nor human. Many French-Canadian papers denounced such thinking from the point of view of a moral vision of international life.

In short, if we have been isolated from something, it is from official propaganda. But there is nothing isolationist in realizing what war has become, and what an atomic conflict would be, or in contrasting the destruction that would be caused by such a war with the annihilating benefits that would be gained.

These are the themes that have been treated and developed at much greater length than I can show here in a good part of the French-Canadian press over the last two months. And this analysis has been carried on precisely in those sectors that have been most open to attack by Anglo-Canadian critics.

Which is to say that reality corresponds in no way to what is claimed to be an accurate picture of the situation.

The trickery that is applied in this process is working to disunite Canada and to provoke tragic misunderstandings.

No one is asking English-Canadian papers to adopt the point of view of the French-Canadian press without believing it. But they might treat it as they would any other source of information—accurately.

It is very unfortunate to see old prejudices aired in a press that reaches more than half the Canadian population. *Traduttore, Traditore* the saying goes, but we see no need for translators to turn traitor, in one direction or the other.

November 27, 1948

A Bird in the Hand

Appeals to the Privy Council have, to all intents and purposes, been abolished. The ancient regalia has at last been relegated to the past. Now we will be judged in the highest court of the land by Canadians, and not by foreigners. Alleluia!

It is a victory for Canada. It might have been a total victory. Each provincial state might have received without restriction its own part of the imperial prerogatives. But since the Supreme Court, a tribunal of federal origin, will be our ultimate judicial resort—even in constitutional matters—Ottawa has been provided with a powerful means of action against the provincial states, perhaps even with a means of weighting the constitution in its favour. As I have already said, there is no cause to fear automatic injustices or partisan judgements, but there is real reason to fear that the federal government, like Roosevelt's in the States, will see to it that the dominant mentality in our highest court will favour centralization.

So once again we are headed in the same direction, with Ottawa gaining power at the expense of the provinces. Mr. Saint-Laurent seems to accept this orientation and offers French Canadians more stable constitutional guarantees in exchange for gravely diminished provincial rights. But is this transfer, even if the "guarantees" are serious, a good deal for French Canadians, or just some kind of a horse trade?

Political decentralization is justifiable on several counts. It places the authorities closer to the people, and makes them better able to respond to the people's needs. It tends to forestall the arbitrariness of the single state and consequently protects the liberty of the individual citizen by more widely distributing responsibility.

That is probably the most valid justification for Confederation. It follows that any attempt at centralization, unless it is technically necessary, is a mistake and an error.

But in fact I do not believe that Confederation was set up to respect those principles. Why indeed was the federal system chosen in 1867 against the will of Sir John A. Macdonald? Macdonald himself reveals the reason in this frequently quoted passage:

Lower Canada, he wrote, "would never have consented to legislative union. French Canadians would have been in a minority and possessing a language, religion, and a nationality different from those of the majority, they were perfectly aware that with the coming of union with the other provinces their institutions and laws might be assailed and their ancestral associations attacked and endangered."

French Canadians had just gone through the experience of Union. Despite Lafontaine's inspired manipulation of the system, it had proved to be a bad one for French Canadians, running counter to traditions that had been current since 1763. In fact, with all our will we had aspired to political independence. Since complete political independence no longer seemed possible in 1867, we had resigned ourselves to Confederation, where, at least in internal matters, we would possess our own autonomous state of Quebec. But we would have revolted against legislative union. "Lower Canada would have risen against it as a single man," Macdonald writes in his memoirs.

These debates have often been reopened since 1867. And each time reaction from Quebec has been the same. We have never consented to cede those rights which allow us to lead our own social, economic, and cultural life.

Has the situation changed fundamentally today? I do not believe so. Certainly technical progress means that some questions are stated in other terms, and new questions have sprung up. But our people remain the same minority that still finds its lifeline in its own political institutions.

The facts are simple. Thanks to Confederation we have a state within which we are a majority and where we can take the political initiatives which best correspond to our own ideas and interests. Whenever the state of Quebec is diminished, to that extent we lose the possibility of autonomy. Quebec is the political reality to which our destiny as a people is tied.

In comparison with this tangible assurance, what is the worth of constitutional guarantees at the federal level? Obviously those of us who have so often fought to obtain or preserve these guarantees do not despise them. But precisely because of our experience, history has shown us their limits. We believed that minority rights were well protected by the B.N.A. Act; experience taught us that articles of a constitution are subject to interpretation, that they are very flexible and fall into disuse when political force is not there to back them up.

Experience has shown us that to abandon rights in Quebec in order to recoup them in Ottawa is often to release a bird in the hand for one in the bush. Claiming to give us in Ottawa what is snatched from us in Quebec is like exchanging gold reserves for paper currency at a time when everyone is threatened with devaluation. And all Mr. Saint-Laurent's good will cannot eliminate the risks of such a transaction.

But this is to argue, we are told, as if demographically the position of French Canadians were fixed forever. Is it not possible that in the next thirty years we may in fact become the majority in Canada? It's a possibility, although many overpowering factors may upset the statisticians' calculations before that day comes.

Even if it did, that would in no way change the nature of the problem. No one knows who will make up the majority thirty years from now. But we do know that there will still be a minority and that the political regime will affect it. Perhaps, if demographic predictions are realized, our English-speaking fellow citizens will turn out to be the most ardent defenders of federalism. In that case they would have the rights we exercise today, and they would find the need for guarantees beyond those promised by such and such a legal clause, just as we do today. The existence of one or several provinces over which they would exercise real control would then perhaps reduce the temptation to join the United States which, as André Siegfried has shown, they would inevitably experience in the circumstances.

But all that is pure conjecture. Let's stay with present realities.

If we are given a choice between a regime that becomes more and more centralizing though offering more formal guarantees, and the federal system, we are without reserve in favour of federalism.

It is an abuse of language to hear the centralizers called federalists. In fact they are destroying Confederation, which is a regime of balance between governing powers. We wish to see this system re-established and we will not fall for the horse trade.

September 30, 1949

Saint-Laurent Gets Popular "Approval"

The North Atlantic Treaty is Canada's major foreign commitment since joining the United Nations. Though one may remain convinced that the former is in direct contradiction to the latter, that is beside the point. The Treaty is now the corner-stone of our foreign policy. The negotiations which led up to it, the vote in the Commons which endorsed it, and the meetings of the Atlantic Council were all given full news coverage.

About a month ago the Gallup poll asked Canadians: *Is Canada a member of the North Atlantic Treaty Organization?* Out of every 100 persons asked, 5 replied no, and 30 said they didn't know. With the help of such a question, one should be able to trace certain tendencies with relative ease.

It appears then that two Canadians out of six are either convinced that we are not bound by the treaty or don't know whether we are or not.

If so many of our fellow citizens live in such ignorance of a fact that official propaganda has played up so emphatically, what of events that take place in the shadows?

It is said that the Canadian people almost all support Mr. Saint-Laurent's foreign policy. If this is exact, it must be admitted that the unanimity is recruited in vagueness and ignorance. Such approval can hardly be considered anything but negative. It would have to be said that the people support Mr. Saint-Laurent's politics but without knowing what they are.

That doesn't scandalize me particularly. Foreign policy has become so complex that to follow it, the average citizen in our democratic societies should be a graduate in political science. Our engagements have become trans-planetary. The worker in Winnipeg, the Quebec farmer, or the miner from Nova Scotia is almost expected to have personal views on Korea and Iran, on Germany, Malaysia, Formosa, and Yugoslavia, and on our relations with these parts of the world.

When one starts to tune in, the cacophony of propaganda becomes stupefying. Two explanations, at least, are put forward for every event, and to disengage the true from the false you would have to have access to information that even the specialists don't possess.

Besides, the man in the street is not really touched by an event until such time as it intrudes on his daily life. Municipal politics are within his grasp, but even provincial affairs often seem to him to be a tangled mess, and as for international commitments . . .

But what can he do about it? Listen to the brand of propaganda that shouts the loudest. This way, attitudes harden that are highly debatable not to say absurd. The labour unionist becomes, without knowing it, an accomplice of Syngman Rhee . . . sociological influences are so strong that they paralyse even those who are capable of personal thought and action. And of course there is always the interplay of large vested interests, and different varieties of cowardice and apathy.

In short, even in western democracies which claim to be highly developed, the sector that is truly democratic is infinitely small. Economic forces tend to foster ignorance and conformism.

Think of the Korean conflict and its repercussions in Canada.

In Ottawa, the four parties are in agreement on the essential points. There are almost no independent opinions. One has the impression of an immense machine that has eliminated all human and living concerns.

The press at large joins in the general chorus. If one attempts to preserve a vestige of reason and speak out as an individual, language becomes so shifty and complicated that one despairs of inspiring the least action. We are all delivered up to a kind of automatism.

Yet without the magic dust of the propaganda fairy it is impossible to imagine such unanimity. Theoretically such singleness of vision is unbelievable in a society of free men.

Take this fact for example. In all the Anglo-Canadian papers I have read, there has not been a single even slightly serious study of American policies, despite the fact that many Canadian editors are capable of some assessment and that American columnists in the same papers have been severely critical. That borders on absurdity.

What is the cure for this grave sickness in our democracies?

To constitute a new political force is an enterprise that many of us know to be extremely difficult. . . . It is almost as long a process to set up a counter-current through an independent press. Man continues to remain alone face to face with the "mind-engineers".

The only hope lies with organized movements. Professional associations and other groups, without getting "involved in politics", probably have an important role to play. And they have an obligation to enter into a field which hitherto they have considered to be outside their range of action.

They have the means to follow developments. They can predict the consequences of distant interventions. They, like everyone else, will suffer the consequences at any rate, for what would become of them in the aftermath of World War III?

They alone, by using the power they have already acquired, can exert some resistance and form a body of opinion. In a democracy their responsibility is evident. They can prevent us from plunging over the brink.

September 5, 1950

After Fifty-Seven Years of Political Fidelity

No one could say that Quebec lacked a sense of continuity in politics.

On the provincial level we elected the same party from 1897 to 1936—thirty-nine years of unbroken fidelity. From 1936 to 1944 the parties alternated. For the past nine years we have been caught up in a new political allegiance.

In federal politics the pattern is even more striking. Quebec's marriage with the Liberal party dates from 1896. There were two serious domestic flare-ups, in 1911 and 1930. Not once during the last fifty-seven years, however, did the Liberal party lose its majority in Quebec. Three more years and it will be our diamond wedding anniversary!

This disturbing political phenomenon has specific causes. We aren't simply creatures of habit. For many years there were good reasons to prefer the Liberals.

Still one can't help wondering if remaining chained indefinitely to the same party doesn't entail more inconveniences than advantages.

We live under a two-party system which has survived two wars and a depression. For my own part, I am not excessively enamoured of it. But the majority of Quebec voters seem attached to it still, and in all probability it is under this system that the next federal election will be held whether we like it or not.

The system is a valid one as long as there are really two parties, as long as the group in power feels that it is truly faced with the threat of a possible successor. If one of the two feels all-powerful in a certain sector, it may very well neglect a region where it none the less draws its strongest support.

The Liberal party has demonstrated this twice in the last twenty years. It formulated war policies that ran totally against popular sentiment in Quebec and yet it was returned to power with large majorities in 1940 and 1945. Why? Because the Conservatives offered no real alternative and because Quebec did not believe in the solution proposed by a third party.

Since the war, two major questions have dominated Canadian politics: foreign affairs, that is the cold war—concerning which the Conservatives are identical twins with the Liberals—and federal-provincial relations. Here once again the federal Liberals run counter to Quebec. Their policies are unconditionally centralizing and thereby constitute a continued threat to the political future of French Canadians. Yet Mr. Saint-Laurent in 1949 carried off the greatest victory the Liberals had even known—just after Mr. Duplessis had done the same on the provincial scene.

This extraordinary situation allows Mr. Saint-Laurent to decide his political position without worrying too much about reaction from Quebec. Besides, he offers us certain consolations. He speaks in French very often. In the federal services he has won advantages for our language as undeniable as they are incomplete. It should be added that these gestures of his are a matter of personal conviction and it must be understood that I do not call his good faith into question.

But in the present situation Mr. Saint-Laurent is free to lead Ottawa's fight against the provinces without giving more than passing consideration to what Quebec thinks about it, even though Quebec usually elects the majority of his party members. The Liberals are convinced that on the federal level Quebec voters simply have no other choice. Whatever they do, they are sure their province will not vote for Mr. Drew.

That's an unhealthy situation. That's where we begin to pay for our excessive fidelity. That's what's got to change—if at all possible.

But at this point we are not the only ones involved. To be able to change you have to have some alternative solution to change to.

To start with, Mr. Drew did not pay much attention to the status of the provinces. Then the exercise of power in Ontario gave him a more realistic outlook and he became one of the champions of provincial autonomy. In his new role as leader of the Conservative Opposition in Ottawa he has often appeared more hesitant and has fallen into self-contradiction. It appears then that he is not a doctrinaire federalist and his party is widely split on the issue. But for the past year he seems to have pulled himself together. His major policy speech last November was firm and farsighted, and the only way Mr. Saint-Laurent could reply to it was by reaccentuating his own centralism. Since then the Conservative leader has corrected certain previous errors in his views on federal aid to education.

And yet that is not enough. Mr. Drew's attitude appears reasonable, but it is too cold. He won't stir up Quebec simply by making statements of principle. He will have to show that he is a decentralizer at heart and launch a real campaign with the help of workers here.

Only then will Quebec voters feel that there is an alternative to the Liberal party. That won't mean that the Conservatives will have won the Quebec election, but at least they will have become an eligible alternate choice.

February 12, 1953

We Are the Vanquished

The shock value of this document is considerable. It's not every day that one reads a brief whose message is so new. And it is rare indeed when such astonishment is inspired by an association that has reached the venerable age of the Saint-Jean-Baptiste Society of Montreal.

The report in question was presented Thursday by the Society's president, M. Eugène Thérien to the Tremblay Commission. It is one hundred pages long, the first half being an interpretation of the history of Canada, the second an examination of the practical consequences of applying the new thesis.

The close relationship between the ideas expressed here and those of M. Michel Brunet, professor of history at the Université de Montréal, is so evident that it would be dishonest not to point it out. M. Brunet certainly must have collaborated in compiling this brief.

How can I best summarize something that is already a synthesis of history?

The basic idea is this: We are a vanquished people. And we remain vanquished. The saying that in Canada "there are neither victors nor vanquished" is nothing but a piece of amiable flattery addressed to French Canadians, or else an opiate designed to lull them in their mediocrity.

We are and we remain a vanquished race.

There's nothing new in that, you'll say?

But there is, first because of a shift in accent, and second because of the importance given certain factors in the new explanation of our history.

For after this basic declaration you would be wrong to expect pious jeremiads and nostalgic complaints. The report's language is hard. Its tone is realistic. It speaks in modern terms.

The effects of the defeat of 1760 still weigh on us. What were they exactly?

Before 1760 New France was a solidly and harmoniously organized society possessing structures which fulfilled "the needs of a young and dynamic nation in full development". In particular it possessed a capitalist bourgeoisie, "the class of entrepreneurs which every society needs to develop normally".

The conquest drove away this type of ambitious and enterprising man. The rare ones who remained were obliged to play secon-
dary roles. French Canada was decapitated. It lost its capitalist
bourgeoisie, its educational system (which it was only able to
begin rebuilding a century later), and its political and social
framework. What remained was the cell of the parish, an impressive structure but insufficient to the task. "The immense majority
of the population were condemned to live the lives of backward
peasantry." When they freed themselves from this condition they
became condemned "to exile in urban centres where the main-
springs of economic life were concentrated in the hands of the
English minority in Lower Canada."

There were political conflicts. The Saint-Jean-Baptiste Society's report does not consider them very important, for behind
the battles and agitation the real control remained in the hands
either of the metropolis or of local sources of wealth, both of
which lay outside our sphere of influence. But we were not aware
of this fact. We joyfully accepted the compromise of Union and
later on of Confederation without understanding what was happening. We were only too happy if we could go on speaking
our own language and practising our religion. For, says the report,
"a people placed in the difficult conditions that had been those
of *les Canadiens* after the conquest can never have more than a
diminished political program."

But all that is far behind us, you will say.

"No," the report answers implicitly. All that is planted within
us, has become our very substance. Our present very deeply
rooted economic inferiority, our lack of intellectual curiosity, the
parsimoniousness of our demands on life—these are social and
psychological realities which come down to us in direct line from
the conquest.

If space permitted, we should quote here some of the facts
cited by the author of the report. They show how he refuses
to give the least importance to emotional reactions and lyrical
outpourings. He expresses himself like a sociologist. When he
says we remain a vanquished race he doesn't say it like some
romantic sniveller but like a clinical diagnostician who has just
finished examining his patient.

We were not, of course, alone in Canada. The control that

slipped through our fingers was grasped by others. The building of today's Canada began in 1763 on the ruins of New France. It was the product of British imperialism and the English commercial and capitalist class, particularly those who settled in Lower Canada. This class, gaining in wealth, came through the period 1791-1840 intact. The idea of the Union of the two Canadas was its inspiration. Under this regime it became energetic and creative and began to equip the country industrially, which resulted in rapid growth. It accumulated riches and a wide experience in big business to which a sense of leadership was added as a natural complement. Then it grouped together the British colonies and in 1867 succeeded in laying the framework of modern Canada.

"This nation-state built up against the United States constituted a victory for British nationalism over the individualism of the old English colonies in North America." And also over the former French-Canadian colony.

Provincialism did not die overnight in the new Confederation. From feeble and poor beginnings, the provinces grew in importance and until 1929 proved to be jealous of their rights. Under the shelter of this generalized provincialism, Quebec was able to conserve important prerogatives "which, for that matter, it used very poorly for it had a government that was traditionally neutral, a government that was afraid to govern." The zenith of provincial power was reached in the period 1921-30. Then the Depression and the Second World War sounded the knell for the provinces. The central government acquired an extraordinary influence. "It has proved over the past ten years that it is as strong as that of any unitary state." Only Quebec continued to resist. The eight other provinces accepted the new order, and their political leaders, their intellectuals, and their businessmen followed suit. Canadian nationalism was victorious. But . . .

But was it really Canadian nationalism?

Not according to the Saint-Jean-Baptiste Society's report. The victorious nationalism was Anglo-Canadian or Canadian, not *Canadien*. Ottawa became the capital of the Canadian nation, not the *Canadien*. French-Canadian influence in major affairs of state was close to zero. The author cites many examples to back his argument and in particular two disgruntled testimonies from Chapleau and Cardin.

Does this mean that for French Canadians considered as a group the future is a sinister one? No. They retain an important constitution. They retain the provincial government of Quebec. This must at all costs be defended. This must at all costs be endowed with political policies that are positive and dynamic. The report sets out the main lines for such policies in fifty pages and then concludes:

> It is essential that French Canadians realize that they form a nation-state. Just as Anglo-Canadians rely on the central government to be their natural political pole, so French Canadians must learn to consider their provincial government in Quebec as the legitimate guardian of their nationality. They will have to make it a great modern government fully conscious of its heavy responsibilities and possessed of the will and the means to discharge them.

The reply to this challenge lies in the hands of the present generation. "THOSE WHO COME AFTER US WILL NO LONGER HAVE THE FREEDOM TO CHOOSE."

This thesis, like all historical theses, is subject to debate, but it has an undeniably modern accent. It has drive. It stimulates. Its author, whoever he is, owes us a more detailed development of his thought, for it is only after this that we will be able to judge its validity. It borrows a great deal, which is natural, from predecessors like l'Abbé Groulx, but it changes the emphasis and the highlights. It is occasionally very black and one is sometimes prompted to ask whether a program of action can ever result from it. Yet the author is extremely vigorious in his demonstration of the possibilities of action.

The Saint-Jean-Baptiste Society should be commended for presenting these views, many of which are new. It should make them available to the public at large. I feel that the publication of the complete report is a must.

May 18, 1954

Have We "Arrived"?

"I think French Canadians are unnecessarily worried about their independence. . . . French Canadians have arrived, and don't realize it. They're fighting a battle they've already won."

That is the opinion of Nova Scotia's extremely sympathetic Premier, Mr. Henry D. Hicks. . . . But is it true?

Such a statement is a kind of testimony. We are happy to learn that an Anglo-Canadian believes that our national future is assured. That will perhaps encourage him to respect it as a living fact, and not just in Quebec. Acadians in Nova Scotia will doubtless be glad to learn from their Premier that French Canadians "have arrived". But there may be serious reasons why they have not "realized" it yet. I don't think that their problems have all been solved, or that they have the impression that they are fighting a battle that is already won. I don't believe they feel at home in Nova Scotia where the number of French speakers has diminished at the same time as the number of "Canadians of French origin" has been on the increase.

The same thing is true, for that matter, in all other provinces. Where, except in Quebec, can we say that we are perfectly at home as French Canadians? Where else do schools accord us the rights that in Quebec we give to our Anglo-Protestant minority? In which provincial legislatures is French officially accepted?

Have we "arrived" in most federal ministries? Or in the majority of federal agencies, the C.N.R., Air Canada, or the National Film Board?

Have we even "arrived" in the English restaurants in downtown Montreal? The other night I had a strip torn off me by a waitress to whom I insisted on speaking French. "We're not supposed to know French in the west end," she told me as a last resort. She was only repeating what many French Canadians have been led to believe.

Not all, of course. But a Toronto M.P. who has the elegance to speak French in Parliament is not going to change the climate of everyday life much. A handful of intellectuals who are really generous and understanding are not going to modify singlehanded an atmosphere that is heavy with hostility towards French.

That's not the worst of it. It's our very life that we feel threatened as it has never been threatened before.

For while Mr. Hicks and other well-intentioned Anglo-Canadians declare us victors, we know all too well the many unresolved problems that come from going through an industrial revolution that has been governed by foreign capital and technology.

In the past we were not so numerous, but history had isolated us already. Farmers cut off from the outside world spoke their own language amongst themselves, heard it spoken on the lips of their priests, their doctors, and their notaries. Those were hard times to get through, for the life of a minority is never easy, but at least this isolation, which impoverished us in every way, served us, too, as a protective shell. Now, even if we wished to preserve it—and we do not—such isolation has become impossible. Our agricultural civilization has become an urban one, and in the cities the control of economic life, and its basic requirements — which have never been in our hands — are less and less French.

Mr. Hicks pronounces us victors at the very time when many French Canadians are asking themselves whether the struggle is worth it after all, and when others have even ceased to ask such questions. We have reached the heart of the most serious crisis that has ever threatened us.

I am convinced that we will surmount it as we have surmounted others in the past. But not by kidding ourselves. Not by telling ourselves that "we have arrived" or that we have reached salvation harbour and that it's time to take a little rest.

The autonomy of Quebec is, in the present state of affairs, an evident necessity. At least M. Duplessis will have deserved credit for conserving it for others who will know, I hope, how to use it.

That is why we are glad to realize that Quebec will not be alone now in fighting federal-provincial battles. For Mr. Hicks' constitutional options seem close to ours, even if they are inspired by quite different motives.

March 11, 1955

Can a French Canadian Feel at Home in Canada?

I had often wondered whether in Vancouver, a city I had never set foot in, I would still feel that I was in my own country.

Well, a month ago I spent eight days there, and now, churned up by contradictory impressions and confused emotions, I wonder still.

The first thing that strikes you is the incredible distances. You had seen them on the map. But to actually cover them, mile by mile, is quite another matter. And if it were only the distances. . . . There are all those walls to get over too.

For hours on end Northern Ontario stretches out below you. Seen from the plane, the extreme poverty of the land resembles the half-forested solitudes of Ungava: rock, thin soil, microscopic trees you can hardly make out, and water, unendingly, as far as you can see. This desolate land of Cain still conceals unexplored riches, but I feel that man will never choose to settle permanently here.

Then it's the Prairies, that long strip of black earth whose fertility dominates the landscape.

But suddenly you are flying between awe-inspiring escarpments, man is left behind again, and you penetrate the Rockies. One is filled with retrospective enthusiasm for the builders of the first railroads, with astonishment at such a clearcut victory of the human will at a time when the technical means at man's disposal were still so limited. But that doesn't in any way change the fundamental fact: the physical barrier remains. It takes its toll still. To go from east to west when nature says north-south means violating the normal course of things: you must pay in effort or in cash.

I don't remember who it was observed that to cross Canada was to run a regular obstacle course—and what obstacles! You have to go over them yourself to realize their almost impenetrable solidity. And sometimes one wonders despite oneself if this country, this permanent victory over geography, doesn't remain, after all, a fragile and precarious man-made creation, a sort of false direction imposed on history, which at some later time a more sensible historical impulsion — or one preoccupied only with wider markets, material comfort, and easy solutions — will correct without too much trouble. The thin ribbon of the railroad is like a toy that a child has set up on a table and that adults with their passion for order will soon put away again.

And yet the ribbon has been there for three-quarters of a century. Other networks, less tangible ones such as radio, have been added to it and bind us together. It is impossible not to recognize the fact that what was merely provisional yesterday has now taken on an almost definitive character, that what was once just the result of an almost crazy dream has now become a habit and a tradition that men have become permanently adapted to.

Yes, all that is, it seems, my country.

Not only did no one ever ask for my passport (which would have happened a dozen times covering an equal distance in Europe), but no customs officer mauled my suitcases or asked me to sign some form or other. Of course I knew they wouldn't from the start. Somehow, obscurely, at each major obstacle something inside me expected the man in the peaked cap with gold braid on his sleeve to symbolize by his presence that I was changing countries. The symbolic man never appeared, and I felt neither fear nor shame. The childish and irrational fear of the man in the peaked cap corresponds, I conclude, to no observed reality. Here I am, 3,000 miles from Montreal, and I go on living under the government of Mr. Saint-Laurent. The same federal laws bind and protect me. As a Canadian citizen this is still my home.

In Winnipeg, Regina, Calgary, and Vancouver, I discovered the expected things. There were, of course some surprises. I didn't imagine that Prairie gumbo was so black, or that Manitoba was so treeless, or that the air was so light and buoyant in Calgary. I wasn't quite aware that Vancouver is one of the most beautiful sites in the world, a regular Sleeping Beauty of a city, suddenly aroused from a sleep of centuries by the rough hand of industry to fulfil its age-old destiny and become a great metropolis. Those are typical traveller's surprises. There were others, deeper ones, that I will speak of later.

But I knew that I would discover these cities, and obediently, one after another, they appeared to me and I felt them mine, because I knew from the start they would be.

It was all due to what was suddenly revealed to me as the sublime power of the school textbook. Because you once read in your illustrated geography book, "Victoria, on Vancouver Island, is the capital of British Columbia, one of Canada's nine provinces," because you stocked that in your memory so many years ago, a city where you discover old English ladies, a British Parliament, Social Credit ministers, but also magnificent flowers, immediately seems Canadian to you. You had seen its picture in the illustrated geography of your childhood. So you arrive with a sense of ownership. The city is yours. You are like an heir who has taken a rather long time to visit his most distant possession, but it belongs to him just as much as the rest.

But it wasn't just the childhood textbooks. Later in life, in a little station in the Laurentians, waiting for the train, you stared without really looking at those sooty old frames hanging on the wall which contained pictures of Banff and Jasper, inviting your visit. You knew those places were part of your country. Your mind was elsewhere, you were preoccupied and in a hurry to get to town, yet those images left their trace in you, and when you recognize them now you know you are still at home.

And then there were those nights of federal elections. You would follow the results on the radio. First came news from the Maritimes. Then Quebec and Ontario. After that you had to wait, and then the Prairies' report came in. Then you had to wait some more. And if it was one of those doubtful contests when the fate of the government remained in suspense until the very last minute, you began to feel impatient, frustrated, anxious, angry. What would Alberta say? Then Alberta would bring in its verdict. But you would have to wait very late for the decision from far-away British Columbia, far away in every sense, far and perhaps even foreign, concerned with other problems, but whose elected members would sit in the same Parliament as yours, and would spell the victory or defeat of the party you preferred. Finally its voice would come through too, from the depths of the night.

And the next morning you would realize that sentiments that didn't entirely concern you tied you to distant British Columbia whose political opinions exert a definite influence on your life.

Naturally those long radio vigils didn't tell you anything about the mist that hangs over Vancouver as I write this, or its luminous fiords, or the mountains that crown its skyline. But you shouldn't underestimate their effect. You felt they wouldn't count for much? Well, you were wrong. They do.

Even though the impressions are still pretty superficial, you find other links. From Winnipeg on, for example, people speak aggressively about "the East". The unpleasant thing is not the aggressiveness, which I find healthy and normal, but the way they artificially lump together Ontario and Quebec as though they formed a single region, when in fact you feel so little sympathy for what happens west of Ottawa. What's going on? When you've spent a good part of your life fighting Ontario, when you feel absolutely no connection with St. James Street, they see you from so far away that they take you for the shadow or extension of your oldest, most intimate enemy. That's a bit too much. You feel yourself swallowed up, annexed. You say so, you complain bitterly. And then you discover one of the most refined pleasures of being Canadian: Everyone gangs up to run down Toronto.

But unfortunately it's not all that simple. On the other side of the coin there's the problem of languages.

For a French Canadian the linguistic barrier begins in Montreal. You just have to cross a couple of streets or sometimes only step outside your own front door to hear English spoken. So it's an old habit with us. A French Canadian doesn't feel he's in a foreign country just because people are speaking English around him. And yet as time goes by, he begins to hear nothing but English. Almost nobody knows his language. Caught at a disadvantage, he has to make do as best he can in a foreign idiom. And it goes on and on. Finally it becomes really tiring. If he is not perfectly bilingual he is often only half understood. People get impatient. His accent seems objectionable to some of the people he talks to. So he ends up feeling like a foreigner because he is treated like a foreigner. Is it any wonder then if he suddenly begins to feel ridiculously upset because at the next table he hears a waitress speaking English with a French-Canadian accent?

But there are worse things. Later on I will have occasion to

148

speak of English-French relations in Canada. It won't be an easy
subject, and even if one makes as careful observations as possible,
it is difficult to arrive at firm conclusions. But what I am concerned
with for the time being is first impressions.

On the surface, then, what Vancouver seems to represent is
a superb indifference towards the whole of French Canada. Not
only does the person you talk to appear to be ignorant of your
problems, he doesn't believe them to be of the slightest importance. He doesn't care to hear about them; doesn't show a speck
of curiosity. In his eyes you, as a French Canadian, are a strange
and somewhat quaint phenomenon. (Notice that I said "as a
French Canadian", for his attitude towards you as an individual
is very cordial, very welcoming. He wants to show you around
everywhere and is ready to put himself out for you much more
than a Montrealer would be.) He goes even farther: As far as
he's concerned it doesn't matter a scrap if you're of French, Czech,
or Japanese origin. On the personal level I didn't find a sign
of racial prejudice. The general attitude is something like: "Let's
all be Canadians. . . . And in that case, why in the devil do you
insist on speaking French?"

I know this oversimplification is very unjust. Some of the university people I met showed such a lively curiosity about French
Canada that they would hardly answer your questions; they preferred to ask their own; their good will was evident. But this
was the exception, not the rule, unless by chance in the course
of conversation some hot issue came up like conscription, or
federal-provincial relations, or the riots that happened last spring
in Montreal when Maurice Richard got suspended.

So I learnt that indifference is more oppressive than hostility.
It flattens you. Wipes you out. You gasp for air. You'd like
to find a good enemy because at least in his eyes you exist.
In the West you barely do at all — at least so it seems.

But is it true? Or have I just expressed the illusions of a traveller
too pressed for time?

November 26, 1955

French Canadians and the West

"You know," he says to me, "there's a French radio station in Edmonton that plays great music."

He's a nice guy, a chance acquaintance, but chance and travel go well together. I was on my way to meet a group of artists when I suddenly found myself talking to this businessman, a little rough at the edges, who bombarded me with questions about Quebec.

"That radio station is right down my alley," he added. "I like the music and since I don't know any French to speak of, I don't hear the commercials."

But he really made me sit up when he asked abruptly with a kind of friendly aggressiveness, "Tell me, will you, what do the French Canadians out here want with their own radio station?"

I stared at him incredulously. What inspired this question, which I couldn't help associating with a kind of secret fanaticism? Up till now the man's behaviour had suggested nothing but warmth and friendship.

"I really don't follow you," I replied. "You tell me that the music on the French station is excellent and that you like music. And if you don't like French you can always switch to three or four English programs, so why should one little French station bother you?"

"No, no," he says stoutly, "you're not answering my question. I'm not talking about my own preferences, I'm asking you why you French Canadians, who are a long way from being the largest minority in Alberta, think they have got to have a radio station all their own when the Ukrainians and the Germans haven't got one."

I was ready to get angry. This way of treating us like a minority the same as all the rest is an interpretation of history that we consider false and offensive. We don't look down on the other minorities, but when an immigrant lands in Canada he should know that he is entering a bilingual country where there are two basic language groups. He can choose between them. The fact that there are French schools and radio stations doesn't give the other language groups the right to have them too. To maintain the contrary is to deny the existence of French Canada and to consider Canada a country with a single language.

But I keep my temper and manage to reply coldly, "Perhaps you can tell me why French Canadians should *not* have a French station here?"

"Why?" he replied without the slightest hesitation. "Because when they do, they show they want to stay a separate group and that gets our goat. In places like this you either speak one language or you speak twenty."

And with that he began to tell me his life story. I was going to hear the same kind of thing many times after that from all sorts of people. I would ask them if there was any special bitterness or anger against French radio in the West. If I asked the question at the start of the interview, the replies would just be vague and polite, but as soon as the ice was broken, people would tell me something like this: "Yes, might as well admit it, people don't like it. They don't talk about it much, it's not all that important, but it irritates them, it makes them mad, or at least it bothers them."

Here is my friend's story. When he was young, he spent some time in remote villages as a teacher. He would arrive at the beginning of the year and find himself in an entirely Swedish community—everyone spoke Swedish. So he would have to teach English to children who didn't know the first word of the language. Somewhere else the community would be Ukrainian, German, or Polish. Those recent immigrants were locked in behind barriers of language. They couldn't communicate with people in the next village. How could you hope to build a country in those conditions? It was like the Tower of Babel. The separate populations had to be brought together by means of a single language, and in the West, that language could only be English.

It is easy to see in such reasoning the theory of the melting pot. The Americans invented it out of sheer necessity. In their case, it suited well because they were not faced with the problem of a bilingual country.

But when your experience has been something like my friend's, you're not likely to turn a kindly eye on a little group that fiercely refuses to be assimilated. What's with them anyway? While everyone else agrees to play the game, here is this contrary bunch who want to stay in their own little corner and won't get into the swing of things. It might be different if they were a numerous minority, or if one of the western provinces was French (or if history had been taught in an exceptionally lively manner). Maybe then Westerners would have the notion of a vigorous French presence here that would have to be reckoned with. But in fact, the French minority only makes up a fraction of the population—and Quebec is so very far away.

So you don't give them the schools they believe they have a right to. And if they manage to create four radio stations in the West (which they paid for out of their own pockets), why, you find that they're really going too far and are setting an extremely bad example for other ethnic groups. And it's really asking for an outsize appetite in altruism and historical knowledge to admit that French has the same rights here as English—and by rights I mean concrete, established concessions and not just those airy principles that float in the stratosphere of "national unity".

This phenomenon is alarming enough by itself. Yet I have been told, I don't know how many times, that the problem is graver still and that it takes root in religious sentiments. Many people conclude that in Canada it is religion far more than language that divides us (though isn't it really due to historical links between the two?) I find the analysis convincing, for the opposition to French in the West antedates by a long time the arrival of the New Canadians.

It is based on the following oversimplifications. The average Anglo-Canadian is convinced that the Catholic Church dominates all activity in Quebec. The Church wishes to expand. It plans to do so by means of French Canadians, good Catholics who raise large families. It follows that the little irredentist groups in the West are the forerunners of a massive French invasion conceived by the Church. The radio stations are one of its tools.

It goes without saying that in this day and age such views are pure fantasy. There is nothing to support them beyond the overly optimistic declarations of a few French Canadians very young in years. The French-Canadian groups in the West, on the contrary, are keenly and painfully aware of their own fragility. Many of them view the conditions of their survival with real alarm. So for the powerful Anglo-Canadian majority to think of them as dangerous conquerors is to play the elephant terrified of a mouse.

In addition, English-speaking Catholics are somewhat less than enchanted with the idea that the Church's conquests are to be made in French. This results in serious tension between Catholics which I felt strongly every time I met English R.C.s. On the other hand, French Canadians complain about their situation inside the Church. They say that in several parishes where they make up the majority, English-speaking priests preach and hear confession in English, which is an injustice.

I tried to explain my point of view to my new friend. "When you state your dissatisfaction with the existence of French radio in the West, do you know what you're doing? You're working for the separatist cause in Quebec."

"I don't see how that is."

"Well, you're saying that French Canadians can't live *as French Canadians* in other parts of the country."

"But that's not true," he says, "I like French Canadians."

"Yes, I know you're not prejudiced. You're ready to welcome us warmly as long as we speak English."

"Come on, don't exaggerate. We let French Canadians speak their own language. Only it's irritating . . . "

"That's just it. You don't really accept French Canadians as they are. It's enough to convince many people in my province that despite all the hypocritical clichés about national collaboration, the only place that a French Canadian can really feel at home is in Quebec. And if Quebec is the only possible place to live, why should a French Canadian be interested in the rest of Canada! Why shouldn't he want to make Quebec his true home, for himself alone?"

December 19, 1955

A Province That Turns
Its Back on Us

I spent eight days in Vancouyer. The sun came out twice, first
for an hour in the afternoon, then for a whole day. And it wasn't
the rainy season.

But to begin with I want to evoke that English distinction
between "love" and "like", which will save me from having to
say, *"J'ai aimé Vancouver."* Its humidity is soothing after the exciting air of Calgary. In the dampness flowers become beautifully
coloured, trees grow immense, and man seems to relax. When the
sun does shine, the city, ringed by fiords, appears with its encir-
ling crown of high mountains which, though quite far away,
seem near, yet do not close in on you but rather gently lift your
eyes to the radiant sky beyond.

The clouds are never the same. One day they will imprison
you in your street, cutting down visibility to almost zero. You
feel the proximity of the thousands and thousands of miles of
the Pacific Ocean. If this fog lasted, I must admit that after
a month it would be dismal. But the next day the clouds rise
a little without disappearing and you guess the presence of the
bay, the first hills, and the lush vegetation of the park. Later
on they lift a little more and the first mountains appear, their
summits lost in a vaporous grey-white mist (I would never have
believed clouds could take on such fantastic shapes). And yet
you wish the sun would come back; days pass and the clouds
still hang heavily around you. You wonder, "Has it disappeared
forever? Will the sun ever come back to earth?" And just when
you are about to give it up for dead, it returns in glory, lighting
up a natural scene that is vigorous, clear, and vast — a site predes-
tined from all time for a great city.

Then you begin to understand. In this country they don't need
as much sun as in other places. Remember those lines of Rostand?

    . . . O sun, you without whom
    Things would not be what they are.

Here, things can afford to exist as appearances. It is enough
for the sun to come out from time to time to show what they
might become.

You could scarcely say that the citizens of Vancouver were
insensitive to this magnificence. They seem convinced that their
city and their province are truly the most beautiful in the world.
They pity you for not being able to live here with them.
Sometimes they even seem to think that if you don't, it must
be due to foolishness, impotence, or pure bad will. Are they
entirely wrong? If you could choose your city as you choose
your tie, wouldn't we all go and live in Vancouver? Think about
it. One of my hosts picked me up downtown in the middle of
noon-hour traffic. In five minutes we had reached his club over-
looking a mountain fiord. From Montreal, to find such a meeting
of mountain and sea, you would have to travel five hundred
miles.

Anyway, perhaps because of this, the British Columbians I
met seemed to me the most self-confident of Canadians. And
it wasn't just a question of landscape. Their newspapers and
their conversation reflect the same state of mind. Does it smack
of regionalism? It would be mean to say so. Let's just say that
having so much to accomplish in such charming surroundings
they haven't much time to think about what anyone else is doing.

British Columbia resembles Great Britain in three respects:
both have a British name, both have wet climates (at least on
the coast), and both are islands. British Columbia an island? Yes,
but a special kind: the province is not surrounded by water,
but the result is the same. Even if it is not technically correct
to call it an island, at least it is a self-evident fact that its inhabitants
are insular. The province is cut off from the world first by the
Rockies (which make, with the Laurentian Shield, a double barrier to the east), then by the Pacific Ocean (but what a prodigious
future it promises once the Bamboo Curtain is raised), third by
the political frontier.

Which of these barriers is the weakest? The political one certainly. That may explain a slight confusion I experienced. When
I was a schoolboy I was taught that British Columbia was the
most British of the Canadian provinces. More recently it has
been described as the most Americanized. Perhaps both statements are true. In Victoria you meet ghosts of the imperial past

and there are some in Vancouver, too, though less conspicuous. But as far as television, sports, and business are concerned, the American influence is dominant.

This expression may, however, be misunderstood. When I say "American" without thinking, I see New York and Hollywood and a hundred million robots in between. On the Coast, a new notion, which was only the skeleton of an idea before, begins to put on flesh and blood. It is that of a well characterized region, the Pacific North-West, as different from New York as it is from Toronto or Montreal, less aggressive, more relaxed, more human, an area whose economic interests often contradict those of the East and whose future power is assured if Asia reawakens and opens her doors to trade.

This part of the continent turns its back on us. I deduce this by several signs, and in particular by this one: I know no other province more indifferent to the fate of French Canadians, and believe me, open hostility is more comforting to man's heart than this serene and Olympian indifference. Yes, they are aware, of course, of the existence of a group of Canadians who speak French among themselves, but that's in the East, so far away that one doesn't have to be concerned with their problems. My arrival and my accent brought the problem a little closer. The people I spoke to, politely and hospitably, took the trouble to notice it. They would say: "A very curious phenomenon. But I don't understand why you cling so desperately to your French."

Others, more straightforward, would ask, "Why can't you just speak English like everyone else?"

It was a piece of advice, not an insult.

If I tried to explain why—saying, for example, that speaking French is a very old Canadian custom in my family, going back without a break to 1680—I would feel, after twenty seconds, that they had begun to think about something else.

Only one question interests them: schools. They detest separate schools. All their political parties fight them. If you talk about the rights of French Canadians, they reply — half in jest, making a joke on Quebec, and half by conviction (and this is the half that counts)—by invoking provincial autonomy. "You have your rights in Quebec and we leave you alone. Let us work out our own problems here as we see fit." In circumstances like these it's not surprising that a man like Father Bélanger (a beleaguered

French-Canadian priest whom I had the pleasure of meeting) needs help.

I spent eight days in Vancouver. By the end of my stay, such is the spell of the geography and of the human environment, I began to think like a British Columbian. For example, sixteen years ago I made a brief visit to Winnipeg and thought myself then in the heart of the West. Now, from Vancouver, I would have snubbed Winnipeg as almost being part of Ontario. And as for Toronto, it seemed to me lost in the suburbs of Montreal.

So it was high time to return home.

Before leaving I expressed my reactions to a journalist and a politician. Both of them protested, "You must never think that we're not Canadians. Any idea of separation is dead and buried. Everyone here believes in Canada and nothing but."

"Yes, but what do you mean by 'Canada'?"

"Well... naturally... when we think of Canada," said the politician, "we don't particularly think of places like Montreal or Ottawa or Toronto or Winnipeg..."

It seemed to be difficult to define. What I finally grasped was that for these men and others like them, Canada was first of all British Columbia, a British Columbia sheathed with a protective shield that stretched as far as Halifax. If they weren't interested in French Canada, it wasn't out of spite, it was just that Quebec was such a distant part of the protective shield. Their omissions were impartial. They would even include Toronto if Toronto weren't the seat of the big bosses and the city everyone in Canada feels it a social necessity, and even a precious part of Canadian folklore, to downgrade as much as possible.

Isolation? In B.C. how could it be otherwise? The economic and political centre of Canada is situated in the East. Even today it's quite a long trip for a Vancouverite to go to Calgary. His own economic interests keep him on the Pacific Coast.

Besides, British Columbia is rich and knows it. It pays the best salaries in Canada. Its social legislation is more advanced than that of many other provinces. It has the best school attendance record from elementary right up through university. Writers and artists make up a closer-knit group in Vancouver than in any other Anglo-Canadian centre. The climate is clement, the scenery majestic. These advantages and the consciousness of possessing them are manifest in the psychology of the people. And isn't it a reassuring thing to meet Canadians who are sure of themselves?

There is just one outstanding problem: how to make a country out of all those scattered parts. . . .

December 21, 1955

Anglo-Canadians and Canada

There is a tiresome image that has been pestering me ever since I began this series of articles on the Canadian West. It is that of a stranger who comes to discover, to study, to define, and to judge Quebec in three weeks. Once back home and safely out of our reach, he liberally spreads scandals about us without leaving us the least chance to reply. He does not think of us as a real subject for study but as an opportunity to exercise his wit and to flatter the prejudices of his readers.

This ghost has been haunting me because I am afraid of resembling it. So once again I am warning you against myself. In six weeks one cannot possibly learn to know four provinces which, despite their youth, have quite a bit of history behind them and an infinite number of problems to solve. I've given you my impressions, impressions that I have felt very deeply and that I have tried to verify, but they remain, just the same, pure impressions that are often contradictory.

I have spoken to you, for example, about the irritation that the presence of French radio stations on their territory causes citizens of the Prairies. Though this feeling is very real, you should not conclude that it is shared by everyone. Nor that all British Columbians happily shun the rest of the world. Everywhere I went I found university circles and groups of artists and individuals whose thoughtfulness and absence of prejudice made them open and friendly.

These milieux are not always in very close touch with one another (or with the rest of the community). How many times have I heard university professors deny that there is any hostility towards the French language. They weren't trying to deceive me, I'm sure. But they hadn't done any analysis of the situation, and old antagonisms that live on in the hearts of thousands of people rarely find a chance to express themselves. Since they live among their own kind, these academics and artists attribute to others feelings they experience themselves.

Would it be safe to suppose that having accepted our existence they also accept all the practical consequences of that fact? Far from it. Even if they travel more than most, French Canada remains a very remote reality for them. Many of our attitudes remain strange to them and those of us who act as informal ambassadors among them (and we are very rare) often reinforce the illusions they have about us. Except for a few researchers (specialists in French-Canadian affairs who often know as much or more about us than we do ourselves), they don't leave much room for French Canadians in their considerations. In general they are very consciously Canadian but they don't always realize that the Canada they dream of is an English Canada.

I have just asserted that this intellectual élite is very Canadian in outlook. This statement deserves to be examined more closely. What exactly does it imply?

There is not the slightest hesitation in their minds. They want to see Canada continue to exist despite the difficulties and sacrifices that its continued existence may entail. If Canada implies a constant struggle between geography (which draws us into the north-south axis and into close relationship with the United States, which tends to disrupt the political framework) and history (which by a constant effort of will maintains East-West relations and hence preserves our country), they are decidedly on the side of the history.

Why? Well, that is not so easy to say. These Canadians consent readily that they are part of the North American continent, but they want Canada to remain a distinctive separate country and are not ready even to entertain the hypothesis of a fusion between Canada and the United States.

First they prefer our political and judicial system and esteem it to be clearly superior to that of our neighbours to the south. They like the role of moderator in international conflicts that Canada has assumed, and even if they are prone to joke about the monotony, greyness, and cautiousness of their country, they like the feeling of reserve, of exercising the wisdom of a small nation sheltered against the temptations of grandeur, of scorning useless breast-beating. In short they like not being Americans.

There are some anti-Americans among them, but for the most part they like our neighbours. Only, Canadians do not intend to resemble them in all things, and they wish to preserve a certain savour which, by contrast to Americanism, might be called European. They do seem determined to endure and I think the man in the street reacts the same. Basically this might be called a British characteristic. English Canadians are not British, but their most vital roots are more British than American. The impetus given by the Loyalists has not been completely exhausted.

In this perspective French Canada may seem to represent a dangerous otherness. In the same perspective New Canadians ought to be rapidly assimilated, and it appears that to a large extent this is the case. But I am not quite sure that things are as they seem. For to assimilate New Canadians very quickly is to cut their roots, and a man who starts off from zero again might just as well become an American as a Canadian. Such political indifference is dangerous, and I felt it very strongly in the West.

There's another thing. The wish not to resemble someone else and the fact that gradually you begin to resemble him anyway are not so contradictory as they may seem. As far as popular culture is concerned, the distinction between Americans and English-speaking Westerners is very slight. Canadians are bound together by their economic interests and their political system much more than by any community of culture. That, too, is a danger and gives our country a kind of adolescent fragility.

Let me explain with an example: Radio, because its network stretches east-west, works for Canada. To accomplish that required strong intervention from the central state. The support came and the plan succeeded. Whether they like it or not, for better or for worse, most Canadians listen to Canadian radio. But with the coming of television and its technical limitations, geography reasserts itself. In Vancouver, as in Toronto, most viewers watch American television, feel perfectly at home with it, and even prefer it to our own. "It hasn't got anything to do with political loyalty," they will tell you. "We are just Canadians watching American TV because it's so much better." All right, but this split in personalities won't, perhaps, last forever. We have to pay a heavy price to keep our country intact (I think of railroads, tariffs, and the fact that the smallness of our home market condemns us to be an exporting country). We will only consent to go on paying the price as long as we feel, and want to go on feeling, different from Americans.

I know that I am intermingling two questions: Anglo-Canadian culture and the political existence of Canada. It may be that through the love of their institutions and by the strength of their socio-political structures, Anglo-Canadians can maintain a country here. But what would be the sense of such a country if everyone in it believed wholly in THE AMERICAN WAY OF LIFE? Why would we pay so much for the liberty of living on our own side of the border the lives of second-class Americans? Doubtless the leaders of our widespread village would prefer to be top dog here rather than something less in Rome—I mean Washington. But mightn't the promise of an improvement in the standard of living prove to be more powerful than the obligation to keep the mighty of Toronto, Montreal, and Ottawa in their financial and political seats? Why pay more for our cars, refrigerators, and shirts when all we're paying for is the preservation of a certain set of political structures?

It will be understood that I am speaking of what may lie in the future, of the rapid evolution that men seem to undergo here, of possible crises to come, and of the realignments of interests that might result. These worrisome thoughts which have been stirred up by my trip west have no immediate cause. Everyone today says he is happy to be Canadian even if Anglo-Canadianism is somewhat difficult to define. The central government gives the impression of relative strength, and, whatever one says, the provincial governments are full of vitality. Immigrants rush to become Canadian citizens. The United States fascinates us, frightens us because of its mass, and disturbs us because of its foreign policies. We seem to be, compared to the giant monopoly, a small independent company whose finances are sound and whose energy is apparently undiminished. Fusion is not for tomorrow.

December 22, 1955

One Hundred Pages by Pierre Elliott Trudeau

In the preface and epilogue he has written for *The Asbestos Strike*, a collection of essays published last spring by *Cité Libre*, M. Pierre Elliott Trudeau provides us with a hundred pages that will be talked about for a long time to come.

The introductory chapter, entitled "The Province of Quebec and the Depression", reviews economic and social factors and the reigning state of mind in influential circles and institutions during the last half-century. In it M. Trudeau defends a thesis which might be summarized as follows: "By their prejudice and ignorance in socio-economic matters, Quebec nationalists have long prevented their intellectual élite from seeing the dramatic changes that our people were living through, changes which amount to a real industrial revolution. When they did happen to recognize certain features of this change, the same prejudices and the same incompetence prevented them from proposing viable solutions to the problems it raised."

Stated in these terms, the thesis is partly true. But M. Trudeau gives it a particular twist by his constant aggressiveness, by the emotion that sets his pen trembling and imparts to it a ferocious irony, by setting down certain nearly absolute postulates with which to judge other postulates, and by generalizing habits of thought which crop up, unconsciously, when he is criticizing or dismissing other tendencies to generalize.

This raises a preliminary question which I would like to discuss today: Are these pages history or polemics?

To be fair to M. Trudeau and his victims it should be forcefully stated from the start that the matter in hand is a downright attack. Yes, it is polemics, and the quality is excellent: well-informed, intelligent, competent, and formulated in a style that is nervous and quick. The writer wields a wicked blade that flashes and whistles through the air with lethal precision and leaves a trail of severed heads behind it.

The corpses, however, are not really dead. M. Trudeau truly slaughters the creatures he presents to us, but they were not really real to begin with. For that matter, he knows his description of them is incomplete and faithfully warns us of the fact. In a brief funeral eulogy Caesar salutes those who are about to die. He intends, he says, to speak of them only from the economic and social point of view. "And for that reason I will have no scruples about exposing those elements of nationalist thought which encumber us at present and which impede decisive and free action." We are going to witness a regular clean-up operation.

Permit me to regret the fact. M. Trudeau's work is based on a vast amount of reading; his attempts to synthesize it are noteworthy and often obtain remarkable results; his thought is clear and lucid, his analysis pointed, keen, and simplifying by nature. I only regret that when he was so well equipped he did not write a chapter of history for us. His pen, however, portrays everything in two dimensions; his portrayal of men and doctrines sacrifices depth. Trudeau comes at them all like a partisan journalist attacking his adversaries sword in hand. Shock treatment seems to be the effect constantly sought after, to the detriment of an intelligent reading of real and fully explored events. Trudeau gives the impression that he has spontaneously chosen those elements which by today's standards seem the most absurd. One might say that from this point of view he has collected an anthology of idiocies.

His study in no way resolves the principal problem that it poses. On the contrary, it makes it a great deal foggier. In his introduction he writes that "history hardly ever takes any sharp corners, and the forces that condition the present always spring from the past." One wonders what past those who seriously approved the Asbestos strike went to for inspiration? How were such social imbeciles, whom he describes for a hundred pages, able suddenly in 1949 to see the light as soon as the strike broke out? What mysterious reflex action or what incongruous illumination prompted them? It is embarrassing to be asked to believe that such stubborn, heavy stupidity was capable of perceiving "the truth"—even if this truth came to them by the operation of some messianic message from the labour movement—a possibility, incidentally, that Trudeau is careful to skirt. The only allusions to the long development that did in fact take place in men's minds, often through a lengthy underground preparation, are made in a mention of "the rare centres of free and realistic thought" in the province (page 11), and in references to a few "exceptional" experiments (page 394) and to the reawakening provoked by the war (*ibid.*). That is quite insufficient, and leaves us with an unexplained phenomenon. This omission alone shows that the dice are loaded or at least that the presentation must be read as polemics.

What makes this all the more striking is the fact that I have just read in manuscript the thesis of an Anglo-Canadian intellectual, Mr. Michael Oliver. It treats the same period and the same climate of opinion. Its general conclusions resemble those of M. Trudeau, but the spirit in which they are drawn is very different. Mr. Oliver is not content to disengage general tendencies; he studies their genesis and stresses divergences from them. He recreates an atmosphere and paints men as they are.

Undoubtedly Mr. Oliver's over-all purpose led him to make a more careful analysis. There is something ambivalent in M.

Trudeau's intention, which is an intellectual effort undertaken at a time of crisis and with a view to inciting action. This explains the dynamism of M. Trudeau's pages and their dramatic quality, but also the partiality of the truths which he deduces or constructs. It is a case of today's "left" judging yesterday's "right", which explains his reverse dogmatism and the sometimes inhuman rigour of his illustrations and his emphasis. Perhaps this stems, far back — very far back in regions of feeling where clarity of thought never shines — from a kind of labour-inspired neo-romanticism that rejects the old ecclasiastical romanticism of the pastoral directives which his generation and many preceding ones venerated. Hence the revolt and the scorn and the fact that emotional elements run away with the argument.

But it seems to me that the author's constant aggressiveness — which delights most of his contemporaries — has its origin somewhere else. Michael Oliver speaks with a certain detachment. Pierre Elliott Trudeau can slice and separate out all he likes; his very determination to break away indicates to what an extent he feels involved in the still-recent past. He is a French Canadian deceived by his own kind. His research brings him face to face with a "monolithic" presence which intellectually he rejects, but which wounds him in his innermost being. I think he is ashamed to have had such ancestors. This feeling is so strong that he has to make a really laudable effort to be honest towards them. While Michael Oliver makes some pleasant discoveries on the way, I think I find in Trudeau the sign of a bitter deception, a contrast which comes from the two writers' very different points of departure.

As long as we understand that it is polemics we are dealing with and not history, I can say that I wholeheartedly praise Trudeau's courage. He sets out his disgust and his differences of opinion in black and white instead of burying them somewhere deep within himself. It will do a lot towards clearing the air to squarely confront issues which have for so long been treated as taboos.

II

The most valid idea in M. Trudeau's attack is his condemnation of a long-standing error: the incapacity of the French-Canadian intelligentsia to recognize the phenomenon of industrialization. There is nothing new in the discovery itself. The "agriculturalist" error has been analysed and condemned before, notably, among others, by the new school of history at the Université de Montréal. M. Trudeau associates it with nationalism. Historically, it is true, the nationalists had shown themselves to be more agriculture-minded than most. But there is no logical link between the two tendencies. The first person to have foreseen the industrial future of the province was Esdras Minville, and furthermore, the history school at the Université de Montréal is incontestably nationalist. It was the whole society that refused to accept a reality that seemed to be dangerous and evil.

If M. Trudeau had been a student of history, it would have been interesting for him to have shown how this error persisted. As a polemicist he judges it harshly and demonstrates its practical consequences. These were sterilizing. Most other recent "errors" stem from this source as well as from the incompetence of our intellectuals in social and economic matters. It is striking that with three or four exceptions — in particular M. Minville and M. Angers — all the nationalists whom Trudeau calls to the stand to speak on social and economic problems are men whose intellectual discipline is in other fields and who are, consequently, "amateurs" in the socio-economic domain. That amounts to saying that we have taken a long time to equip ourselves with experts, which surprises me less than it does M. Trudeau.

He insists on the suffocatingly provincial nature of our society. We had our taboos, it is true, and an immoderate passion for unanimity, reinforced by the fact that ideologically we were situated on the right and loved to set up the cry of "Give us leaders!" Personally, I don't believe such leaders would have been very well served, for the society was, curiously enough, made up of individualists. But at least the cry went up for them loudly, and M. Trudeau demonstrates this forcefully.

But a more exhaustive analysis of the minority concept might have explained why. We are not the first group in the world who, in order to survive in difficult conditions, cut itself off, rigorously hewed to its basic ideology, and pitilessly excluded all foreign elements. M. Trudeau notes this. He calls it a "Security System". Then he forgets it more or less and chastises every incidence of intolerance that he meets on his way. God knows there was no shortage of them. M. Trudeau doesn't miss one.

A detailed analysis of his thought, confronting it with appropriate texts and an experience of the period, would take more time and space than I now have. I will have to content myself with pointing out several examples that show how M. Trudeau simplifies to an extreme and how his hostility, even at the very moment that he is making an astute analysis of reality, tends to accentuate one side of the question to the point of caricature.

I don't choose my examples at random. I choose those that best illustrate how he distorts, or those that I know from first-hand experience. It is a question not of his dishonesty but of the passion of his opinions, which to my mind leads to an oversimplification.

During the Depression l'Abbé Groulx wrote: "I do not claim that if we had captains of industry and financiers among us we would be socially better off. But social ills would remain social ills, and the passionate element which dangerously inflames them would be absent." Trudeau comments: "As if to say that a native capitalism would have spared us all difficulties that might be accompanied by a 'passionate element'." That is easy irony. Trudeau implies that for l'Abbé Groulx there is no passionate element in social ills themselves. Does he seriously believe that this represents the historian's thought? What l'Abbé Groulx meant was that the nationalist question risked inflaming a conflict which we knew at the time to be acute everywhere. Trudeau's literalism belongs to the literature of combat.

Of the school of social sciences at the Université de Montréal, Trudeau writes: "The professors had no guarantee of tenure and the great majority of them had never published anything to demonstrate their competence in the social sciences." That's true on the whole, but where would we have found really specialized professors except abroad? It would be most obliging if M. Trudeau would draw up a retrospective list for, say, the years 1920-30. He continues: "Courses were given in catch-as-catch-can fashion with the collaboration of a few good souls and the chance participation of a number of visiting firemen." Let us pay our respects to the visiting firemen in passing, and absorb the criticism. Edouard Montpetit was the first, in private, to recognize the "amateur" character of part of this teaching. Its mediocrity had nothing to do with the "racial" considerations which M. Trudeau lends it, in a reflex which has become a professional tic. It resulted first of all from the intellectual poverty of the milieu and from the financial penury of all our non-professional faculties. Specialists could only be obtained by sending young students for long periods of study abroad or by importing foreign experts, and then by offering the former a decent salary and a job teaching in their specialty. Either system was expensive, and no one was ready to foot the bill. In a society which had always done without economists and sociologists, it wasn't easy to plead the necessity of having them. If Laval succeeded in 1938 in founding a social science faculty, it was thanks to the personal gifts and extraordinary initiative of Father Georges H. Lévesque. And the fact remains that even in 1956 most of our faculties where research and pure science are pursued are vegetating, not because of nationalism or even because of incompetence, but because of insufficient funding and the lack of a proper intellectual climate. The politicians are the ones to blame. M. Trudeau acknowledges this (pp. 18 and 19) but all the weight of his attack is directed against others.

And here, finally, is all the author finds to say about co-operative ventures in French Canada. After a brief tribute to the Caisses Populaires he writes: "But if the co-operative movement met with a certain success in the country and among fishermen, it failed miserably in the towns. This institution presupposes a sense of democratic responsibility and of collective ownership, two notions which the fear of socialism—especially in the cities—obliged us to stifle systematically." What does that mean? That the general climate in our milieu favoured neither the sense of personal responsibility nor that of collective ownership? It's true. But it is also true that the propaganda for co-operatives acted as a democratic ferment and as an initiation to other forms of ownership. In the country the propagandists were treated as Communists. In the circumstances it must be said that they achieved remarkable success. Does it hold, as M. Trudeau suggests, that the atmosphere was less authoritarian there or that the fear of Communism was less?

As for their failure in the cities, it was not only due to the reasons he mentions later on. I would single out in particular the constant lack of interest that unions showed in the movement. That is understandable, but it is none the less a fact.

III

Now let's move on to political issues. Here again one recognizes the offhand manner and the annoying superiority of tone that Trudeau adopts in the presence of developments which have not perhaps been fully realized long but which just the same have been slowly and painfully achieved. That is the accent he takes when he speaks of l'Action Libérale Nationale.

He rarely allows us to measure the decades that are necessary for a society, any human society, to re-orient itself, to discover and assimilate one tiny truth. The tempo of a social milieu is not that of an intellectual, and to clearly establish the effectiveness or ineffectiveness of any political or social action, one must carefully mark the point of departure and the point of arrival.

L'Action Libérale Nationale was in a vital way our C.C.F. It was nationalist (but national socialisms do exist), much more diffuse than the C.C.F. because its doctrine was less well integrated, and more confused too, because politicians had a hand in it. M. Trudeau alludes to this several times when he judges our social ideas. Then he devotes exactly thirteen lines to the political side of the movement, while according twenty-eight to Social Credit. I would not employ this curious statistical method if M. Trudeau had not set the example himself on several occasions. Now, one can understand precisely nothing about the A.L.N. after these thirteen lines. The economist Trudeau leapfrogs over it. He gives no idea of the great anti-trust movement of 1933-6 which shook the province and aroused so many anti-capitalist hopes. He never even hints that thousands of people, spurred on by nationalism and by revolt against a corrupt government, reached a certain degree of radicalism and began to discover some aspects of the industrial geography of the province (even though "back to the land" remained the dominant concept). The result, no doubt, was a failure since at the end of the road was M. Duplessis. When that came the men who had launched the movement abandoned it.

"It was a great deception. But since French Canadians study politics with their feet, the same men were to commit exactly the same errors a few years later." Once again the historical portrait is turned to caricature. The Bloc Populaire chalked up many errors because it lacked an organization and a political doctrine, but it did not commit "exactly the same errors". It is also quite irresponsible to judge a political movement exclusively by its platform, simply by selecting dissimilar elements in it and clashing them together. I do not see a single reference to the parliamentary action of Le Bloc, where it certainly revealed itself as much as in a set of pompous documents. M. Trudeau, who would be quite ready to weigh out fly shit if he thought it would make the nationalists smell worse (see for example the full page devoted to a brief presented by the Société Saint-Jean-Baptiste), in Le Bloc's case passes abruptly on to Social Credit; the tone changes and the author becomes suddenly almost understanding.

"It is important to distinguish clearly between Catholic social morality as developed by certain Popes who were particularly attentive to the upheavals that have wracked modern societies, and the social doctrine of the Church as it was interpreted and applied in French Canada." So we were to have "our own" Catholic social doctrine, just as we have our own maple syrup. The formula is neat but it scarcely corresponds to reality. Apart from a few indigenous patterns (like our enthusiasm for small industry), the movements M. Trudeau is talking about were common to all Christian Socialists of the period—corporatism principally, but even the "back to the land" movement, co-operatives, and Catholic labour unions. The author had only to think of what was being written at the time on these same subjects in France and Belgium.

In reality the "Church's social doctrine" in Quebec was only "our own" by the emphasis we put on certain questions (such as return to the land) or by certain applications we made of it (for example, our insistence that we obtain such and such a measure from the provincial government rather than from Ottawa, a type of question that never arose in non-federal states). As for the rest, we were slavish imitators. Not perhaps a very glorious role, but it drastically deflates M. Trudeau's "our own".

Corporatism in particular had an intense vogue in France and Belgium with Catholics of the right and centre. *Les Semaines Sociales de France* published a great deal on it. This doctrine, far from being part of our peculiar folklore as M. Trudeau believes, is to a large extent the reflection of attitudes that were French, Belgian, in certain cases Portuguese and Austrian, even Italian. This does not in any sense alter any fundamental questions, but it reveals the author's passion for hunting out highly particularized blemishes, a sort of inverted nationalism that he frequently falls prey to.

I will take my last example from close to home. It is well known what exposure was given to labour problems when M. Gérard Filion took over the editorship of Le Devoir. "Police-stick justice" was a phrase coined in 1947, two years before the Asbestos strike. Close coverage of the labour scene was a conscious and concerted part of editorial policy. Soon M. Gérard Pelletier and then M. Fernand Dansereau were specially assigned to follow the problem closely. That won us relentless enmity and incomprehension in some quarters, as well as warm support. I'm not asking whether we were right or wrong, I'm just stating a fact.

In a chapter in Trudeau's book entitled "The Strike and the Press", M. Gérard Pelletier sums up very justly the attitude of Le Devoir during the Asbestos strike. M. Trudeau speaks of it too. But he only mentions Le Devoir's connection with two other strikes, the meat packers' and the Devoir typographers' strikes, both of which we were against. Framed up this way, our attitude during the Asbestos strike takes on the complexion of a passing fancy. Our real labour policy, according to M. Trudeau, was one of "social immobility", a judgement based on two citations when two hundred others would have proved the contrary. Is the reader really expected to believe that "in social matters" we aligned ourselves "more and more with conservative elements"? At this point M. Trudeau's simplifications trail off towards the absurd. One can understand their sentimental genesis: his essay was written just after the strike at Le Devoir, when certain of our friends believed that we had veered back to the extreme right. M. Trudeau indicates a similar interpretation in a note where he charitably allows that Le Devoir's social policy is not quite that of Notre Temps.

After this discussion, does it seem contradictory to say that M. Trudeau's essay is a document of great positive value? The author lays charges; he wants to see heads fall, and we have noted that his guillotine functions a little arbitrarily. But time after time, just after he has made too harsh a judgement, he lays bare a new truth, or at least one which few minds would have had the courage to formulate. That is why, when one reads his essay straight through at one sitting, according to one's frame of mind it seems either crushing or liberating. Both reactions are inherent in his prose, which is incisive, probing, and indiscreet.

If I judge these pages to be a good tonic then, it is because they take as their principal target some of the permanent weaknesses which we always wish to close our eyes to. For example, the slowness of French Canadians to tackle social problems in themselves; the tardy and often unrealistic character of their legislation in this domain; the chauvinism and grotesque boasting that accompany it; the almost universal incompetence in economic matters; and the mental sloth that makes us prefer a ritualistic repetition of old formulas to basic research. All that can be explained, but it also exists, and it is M. Trudeau's role to expose it in painful relief. When the author frees himself from immediate problems he can create striking historical perspectives (pp. 394-5). He has written some excellent pages on the religion of authority in our politics which casts doubt on the quality of our faith in a democratic regime and our adhesion to it. The best part of Trudeau, besides his technical competence, is his love of liberty: he is prepared to run its risks as well as claim its advantages. A remarkable personality has been revealed.

October 6, 10, and 11, 1956

What Sauce Would You Like To Be Eaten With?

Several French Canadians recently appeared on a panel on English television discussing whether provincial autonomy is essential to preserve French-Canadian culture. Towards the end of the program, the host, Mr. Frank Scott, asked them the following question: "Where does the greater danger lie, in centralization or in Americanization?"

I would not like to misinterpret Mr. Scott, for he has a clear and subtle mind which is never simplistic, but if he asked this question, is it not because in the opinion of many Anglo-Canadians it points up a dilemma? Centralization is for them the best way to combat Americanization.

The roots of this attitude strike far back into the past. Where, for example, did Confederation come from? On the Anglo-Canadian side, the wish to protect the British colonies in North America against the enterprising dynamism of the United States was certainly one of the essential factors. All historians agree on this. All also recognize the fact that Sir John A. Macdonald wished to see established a strongly centralized Dominion, for a state in which sovereignty was exclusively invested in a central authority seemed to him the best protection. The insularity of the Maritime provinces, but above all the opposition of French Canadians prevented the Conservative chief's project from taking the shape he wished. Canada exists first of all thanks to the British fidelity of Anglo-Canadians; if it exists as a kind of Confederation, it is due mainly to the French fidelity of French Canadians.

In English-speaking provinces, regionalism has become less intense. Infatuation with provincial autonomy does not exactly intoxicate anyone, either in B.C., where it is openly advocated, or in Nova Scotia, which is traditionally preoccupied with local problems. In fact, political regionalism is practically moribund almost everywhere. And if it appears so vigorous in Quebec, that is because it is not so much a feeling of regionalism as one of having to defend a particular culture.

For the average Anglo-Canadian the existence of the smaller provinces is simply absurd. Take the tiniest of them all, Prince Edward Island. Its population is smaller than that of Quebec City alone. It is an island of extremely modest dimensions. It would have been totally incapable of creating a viable system of social security. Having its own radio and television would have been unthinkable. It can neither build up nor maintain a full-scale educational system. And we are far from exhausting this catalogue of its incapacities.

Whoever tried to defend a tradition of autonomy for this province would chain the island to the parochial narrowness and condemn it to the poverty of its limited means. Try out the kind of declarations we make in Quebec down there—they sound absurd. Move up the scale a little and try them in a province like New Brunswick—it may be a little less ridiculous to talk about a certain type of autonomy, but on the whole it still sounds silly.

What, in the eyes of Anglo-Canadians, are these small and medium-sized provinces? A collection of scattered weaknesses. They would never have been able to do alone what Canadian television has done: build up at least a kind of protective barrier against American TV. In this sense centralization has been a way for the small provinces to fight against Americanization. And the same is true in education.

In our eyes, however, the problem is very different. When you ask someone from Quebec which constitutes the greater danger to his culture, centralization or Americanization, it's a little like asking a father which disease he would prefer his children to catch: "Which in your opinion would be the least dangerous, scarlet fever or diphtheria?"

In the present state of our medical knowledge, scarlet fever—that is, centralization—seems to us to be the less noxious. But the truly mortal malady would be a dose of scarlet fever on top of a case of diphtheria—that is, centralization on top of Americanization. For one isn't necessarily the antidote to the other. In fact, just the contrary.

It's always the same old problem of which sauce you'd like to be eaten with. "But what if I don't want to be eaten at all?"

The most precious thing that provincial autonomy has given French Canadians is a territory where they can live as a majority and where they can create their own institutions. In a very relative way they are able to live here the experience of self-government. It doesn't always suit them very well. But its value is irreplaceable. If this container should fail them, their cultural life, like a liquid, would seep away on every side and they would risk losing the most essential part of it. (I speak, of course, of their national culture.)

So when all is said, the reply to Frank Scott's question is diametrically opposed if your culture is English or French. The Anglo-Canadian finds in Ottawa, on a larger scale, what he already has in his provincial capital. In Ottawa the French Canadian is, by definition, in the minority. In the eyes of the former, centralization appears to be a rampart against American influence; in the eyes of the latter, it spells the ruin of his best line of defence.

Since this is so, isn't it time to think about restructuring Confederation? Would it not be realistic to think of the Canada of tomorrow as a federation grouping five great provinces: the traditional ones (British Columbia, Ontario, and Quebec), and two new ones (the Prairies and the Maritimes)? Or should we be searching in the direction of a true double system where Quebec alone would constitute the second half of a new régime? And are other solutions feasible?

The fact is that if both sides were to put their cards on the table and stop bluffing, French-Canadian and English-Canadian positions would be seen to be squarely antagonistic. It would be just as well to recognize that honestly and to begin, in all modesty, to seek out a viable solution.

January 13, 1958

How To "Weld" Us

In Toronto last week Mr. Diefenbaker claimed to be hunting for "a way to weld together" Canadians of every origin. He has always worked to further this unity, he reminded us, and his efforts "were crowned with a certain success in 1946 when citizens were authorized for the first time to be registered in the Canadian census without indicating their ethnic origin".

This is a restatement of some of the ideas that Mr. Diefenbaker expressed in his *Maclean*'s interview before his electoral triumph. We pointed out then the ambiguity of some of his pronouncements, which seemed to be pointing towards "melting pot" politics. The Prime Minister gave them an almost mystical accent, in which we thought we could decipher the trace of painful experiences that had marked his own childhood. In Toronto, Mr. Diefenbaker took up this theme again in less passionate terms: "Every one of us, throughout his life, has a particular project which he holds dear. Mine, because I was of mixed origins, was to obtain Canadian nationality."

Should we interpret this declaration in a restricted sense? Does Mr. Diefenbaker only wish by it to foil some census-taker's question which he finds offensive and wrong? Or does he wish to unite Canadians more closely politically, and what exactly does *that* mean to his way of thinking? How far does the unity he is seeking go, and does it risk interfering with a particular culture—our own?

If it is only to be taken in the restricted sense, Mr. Diefenbaker is talking about a battle that has already been more than half won. The question about ethnic origin disappeared from the "intermediate" census in 1946. And it was not reintroduced in its entirety in that of 1951.

At that time, in 1951, the editors of *Le Devoir* demonstrated that this modification was, in scientific terms, a regression. The Dominion Bureau of Statistics had enjoyed a high reputation throughout the world. I can remember hearing André Siegfried praise it in the precincts of Le Collège de France more than twenty years ago. The famous geographer cited the wealth of information provided by our service and, generally speaking, its accuracy. One may thus question why we would decide to impoverish our own sources of information, all the more since the question about ethnic origin has nothing degrading about it. Nobody here is forced to wear a yellow star, or a red or a green one. It is just a matter of collecting information.

Information like this can be useful to others beyond the scientific researcher. It can permit an ethnic group—and obviously I am thinking of French Canadians—to measure their progress or their decline. If for example, we have been able to register the losses experienced by French minorities in this country, it is by comparing the statistics which record ethnic origin with those which record Canadians' mother-tongues. Thanks to them, we can better realize what is happening to us. Why deprive us of such information?

Clearly, knowing such statistics does in a sense have a conservative effect. They might be used to back up certain claims and to give them a semi-official character. By informing the minority about a certain decline they may stimulate its will to live and provoke the creation of new institutions. Such a reaction must seem legitimate except to those who wish to see here a mixing of cultures, which would mean eventually the disappearance of the weaker ones.

And this is precisely why Mr. Diefenbaker's remarks are disturbing. Our country possesses a political structure very different from the one that Americans have chosen for themselves. By and large we have not welcomed mixing races, and we have refused assimilation—two of the acknowledged aims of the cultural policies of our neighbours.

Any unity achieved by cultural deracination would make us dangerously like the Americans. It would lead to the loss of one of our most original traits and one of our principal *raisons d'être*. In the long run, French Canadians would lose in this venture not only their language but also their own distinctive character and their most vital Canadian ties.

The whole subject remains vague precisely because Mr. Diefenbaker's remarks are imprecise. They can be treated as innocuous, and the example he constantly gives when he touches on the subject (the question of ethnic origin in the Canadian census) tends to confirm this interpretation. On the other hand, the solemnity of his tone and the sincerity and gravity of his words lead one to suspect more serious intentions. "A way to weld us together to assure the unity of Canadians of every origin" must mean more than an amendment to the census questionnaire.

The Prime Minister would reassure many Canadians if he revealed to us the true depths of his thought on this question. Failing this, we will begin to feel uneasy when we recall that the C.B.C., the National Film Board, and other important federal services now controlled by Mr. Diefenbaker are impressive tools for influencing public opinion.

June 10, 1958

The
Nigger-King Hypothesis

Last Friday M. Maurice Duplessis had a *Le Devoir* reporter, M. Guy Lamarche, brutally ejected from his office.

The reporter was attending the Premier's press conference. He hadn't lifted a finger, hadn't uttered a word. He was just there. That was enough to trigger Duplessis's anger. "Get out!" shouted the Premier. The journalist, thinking that he was within his normal rights in a democratic country, refused to obey. So Duplessis had him thrown out by the provincial police.

Three different groups of journalists have protested against this behaviour in immediate recognition of the gravity of the situation. A reporter "duly assigned by his paper to cover the Premier's press conference" should be able to "freely exercise his trade". That is the most modest claim that could be put foward by the profession.

On the other hand, the newspapers themselves in their editorial pages have proved to be very philosophical about the matter. Except in two cases, they have said nothing at all. We will not be so insulting as to conclude that they felt nothing. The press is the natural guardian, not only of freedom of expression, but also of that other freedom which sustains and protects the first: the freedom of access to the sources of information. So the expulsion of a reporter from a press conference which was theoretically open to all could not but be viewed with alarm. Let's just say that the papers seemed better able than the journalists to contain their indignation.

For if M. Duplessis starts playing favourites, everyone knows that sooner or later it may be his turn to be victim. What's to prevent the Premier from repeating his *Le Devoir* performance against some other paper? This time it was a press conference, next, by the same principle, it may be a debate in Parliament.

And what principle am I referring to? To the principle of arbitrariness, M. Duplessis believes, and we do not doubt his sincerity, that political power is his own personal property. He uses it as he pleases. His friends receive his favours. Friendly counties get special treatment. Members of the Opposition in the Legislative Assembly deserve in his eyes no more than partial rights; he treats them as if they had not been elected as legitimately as the majority.

M. Duplessis seems to think that it is fair game to starve out the opposition; whether in jobs or roads, schools or bridges, only his favourites are well served. He is now applying this principle to the newspapers. His chosen adversaries aren't even worthy to hear him speak. He has picked out the newspapers he considers to be loyal to him and is beginning to exclude the rest.

Such arbitrariness runs counter to democracy and to the practices of a parliamentary government.

As a rule the English are more sensitive than we are to any infringement on their liberties. That is why M. Duplessis has had a bad press outside Quebec. But the attacks he has been subject to in Ontario or Manitoba have not always been inspired by such considerations; the old prejudices of language and race have often been loudly in evidence. It would be a mistake, however, to explain everything by ethnic prejudice. The British won their political freedom by slow degrees; they are all the more aware of the price exacted; they are usually extremely sensitive to dangers that threaten it.

Usually, I say. For in Quebec this tradition seems to be singularly anaemic, at least to judge by what the English papers in the province have to say about Quebec affairs.

When it's a question of the majority *in Ottawa* trying to gag the minority, why, all the papers protest in chorus and set up a noble din. All the English papers, including those from Quebec, proclaim quite rightly that the government is violating important parliamentary liberties. Urged on by the press, public opinion is galvanized, and the whole question becomes a factor leading, as it did in the pipeline debate, to the downfall of the government.

In the Legislative Assembly in Quebec incidents of this kind are a dime a dozen. Yet our English-language newspapers tolerate them, scarcely ever raising a murmur in protest. Why?

The expulsion of Guy Lamarche last Friday was hard to take. To begin with, the English papers said nothing. Five days later, in the middle of an article favourable to the government, the

Gazette registered a protest, but a chillier statement would be hard to imagine. The next day the *Star* declared that M. Duplessis's behaviour was clumsy but couldn't bring itself to judge it wrong. Why?

The English papers in Quebec act like British administrators in an African colony. Wise in the arts of political science, the British rarely destroy the political institutions of a conquered country. They keep a close check on the nigger-king but they wink at his whims. On occasion they permit him to chop off a few heads; it's just part of the local folklore. But one thing would never occur to them: to expect the nigger-king to conform to the high moral and political standards of the British.

The main thing is to get the nigger-king to support and protect British interests. Once this collaboration is assured, the rest is less important. Does the princeling violate democratic principles? What else can you expect of the natives? . . .

I am not attributing these attitudes to the English minority in Quebec. But it is as though some of their leaders subscribed to the theory and practice of the nigger-king hypothesis. They pardon in M. Duplessis, chief of the native people of Quebec, things they would not tolerate in one of their own kind.

You can see it in the Legislative Assembly. We saw it in the last municipal election. We have just seen it demonstrated again in Quebec.

The result is a regression in democratic and parliamentary practices, the entrenchment of unchallenged arbitrariness in government, and constant collusion between Anglo-Quebec financial interests and the rottenest elements in provincial politics.

July 4, 1958

Inside French America

Americanitis is an old ulcer of ours, a familiar complaint. For years we lived in trepidation at being "an island of spirituality in the midst of an ocean of materialism". We didn't, as you can see, exaggerate the physical dimensions of our dilemma, but we believed we possessed "a supplement of soul" sufficient to re-establish the equilibrium.

Those happy days are no more. It is true that we tried to protect our integrity by a high-principled ignorance of everything that happened "south of the border". Alas, if the frontier was a more or less effective obstacle against certain ideas, it prevented neither men nor things from passing. Consequently we lost more than a million French Canadians for whom even the noblest brand of misery was no longer palatable, and in return imported U.S. capital, refrigerators, and cars.

American influence, though not exclusive, continues to be one of our favourite sore points. Yet the more we denounce it, the more American films we show, the more we go to New York or Old Orchard Beach, the more U.S. magazines we read, the more we pattern our habits on American models. So the judgements we pronounce against Americans, while they continue to be harsh, have suffered some loss of conviction, until today the average French Canadian—the man who doesn't exist though we meet him every day—feels a kind of inner contradiction and is beginning to wonder how much longer he can go on preaching what he has all but ceased to practise.

This old sad theme was recently reworked at Sainte-Agathe. The Canadian Institute of Public Affairs bravely tackled it once again, though, from what one can gather from newspaper and TV reports, in terms that remained rather vague. Vagueness, it appears, is a necessary concomitant of such a subject: it is too vast, too complex; it strains everyone's prophetic powers and throws everyone back on his own fears and hopes.

Observers this time say that what strikes them is a change in atmosphere. One does not find today in intellectual circles in French Canada the hostility once manifested towards American culture. Now that we have lost a little of that really too naïve confidence in our own works and even in our own destiny, we can no longer indulge that cheap anti-Americanism which used to be rampant. Our academies have discovered that American universities exist, produce, invent, and lead in many fields, that good research is done there, that the equipment is magnificent, that collaborators are numerous, and that in comparison to these institutions our own scarcely deserve to be called universities.

At the conference surprise was expressed that so many French Canadians live in ignorance of the leading western power which happens to be our next-door neighbour. We absorb American influence on the "popular" level, which means some of its most questionable aspects, but at the same time we are slow to take advantage of its real riches.

To state the problem in these terms is to answer it already. Who could claim ignorance as a safeguard or as a basis for a political stance? Intellectual contacts with our only neighbour must be pursued.

In addition we have often been in the habit of calling "American" things which are simply modern—the consequences of technical developments which the whole planet is due to experience. They reach us as imports because we didn't invent them; they keep an American flavour because we haven't completely assimilated them. But wherever machines have settled in, these products proliferate and they have nothing specifically to do with Hollywood or policies of the State Department.

In this regard, as in the case of certain other influences which are geographically continental, we are swallowed up in the ineluctable.

The important thing, however, is to preserve our roots. We are, despite ourselves, Americans; despite ourselves part of the twentieth century; despite ourselves neighbours of the United States. But by our origins we remain attached to a great European culture. To forget that would be to act like barbarians. To cut ourselves off from our roots would be to condemn us to desiccation.

To deny one's self in order to live someone else's adventure is, humanly speaking, an exceedingly lame solution.

October 7, 1958

The Logic of the System?

To express surprise that a French-Canadian nationalist is not at the same time a separatist, because it follows in "the logic of the system", is a little like being surprised to learn that socialists are not Communists. "The logic of the system" hasn't got much to do with it.

Nationalism as it exists here is founded on a particular culture which it loves, is determined to defend, and wants to be free to develop. It does not follow that this must lead to a political break-up.

Naturally, a nationalism which is primarily cultural seeks support elsewhere; it knows that culture doesn't live in the clouds but among men, and that men have economic and political interests. If these interests and the institutions that serve them are at odds with the culture, little by little the culture will be abandoned. So nationalism is led to examine such relationships very closely.

Does this mean that politically speaking nationalism must necessarily lead to separatism? The first observation to be made is that except in a few cases, once the enthusiasm of the first discovery is past, most nationalists have not followed that path. Why is this so?

For most it was a question of being realistic. Separatism was rejected once and for all because it was judged to be unrealizable.

The secession of Quebec would break Canada in two. What Canadian government would accept such a misadventure? What party would accept letting Canada go the way of Pakistan? It is impossible to see how such a schism could take place amicably. Would it have to be imposed, then, by force of arms as the Confederates tried to do in the United States? The question seems a little far-fetched. What arms does Quebec possess? A little common sense is enough to remove such temptations in most cases.

There is also the political climate in which we live. French Canadians do not seem ready to imitate Africans or Asians who have resorted to the tactics of the weak—to terrorism and setting up an underground. In the present context and in North America, that solution too, fortunately, seems mere fantasy.

Separation, then, seems impossible to almost everyone. Some go further and assert that it is not desirable. Henri Bourassa believed in Confederation. His nationalism, which was very active, got along very well with federalism. The advantages of having political institutions that were entirely independent seemed to him to be outweighed by the dangers of being cast back on our own resources.

The idea of Quebec separatism is based on the principle of nationalities: that is, each nationality should have the right to organize its own independent state. This principle has caused more difficulties than it has solved. It has spread anarchy through parts of Europe and has added to the risk of war. Practically speaking it is often impossible to apply because it goes against geography, legitimate economic interests, and political stability. There is no guarantee that it will succeed any better in Africa.

There are other facts which are as evident to French-Canadian nationalists as to anyone. We share with Anglo-Canadians two centuries of common history. It began badly and often continued badly, dividing us as much as it united us. But the inverse is also true. Because of it, we feel bound by common concerns.

We feel this more since the ties of Empire have loosened and Canada, not so much in its sovereignty but as an independent power and as a people with clearly defined characteristics, has become more and more threatened by the proximity and power of the United States.

We are not the only ones attached to the idea that Canada must persist and develop distinct from the States. It is perhaps a risky wager; at all events, it will be difficult to win if we remain together, lost if we separate. A small Laurentian state preserving some of the political customs we have come to call Duplessism but which antedate Duplessis will not advance by one iota the culture on which our nationalism is founded. It is in no way a desirable ideal.

It remains for us to organize our common life, to profit fully from the status quo, to defend when necessary that portion of independence and liberty which we have carved out for ourselves within Canada. In other words we must find a formula for collaboration which will keep us from being crushed. It is a difficult task. Facts crop up constantly which show to what degree a whole segment of the Canadian population continues to refuse to accept us, or wants to impose upon us living conditions which amount to eradication. That is just part of the daily struggle.

But to fight hard for a vital and precious autonomy for Quebec does not mean that one shamefully hides separatist sympathies in the inner recesses of one's heart. In the present instance "the logic of the system" resides in the brain of the adversary. Which does not mean that it corresponds to a secret compulsion of Quebec nationalism.

January 14, 1960

Logic and Realism in Politics

Separatists are people who like to write. In general they do it very well. Besides, the separatist position, stemming as it does from nationalism, is one which can be defended very ably—on paper. It is an attitude that is clear, stimulating, and above all "logical". It is the kind that wins over young minds. It is normal, or in any case perfectly acceptable, to be separatist at twenty-five. At thirty-five, it's more problematic.

M. Pierre Bourgault accused me yesterday of having lost "the faith". He means his faith. But just as I can hardly reproach him for being young, he is perhaps wrong to hold me to blame for being twice his age. No doubt he doesn't take such a strictly mathematical view of things; nor do I for that matter. What I mean is that it would be too bad to have lived so long without learning anything.

M. Bourgault asserts that separatism is realistic and that we have ceased to be so. But he is confusing realism and logic.

185

Basing his arguments on realistic observations about the position that we hold within Canada, the separatist logically deduces a solution that has nothing realistic about it, a solution that is neither workable nor livable and which could not be translated into facts. No one has yet shown us how Quebec could achieve its independence. Neither René Lévesque's witticisms, nor allusions (a little dishonest, it seems to me, in the context) to Anglo-Canadians' sense of fair play, nor falling back on the precedent of decolonization, are really arguments. What if forty colonies have recently gained their independence? That doesn't presume in any way that a country solidly constituted is going to let itself be broken in two without resisting.

Quebec is not an island in mid-Atlantic. Its departure from Canada means the death of Canada. I cannot see how a Canadian government could accept without a violent reaction—or at the least a vigorous reaction—the ruin of a country that it has been administering for the past century.

In addition, separatists wish by means of a political revolution to solve a problem that reaches beyond politics and whose present roots stretch into causes that lie outside Canada. I don't expect to convert anyone overnight, I just ask that all elements of the situation be thought through and carefully weighed.

If as a people we often feel in mortal peril, that doesn't come from being a minority within Canada. At one against two we have long known how to fight and resist and move forward. The danger in all its amplitude comes from the presence beside us of the United States—a culture which surrounds us, leans on us, infiltrates us, and is embodied in a people who are numerous and rich. With them beside us, it is no longer one against two but one against thirty. This disproportion would remain even if Quebec became independent.

Is it argued that we would be protected by a political frontier? But the frontier exists already and we know that it doesn't hold out much. Our only protection lies in our lives themselves, in our capacity to live and to create.

It so happens that Anglo-Canadians are caught up in this game too, and that they risk losing their existence as Canadians even more than we do. In this respect they are allies, not out of the goodness of their hearts, nor because of a love of French culture, but because geography and political institutions draw us together.

Thanks to their presence we are seventeen million—instead of six—who are not and who do not want to be Americans. It is not an easy liaison: collectively the results we have produced in either the cultural or the economic fields are meagre indeed. The easy solution is all on the side of Americanization—and it would remain so even within the borders of the independent State of Quebec.

It is true that if the Anglo-Canadian mass helps us, it also causes us problems. The central state as it now operates, whenever it functions and wherever it administers, is a denationalizing force. Take the French network of the C.B.C. for example: on the production level it's French, but on the administrative level it's English. And in most federal ministries the situation is even more absurd and deceiving.

That's what separatism rears up against. As a protest it makes sense: meet refusal with refusal. Perhaps it will make part of the Anglo-Canadian élite realize how scandalous and intolerable we find this state of affairs. But I cannot see how—except by very devious paths—the separatists' revolt can have positive and useful results. I spoke about the deception that young separatists were courting. This view of their future is based obviously on a profound conviction, which is that they are going to run up against a brick wall. I am afraid that at that time, tired of chasing the impossible and used to dreaming in absolutes, they may turn away from solutions which, though not so exciting, remain realizable.

On the political level the main solution consists in using to the maximum those powers that we already possess. It consists in thinking of the provincial state of Quebec as the tool, a less powerful but more useful tool, for realizing a political program which corresponds to our needs and to our way of thinking. This has never yet been accomplished. It is a task which part of the French-Canadian intelligentsia has always systematically refused to accept and which successive governments have spurned. M. Jean Lesage assures us that he will undertake it. We will judge him by his works. But I maintain that such an enterprise is possible. We would be wrong, in the hopes of realizing some Utopia, to turn away from the more modest goal, for it will require the enthusiasm and energy of a whole generation.

March 8, 1961

A Proposal for an Inquiry into Bilingualism

If one had to judge the policies of the Diefenbaker government by the speech from the throne, one would have to conclude that their main characteristic is their refusal to face major issues.

In my opinion, three problems outweigh all others:

1. Economics: the problem of built-in unemployment and the options available in view of Great Britain's plans to join the Common Market.

2. Defence: the decision formally to accept or refuse nuclear warheads on Canadian soil.

3. Confederation: here there are problems far more important than simply repatriating the Canadian Constitution, let alone the question of bilingual cheques.

Neither nostalgic musings nor muteness will solve these problems. It is true, of course, that governments need not reveal all their intentions at the very beginning of a parliamentary session, also that just before an election they may wish to keep back some surprises. If that is the case they will excuse me for tackling one of the three problems conspicuous by its absence from the official document, that of French-Canadian participation in Confederation.

Do I intend to reopen the question of bilingual cheques? Barely. I consider the problem outdated. If it is raised again it will be both too little and too late.

Is it true that the Prime Minister intended to promise them but that pressure from a group of some sixty-odd Tories forced him to back down? Whether this manoeuvre is a sign of stubbornness or of ill-will, I would gladly write off the question of bilingual cheques altogether for the time being, if the government would consent, even without the hope of finding an immediate solution, to examine the problem in all its amplitude.

188

Bilingual cheques is a tardy measure which in no way corresponds to the present aspirations of the French-Canadian people. They have had enough of these little concessions meted out once every ten years. What they want, if their presence within Confederation is truly desired, are reforms much more general in nature.

I am ready to accept that no government today—under a Diefenbaker, a Pearson, or a Douglas—could make these reforms overnight. I would go farther than that: after nearly a century of Confederation no one knows exactly what, in fact, a completely bilingual state could be. Prime ministers succeed one another, all employing the same formulas which in no significant way alter reality, and no one has any clear idea what official state bilingualism should or could be. The separatists make hay out of such a situation. And let's admit it—French-Canadian politics consist in asking Ottawa for a sizeable chunk of the pie while Ottawa politics, according to the election results, consist in doling out crumbs.

Personally, I would like to propose a moratorium on crumbs; no bilingual cheques, no new bilingual labels, no more piecemeal concessions for a while. And instead of them a royal commission on bilingualism.

Such a commission would have three objectives:

1. To find out what Canadians from coast to coast think of the subject. That would perhaps be a good way to lance the abscess. We might as well stop kidding ourselves; there is nothing to lose from knowing the truth. This way individual citizens, different groups, associations, and provinces would have a chance to say how English-speaking and French-speaking Canadians react to the question.

2. To study very closely how countries like Belgium and Switzerland which are faced with the same problems are dealing with them.

3. To examine, again very closely, the role played by the two languages in the federal civil service.

From this mass of facts, the commissioners should be able to disengage some firm and clear principles upon which the government, in its own good time, could construct a policy for bilingualism.

Of course the inquiry must be entrusted to men who inspire confidence in both Canadian communities; they must be granted complete freedom of action, and must be generously provided with the means to pursue their triple inquiry. And let the inquiry last as long as necessary—eighteen months, two years, three if need be.

On the one hand, creating such a commission does not compromise the government dangerously; at the most it means that they recognize that a serious problem exists.

On the other hand there is a growing unrest among French Canadians which is becoming more and more acute. Do people think that it is so unimportant that it can be left to degenerate indefinitely? At the present time no one is doing anything about it except the separatists; the others are content to say that Confederation should be reformed. But nobody says how or to what extent. It is time for action from those who believe in the future of Canada *under certain fundamental conditions.*

At stake is the French language, the language spoken by nearly a third of the population of Canada. At stake is the participation of nearly a third of Canadian people in the life and administration of the central government. I address this challenge not only to the politicians but to the whole of English Canada.

Paris, history reminds us, was worth a mass. Perhaps Canada is worth a royal commission.

January 20, 1962

FROM

Le Magazine Maclean

What If the Liberals Were Only Conservative After All?

Imagine with me, if you will, that we have slept through the last two years.

Suppose that yesterday was February 1959. The "Chief" reigns in Quebec. He has grown older, but his hand is still heavy.

There are some cracks in the plaster. The students have taken a few nicks off him, and he didn't like it. Now he doesn't dare maintain the surtax he had imposed on the Dominicans at Montmorency. The natural gas scandal seemed to shake him and it took him two months to recover his reflexes again. But he bounced back and opponents of the Union Nationale shake their heads and mutter amongst themselves that "The scandal came too soon."

He has aged. The administrative machinery is starting to slip. The Chief must scrutinize each Order in Council himself, for his ministers are poor, inferior creatures whom it is best to mistrust and wise to humiliate—government by humiliation. Education is improving despite him, but in a state of disorder that permits the government to go on being arbitrary. In most ministries the pay is bad and the way they recruit staff is worse. In certain fields government subsidies are as generous as they are capricious. Provincial autonomy is locked up as tight as the Polish art treasures. The Tremblay report has been relegated to the dungeons.

To be sure, things get done. Bridges get built; roads, schools, hospitals, factories, fortunes, and empires get made. . . . A move

192

directed against foreign trusts and capital a few years ago has
now swung around entirely to the side of big business — 1936
seems a long way off! Today the enemy is the trade unions.
Nationalism is only tolerated if it is the chauvinistic variety.
Schools are blessed with due solemnity, and in private the Chief
declares, "I can make the bishops eat out of my hand."

He's hard. He leads. He's alone. There's a certain grandeur
in this solitary decline. When one is sick and old it is not so
much fun to govern any more. But it must be done, it must,
or what would become of the province? He imposes his will.
He gives his adversaries the impression of a strange, impregnable
strength, but his closest friends have watched his hand fumble
for the elevator button. Having seen so much corruption around
him, he plunges even deeper into contempt for his fellow men.

And then in three days, taxed to the limit, after fighting against
the body's capitulation to the very end, he disappears.

He is replaced without an instant's hesitation by Paul Sauvé.
In three months, this man will destroy the most deeply rooted
of the old myths. From now on...

From now on subsidies will be distributed, as far as possible,
according to a fixed scale. From now on universities will have
stable budgets. Colleges will receive regular aid, and school com-
missions too. The government will no longer treat its civil servants
like dangerous incompetents whose chief vocation seems to be
to starve to death. And what about Ottawa? Health insurance?
Probably, after closer study. Who's in charge? Paul Sauvé, but
he also has ministers. And the opposition, somewhat stunned
by this blitz of mildness, will retain its rights. From now on...

The province can't get over it. We had to stand on our heads
so long, it is sheer bliss to find our feet again.

Maybe these reforms won't go very far. And what in the long
run is Paul Sauvé up to? He is giving the province a chance
to make up for lost time. Reforms that public opinion had gradually seen as necessary over the last fifteen years, but which Duplessis had refused, are now being realized without revolution, are
being granted with grace and elegance. Sauvé permits us to judge
the difference between the reactionary turned slightly manic in
old age and an intelligent conservative.

He dies suddenly on January 2, 1960, leaving behind more
hopes than accomplishments. His main legislative program has

not yet been presented to the Assembly, but he announced it in such a way, and his promises were so warmly welcomed, that his successor must feel bound to respect them.

And he does. M. Antonio Barrette, however, lacks Sauvé's ease. He hesitates between two styles. He is heir to two contradictory political legacies and is condemned to be an imitator at best. Moreover—this becomes clear later on—he doesn't completely control his general staff; he reigns but he doesn't quite rule. Under his leadership the Union Nationale sags a little. This may be due to the hidden effects of a latent Duplessis backlash which didn't dare declare itself under Paul Sauvé.

None the less, though the tone is lacking, the Hundred Days go on. Barrette defends Sauvé's legislative program, sometimes using Duplessis's tactics.

But on the horizon a new machine is gathering. The Liberals have realized that perhaps their time is ripe. They take the plunge. What is the explanation for their success, a success that few people foresaw? It came from self-assurance and a campaign program built on that. While the Union Nationale was trying to change its image and was still struggling under the dead weight of its own past and finding nothing new to say, the Liberals were gaining confidence. A political program's value cannot be judged, and perhaps should never be judged, by the direct effect it has on the masses; it is rather a rallying-point for active workers. This one appealed to a clientele that was ready and waiting. It reassured the nationalists, gave a few guarantees to the radicals, and, by its clarity and the solidity of its structure, created an impression of being really serious. René Lévesque jumped onto the band wagon "because of the program", adding his brio and an element of paradox. He showed himself to be admirably well equipped to fend off the heavy storm—plenty of thunder but no lightning—that the Union Nationale was stupid enough to mount against him, instead of training its artillery on Jean Lesage's rapid rise to prominence over the question of autonomy.

Though beaten only by a narrow margin, the Union Nationale falls apart, loses its leader, painfully sets about looking for another, stumbles over its old deputies, loses Montreal, bogs down, makes a lot of noise to prove that it still exists, wonders if it shouldn't take a crack at self-reform too, expectorates, and regurgitates.

The beginning of the Lesage regime reminds one of Paul Sauvé's Hundred Days, though with different points of attack. The new team lays down in principle that it will be true to the latter's program. It promises a full inquiry into the administrative practices of the last few years, begins to reform the Provincial Police, denounces and hunts down patronage. In Ottawa M. Lesage adopts an attitude that is at once very firm and very flexible. Reforms are announced in the school system. We will finally get our health insurance. And to support this program, M. Lesage has given some of the most important portfolios to colleagues who are known as reformers.

Since then the situation has become a little confused and the difficulties have begun.

Sometimes, from the outside, one has the impression of a slowing down or at least of a certain hesitation not only in regard to the means to be used but also concerning the objectives to be reached. Will this government age too quickly? Does it, does the party itself, possess a really lively faith in its own program? I have no doubts as far as men like Lesage, Lapalme, and Lévesque are concerned, but will this yeast be enough to make the dough rise?

Under Maurice Duplessis we had an autocratic government more retarding than simply tardy. For the past seventeen months, three successive governments have spent a good part of their time trying to catch up with the present, trying to readapt our laws to the most obvious needs of today, and trying to conform to the wishes of the man in the street. The Union Nationale made rapid progress in some areas, the Liberals have gone on making adjustments in others. But once the most obvious shortcomings have been eliminated, what kind of government will we be left with? Will the Liberals be content to float, cork-like, on waves of public opinion of the commonest kind?

One problem — among several others — will soon permit us to measure the new government's success. The problem of education.

It is in this domain that the Liberal program has introduced most innovations. It promises a great deal and encourages the highest hopes. Undoubtedly the government was well aware of the risks it ran. The policies it announces will stir up against it the most conservative elements in the province, both inside and outside political circles. These conservatives probably don't form a majority but they do have considerable weight, and in some quarters, influence. The more the government hesitates, the more they will show their teeth and the more savagely they will defend the old formulas. It will take courage and audacity to face them. The Liberals have known that from the start. But in a recent by-election all the political demagogues had to do was sound the alarm to make the government seem to retreat and persuade M. Lesage to declare that his government would never form a Ministry of "Public Instruction". To defend this surprising statement he recalled, on television, what a hornets' nest Premier Marchand had stirred up when he proposed the formation of such ministry . . . in 1898!

If this is nothing but a tactical manoeuvre, there's nothing to get excited about. In that case, let M. Lesage give the province the same thing by any other name and that will be fine. Only one wonders if the way he balks at the name doesn't betray a real fear of the thing.

What we are calling "the thing" is one authority in Quebec in charge of the whole educational process, or, to use the terms proposed by professors at the Université de Montréal, "a single ministry responsible to Parliament and to public opinion for the proper functioning of our system of education at every level". This means an efficient ministry backed by a competent and active Pedagogical Council. Since we are in vast majority a Catholic province, this council will, by the nature of things, be Catholic in one of its most important sectors. But a confessional committee does not necessarily imply the presence of a whole synod of bishops—as many theologians would agree. To achieve the desired result, the government will have to shoulder its responsibilities and govern, and face up to the conservative attack. Otherwise, in this field, and perhaps by contagion in others, it will be neither more nor less than a good conservative government in the Sauvé style.

March 1961

Weak Representation in Ottawa Turns Quebec Away From Canada

Is it entirely coincidental that Quebec separatism has taken on new importance during Mr. Diefenbaker's term of office? I don't think so.

Under his government French Canadians have had no real leadership from Ottawa. They haven't been able to identify with anyone in the capital from their own group. There is nobody there to speak for them. There is nobody to speak to them with authority in their own language from the Ottawa side of the fence.

You may find it an exercise in futility to raise the question of a Quebec spokesman. You will say, and it is perfectly true, that having a French-Canadian spokesmen in Ottawa doesn't much change the realities of the situation, that it doesn't modify the policies of the party in power, that it doesn't win any decisive influence for us. After all, the Canada of today, which we find so unsatisfactory and in which we feel such strangers, is the result of half a century of political history when we did have spokesmen there, men such as Laurier, Lapointe, and Saint-Laurent.

That's true enough. A separatist could even argue that after these "impostors" the Diefenbaker regime is at least honest. At least he doesn't try to mask the facts. (Except belatedly with his bilingual cheques. But that's just the point. That gimmick didn't take; it showed up too transparently as a concession because no important French Canadian would stand behind it.)

But the fact remains that from a psychological point of view the absence of any spokesman from Quebec little by little creates a feeling of estrangement, a sense of not belonging to the rest of Canada or its government.

But let's review some of the facts. In 1957 Louis Saint-Laurent is still Prime Minister of Canada. In the June election Quebec votes overwhelmingly for him, but it is his lone victory and Diefenbaker carries the day in the rest of the country and forms a new (minority) government.

Thereupon Mr. Saint-Laurent quits politics. Mr. Pearson replaces him and the bond which ties Quebec to a single figure in Ottawa is broken. Then the Union Nationale throws its resources behind the Conservatives party. Everyone knows that Diefenbaker will win. As a result, in the 1958 election Quebec performs a sensational about-face; the province accomplishes something that hadn't been seen since 1887: for the first time in fourteen general elections it brings in a Conservative majority.

So here is Mr. Diefenbaker, supported by a strong French-Canadian delegation. On the whole it must be described as being inexperienced and pretty mediocre. We are used to mediocrity. The Liberal back-benchers in King's or in Saint-Laurent's time were not exactly luminaries. But they did have at their head an Ernest Lapointe or a Louis Saint-Laurent. So the question is, who will be Mr. Diefenbaker's Lapointe?

Now the Prime Minister doesn't seem to be in any great hurry to choose someone. Authoritarian by temperament, he doesn't like sharing power. He will have to take his time anyway, they claim, for he scarcely knows his Quebec deputies and he will have to let them prove themselves. Later on they find excuses for him. Is it the Prime Minister's fault if we haven't elected any outstanding men? According to Mr. Jacques Flynn, it's up to the people to choose their own spokesman. In other words, personal prestige is something that must be earned, and it isn't Mr. Diefenbaker's job to impose his choice.

Be that as it may, after five years of Conservative rule no French Canadian has yet been found deserving of a major cabinet post in the federal government.

If it is true that Mr. Diefenbaker has not been able to place full confidence in colleagues chosen for him by the Quebec electorate, then why hasn't he come into Quebec himself to look for someone he could make into his right-hand man? It would have been easy a few years ago. Mackenzie King found himself in a similar position in 1942. His chief French-Canadian collaborator, Ernest Lapointe, had just died. He didn't put very much stock in the politicians around him. And what was his immediate reflex? He singled out a lawyer of excellent reputation but relatively unpopular, Mr. Louis Saint-Laurent, and had him elected in Quebec East, the old riding of Laurier and Lapointe. The gamble paid off beyond the highest expectations. But King had flair and a good sense of politics.

Suppose that in 1959, or even in 1960, Mr. Diefenbaker had conscripted someone like Marcel Faribault in the same fashion and had publicly declared his esteem for him. No doubt he would have in his party today that Quebec spokesman who is so sadly lacking.

The idea was suggested to him several times. If he never did anything about it, I'm afraid it's because he thought he could do without any very strong collaboration from Quebec.

A Westerner, a champion of New Canadians, and a man marked by rather painful experiences in his youth, Mr. Diefenbaker likes to assert that we are all Canadians. But does he believe very firmly in bilingualism or in the role of French Canada in our history? For a long time it has seemed rather doubtful. I believe he thinks of us as the most important minority group in the country. As such, and because the constitution guarantees us certain rights, we must be treated with special consideration. But never as partners on an equal footing.

Of course I am putting my own interpretation on the statements and more particularly on the actions of the Prime Minister, who has never expressed himself in these terms. But it's a legitimate interpretation. Add to this that Mr. Diefenbaker has had to endure the friendship of Duplessis's bunch and one can see that he has good reason to be contemptuous of political practices in Quebec. He seems to mistrust our bad habits and to fear that his government will be peppered with scandals. Considering that some of them stem from his French-Canadian entourage, we can readily forgive his reticence. But we can also reproach him for not having known, when at the peak of his power, how to disengage himself from such company in order to go and seek out, at a considerable distance if necessary, collaborators who would be more worthy of the best traditions of his party.

Unless they can remedy this situation—a difficult thing to do at the last minute—the Progressive Conservative party will pay for this error at the next election, even though the Liberals are also exceptionally weak in this regard.

If Mr. Pearson makes notable gains in Quebec he will owe

it to the mistakes of his opponent rather than to any enthusiasm that his own side generates. He does have a few men of real quality, but not one who has been able to impose himself on the public mind as a leader. It is hard to imagine what role they would play in the inner councils of a Pearson government. As far as a Quebec spokesman is concerned, Mr. Saint-Laurent left no successor. Though Mr. Chevrier is a first-rate debater, this is not the job for him. Mr. Maurice Lamontagne is not an M.P. He made his mark as a theorist of central power and is more interested in economic matters.

Luck began to run out on the Conservative party in Quebec when Macdonald died and even more decisively when Laurier took office. Since that time they have had three opportunities to put down roots here: in 1911, in 1930, and again in 1958. They have never been lucky or capable enough to take advantage of them.

In 1911, collaboration with Henri Bourassa's Nationalists assured Borden, despite Laurier's prestige, twenty-seven seats. But the Borden government turned out to be more imperialist than its predecessor and it bore the brunt of the unpopularity stirred up by the first conscription crisis. His party was crushed and was not to rise again until 1930, when the Depression helped R. B. Bennett to find twenty-four Conservative members in Quebec. But Bennett didn't understand the French Canadians; he didn't know how to choose his Quebec lieutenants. In all, he tried out three of them, which led Louis Dupire to write, waspishly, "What we needed was four aces and we drew four jacks." Bennett's last-ditch concession of bilingual banknotes was a vain gesture; he was soundly trounced in the next election. It was during his government that Quebec's first separatist movement was organized. Was that a coincidence?

Borden, Bennett, and Mr. Diefenbaker all either refused to choose a spokesman from French Canada or failed to move fast enough to find one. Each time Quebec's attachment to Confederation slackened. This was due to many complex reasons, among which the lack of a French-Canadian chief was at once a symptom and a result, but at the same time, this absence aggravated and emphasized the reactions of all the prime causes.

So Mr. Diefenbaker doesn't have full confidence in Mr. Balcer, in Mr. Dorion, or — at least until recently — in Mr. Jacques Flynn?

Neither do we. We share his concern. When faith dries up at the source, one can hardly expect it to circulate.

Please note that my reservations are purely sentimental. I doubt very much that except in very precise areas Mr. King ever really shared the responsibility of government with Ernest Lapointe. As for Laurier and Saint-Laurent, they were prime ministers and, as such, were obliged to think for Canada as a whole; they would never have been forgiven had they shown preference for Quebec. But their presence at the helm flattered the self-esteem of French Canadians. When your group has given the victorious party its star performer, you feel, rightly or wrongly, that you are part of the team. But if your representatives do a mediocre job, why, you turn your back on them.

And that's just what might happen tomorrow.

May 1962

French Canada Is at Loggerheads With Its Intellectuals

In French Canada our intellectuals have had their little hour of semi-glory. It all happened during the first years of TV, perhaps because in those days there was a lot of easy admiration going around, perhaps also because of the profound scorn that Maurice Duplessis lavished on them. He used to call them "poets", or better still, "piano players". When Duplessism was still in flower but had begun to lose some of its bloom, intellectuals in Quebec shone with a certain lustre.

Those days (should we say those happy days?) are past. A succession of minor prophets has arisen to denounce them. M. Daniel Johnson is a late-flowering advocate of "return to our roots". M. Réal Caouette claims that the truth is simple and that the intellectuals complicate everything. M. Jean Lesage doesn't like hearing it said—any more than does President Kennedy—that they are running his show. The nearest they get to recognition comes from some of their old adversaries who, prompted by some remnant of respect, are quick to talk about "pseudo-intellectuals". But since nearly all intellectuals, one after another, have been declared "pseudo", the divinity we used to worship is getting devilishly distant. In the same way, other people—or are they the same?—profess their undying love for the union movement in general but find fault with all working-class leaders. In short, the picture is gloomy, and French Canada is at loggerheads with its intellectuals. But why? Intellectuals aren't exactly knee-deep in the streets, as those who are stirring up hostility against them seem to imply. And what, after all, is "an intellectual"?

For my own amusement these last few days, I have asked everyone I met that question. Precise replies were few and far between. But I got lots of polemics: Your "damned intellectuals" are grouped on "the left", they trample tradition, preach atheism and agnosticism, form a small but active clique that controls Radio-Canada, the newspapers, and the university. To sum up, they are regular devils.

You'll have to admit that doesn't help much. So we'll have to go to the dictionary. *Larousse* says: "Someone who by taste or profession devotes himself to things of the spirit." That should please everyone, but it leaves us in the dark.

Quillet permits us to take a step towards the light: "A person who has a taste or an exclusive taste for things of the spirit."

Oxford gives us a different orientation: "A person having superior powers of intellect (used in English since 1652)." The intellectual then is characterized by the vigour of his mind.

In *Littré* the word is not listed as a noun. I look elsewhere, and under *clerc* (as in Benda's *La Trahison des clercs*) I find: "In former times, by extension from its first sense (a man of the church) anyone who is literate and learned", which comes close to the English definition. But here is another word which may throw more light on the subject. According to *Littré* an *idéologue* (ideologist) is:

1. A person who deals in ideologies (the science of ideas considered in themselves as phenomena of the human mind)

2. In an unfavourable sense, a dreamer in philosphical or political matters

Oh those piano players! Today's intellectual is perhaps a combination of the clerk and ideologist of former years. In the same way that the word ideologist has deteriorated continuously, for it is never used today except in its second, derogatory, sense — the word "intellectual" now tends to designate chiefly the faults of yesterday's true intellectual. The man of action imagines him lost in the clouds; the artist thinks of him, with a kind of respectful awe, as a dry and sterile enemy.

We might conclude, arbitrarily, that the intellectual sees himself as one who, at the price of considerable effort, has acquired the capacity to manipulate general ideas. He does so because he believes in them, but also sometimes simply as a game. To understand his role better, he may be contrasted with the man of action or the technician, men who have a more immediate contact with reality, or with the artist, who approaches reality in a more direct and more intuitive way. The proper sphere of the intellectual is the realm of ideas — ideas which he has extracted from reality or which he has "abstracted" from it. Therefore he may have as true a contact with reality as the man of action, the technician, or the artist, but he achieves it in a different way, which permits him to see farther or more clearly, though the risk of error is also greater when the possibility of verification is dubious.

In this domain there are amateurs and professionals, which is not necessarily to discriminate between them since certain amateurs are very gifted and can move faster and farther than the professional. But in general the latter's ideas are developed with more rigour and firmness. Some intellectuals possess creative gifts, others are merely talented, still others are mediocre — like everyone else, they obey the law of general averages. For that matter, nothing is more difficult than the situation of the semi-mediocre, for, like the disappointed artist, he has the capacity of self-knowledge. The hypercritical intellectual is not always the most self-confident; his stiffness often springs from self-doubt.

Every party, group, and church has its intellectuals. There is Marx but there is Maurras, too. In his own sphere, the theologian is an intellectual and shares the intellectual's struggles and weaknesses. Different currents of thought traverse every epoch, and often one of them dominates the others. But, God willing, in a free world it will never destroy its rivals; it is history that sweeps the debris away.

The intellectual is human and shares all human frailties: prejudices, passions, the drive to succeed, corruptibility, conformism, ambition, snobbery, and so on. To this should be added faults peculiar to his breed: notably an ingrained love of system and a dryness of heart which lead to contempt. The public knows this all too well and what they hate most in intellectual circles is precisely this scornful attitude which speaks only in insulting tones and draws even further apart when it fences itself off behind the barrier of its own pride.

When the intellectual is asked to show some heart, he is not expected, any more than the surgeon, to manifest the trembling hand and the tear-filled eye, for he too operates, cutting into the living flesh, and often his chief function is to be pitiless. Seeing and judging the spectacle of human foibles and pettiness from on high, as he does, is a painful experience and in the long run it weighs down the soul. Proofs that are dazzling to him are difficult to communicate. If his ideas are new, he is left to stagnate in neglect and solitude, or else society lashes out against him. The scorn of "imbeciles" is hard to bear, and he counter-attacks. Which is a weakness. Scorn, not of particular error but of men, is always a human weakness.

Society needs its intellectuals. When a divorce takes place between the two it's a tragedy. A healthy society does not attempt to realize immediately the latest inspirations of its ideologists. As a general rule it does not turn over the reins of power to those whose domain is that of the mind. But it should listen to them respectfully. Even if they speak a difficult or startling language, it should beware of systematically laughing them off or levelling curses at them. Nor should it park them in some ghetto where they will dry out and grow bitter with exasperation. Nor lionize them either, for their work requires a certain remoteness. Between the intellectual and the masses there should exist an intermediary corps—journalists in the main—who too often easily pass themselves off as intellectuals. But one should beware of mixing genres, for except in rare instances each kind should govern its own estate rather than try to conquer its neighbour's.

What I have been describing is, of course, the ideal city. In real life tensions are inevitable. For that matter, intellectuals don't even live at peace amongst themselves. Like everyone else they are slightly cannibalistic and the choicest morsel is often the nose of some colleague and competitor.

The intellectual will never play his full role in a society that rejects or forgets him. Those primates who can only think of the intellectual as a scatter-brained egghead may have well-ordered digestive systems but they repeat themselves uselessly, and meanwhile society degenerates. By his discipline of mind the intellectual sees farther, probes deeper, examines ceaselessly from the base of an experience that is not accessible to all and with a breadth of vision that the man of action rarely achieves. He is not the captain but the pilot. And what ship (even the ship of state) can do without its pilots?

March 1963

Like Father, Like Son

Two widespread faults have been attributed to previous generations: first, the absence of any intellectual stamina, and second, a strong penchant for dogmatism, each weakness sustaining the other.

The dogmatism comes, they say, from transposing religious attitudes to the temporal plane, which results in attributing absolute value to personal convictions which are often as debatable as they are honourable. The quest for knowledge is considered to be purely nominal; truth is deduced from grand, indisputable principles, and patient, humble research in the field of fact is reduced to its most simplistic expression. This is what one might call the "noblest" aspect of an attitude which is usually partial and prone to error.

But other factors are involved. Our society is on the threshold of an intellectual and artistic awakening. Specialists are still rare and creative people even more so. As a result we live in a climate of facility and even of slackness. In days gone by, when a man claimed competence in one particular area, people rushed to him expecting miracles in other fields where he was only an amateur. It was not easy to resist solicitations from one's own milieu, and the young expert soon became a jack-of-all-trades in the intellectual community. Caught up in this game he even lost his initial value. Besides, expertise that is too cloistered is dangerous. The person who is never confronted with his peers and who is consequently never seriously questioned begins to talk like the village pedant and finds it more and more difficult to give his true measure. The end result is an intellectual climate that one could hardly call stimulating. The air one breathes is heavy and dead and the mind drowses, which doesn't prevent it from making peremptory pronouncements.

What I have been summarizing here are objections that have been raised a hundred times over by the younger generation.

I have noticed however that whenever young people do take the trouble to express themselves, they show all the signs of the same old traditional shortcomings. For example, certain representative factions are as dogmatically anti-clerical as their predecessors were dogmatically church-bound. Youthful separatism is almost as repetitive and vague as yesterday's pan-Canadianism. Although the young violently contradict the old ideas, they remain, to a frightening extent, their fathers' sons. Certain positions may have changed but the continuity of attitude is a little disconcerting.

There is no end to their grumblings of disgust and anger. And there is a kind of ritualistic magic in their protestations, just as the religion of their predecessors was tainted with superstition. Matching the svelte theologians of a conservative era, we now have the sulphurous theologians of a radical age. The affirmations of the former lacked backbone, the latter's negations are just as flabby. If you take an antique stone column and stand it on its head, you may think you're an innovator, but it's still the same old column.

Only yesterday we had no cinema; today we have theories of cinema. The art has progressed, but there are still those who wish to give it a moralizing role—yesterday exalting peasant virtues, today, God knows what fad of the moment. The old rigidity has just changed name.

Separatism is at present repetitive and vague, that is to say, made in the image of yesterday's Canadianism. Of course, it is still young and we can hardly expect it to make its first appearance armed from head to toe. One could hope to see it develop and establish proofs of its fertility by tangible signs. And yet, in the intellectual sphere, it seems to put the curse of sterility on even the most open-minded people who join the movement. Its beginnings were generous, but the nervous jitters soon set in, and now condemnation succeeds condemnation, anathemas roll up to heaven, and we are once again besieged by moralists.

In short, although they violently condemn the ideas of their forebears, the young people I am speaking about are dreadfully like their fathers. The positions have changed but it is the continuity of attitude that I find alarming.

But after all, what's so surprising in that? One type of fanaticism gives rise to its counterpart. It is easier to shed one's ideas than one's temperament. Social heredity acts on the masses almost as blindly as physical heredity on the individual. On the broad political scale Taschereauism gave rise to the Duplessism that we haven't quite shaken off yet. From one system to the next, the spirit of the system remains. No one is born with liberal views, one acquires them little by little, by taking pains. And one must also be able to admit to start with that a certain mental detachment is neither scepticism nor indifference, and that it is possible to hold opinions enthusiastically even if they are something less than monolithic.

I may seem to be speaking as though we were the only society to have these problems. Dogmatism, to be sure, has no nationality, although it perhaps finds itself more at home in some countries than in others. When the normal reflex is to call a man a traitor, or more politely "collaborator", because his beliefs are contrary to yours, the style of name-calling reflects on the person who uses it. When such practices become generalized, they signify a refusal to see things as they are, and a refusal to dialogue with others.

In the past, heretics were burnt at the stake; nowadays, while waiting for better times, they are simply burnt in effigy.

Particularly striking among young separatists who have lost religious faith is the fact that they have formed sects that are even more savagely exclusive; intolerance has just crossed the street. It could very easily go wild.

I know there are those who will find the tenor of these remarks conservative. And there precisely is the crux of the drama that is going on around us. It seems that one is condemned to sink ever deeper into the tradition that one is trying to discard; that one is forced to repeat over and over again the same gestures with a seasoning of new words, and to accentuate to the point of caricature traits that we believed we had freed ourselves from forever.

"But isn't it a legitimate ambition to denounce the clericalism of our society, to have new artistic ideas, to propose the independence of Quebec to the French-Canadian people?"

Certainly. However, what I am denouncing is not an ideology but a style, and one that is becoming more and more widespread.

An important debate which will influence all French Canadians is taking place over Bill 60.* Why have these self-styled progressive spirits that I have been talking about waited so long to swing into action? Why have so many of them simply kept silent? Does this legislation seem to them to be divorced from the question of independence? They haven't even taken the trouble to examine it publicly. Their views are practically unknown. That's what I call courting sterility: only looking at one side of things; starting up witch-hunts; paying more attention to form than to content; ignoring day-to-day reality; practising a nationalism that is rigidly formalistic in conception; and every day ceasing a little bit more to belong to the nation they claim to be saving.

October 1963

*Bill proposed by the Liberal government which became law in March 1964, which led to the creation of the Ministry of Education and sweeping reforms in the educational system of the province.

It's Hard
To Talk Across
the Generation Gap

A young university professor tells me: "I'm thirty. In their eyes I'm already a square. They shut themselves up in their own special concerns. They don't need anything from us, except a little technical know-how. They reject everything before them. They're ashamed of us."

A young artist says: "In Canada everything has to be started over again from scratch with each new generation. And generations that used to last a decade or so now shoulder each other out of the way every five years. Those kids are treading on our heels already. As far as they're concerned I'm almost your age."

And from one of the younger generation: "Dialogue is out. You've just got to be yourself, come what may."

If everyone so unanimously speaks and writes this way, it must be true. For that matter, the revolt is now world-wide. It has its own language, its own style, its own uniform almost, and a set of hatreds that all look alike. As far as Quebec is concerned, it is the first time an organization like the F.L.Q. has sprung up, the first time young terrorists have taken to direct action, the first time that theories of violence and hatred have been openly preached here.

But personally I reject this near-unanimity. Perhaps it is the result of ignorance; I used to meet a lot of young people, but I have much less time now and I must be content to read them. It's quite possible that I fail to grasp all the real originality of the generation that is just beginning to express itself; that I don't take their negative attitudes seriously enough. Experience is sometimes a dangerous asset; it teaches us how things and people react as a rule, and leads us to reason from the law of averages, when sometimes habits of thought and action are violently rejected.

This is not the first time I've seen a new generation hatch. The very first time is never much fun. It's the day you discover that you don't belong to the "younger generation" any more. It's a kind of death knell for you. You find yourself promoted despite yourself. Younger men come pushing in behind. They question you harshly. It isn't so long ago that you were saying to the previous generation, "What youth wills, youth will have," and saying that, you had the feeling that history was changing course, and that you were the course-setter, and that the new direction being laid down ran counter to the course set by the old fogeys (out of politeness, you called them the older generation). But now you find that history won't stand still. To believe today's youth, it has veered off on another course and you are one of the old fogeys yourself.

It happened to me with the *Cité Libre* group (who are called "the old men" by the *Parti pris* generation of today) and with the School of Social Sciences at Laval. While my classmates and I had believed in nationalism, the new wave signed its death warrant. It spoke in the name of individual liberty, social values, technical reforms. It rudely challenged "monolithic" French-Canadian nationalism. It was vigorously critical of clericalism, and little by little reformulated the problems of education.

Then there was the *Liberté* group, more oriented towards artistic creation, deliberately impertinent, and more difficult to define. Weren't they in reality a kind of half-generation? Certain of them felt almost as much at ease in *Cité Libre*, while others were more at home with the new wave who accepted them and solicited their collaboration. This is surely a sign that the generations are less diametrically opposed than they claim or than they may seem to be. For that matter, the criticisms voiced in *Cité Libre* and in *Liberté* (the same word occurs in each title—that must mean something) have not been abandoned by today's younger generation. They have assumed them. These questions have lost their interest, because as far as today's youth is concerned they've already been answered. But at the same time, they are part of the general heritage. Read any article in *Parti pris* about politics in French Canada and you can easily identify the sources: Pierre Elliott Trudeau here, Michel Brunet there, and Jean Le Moyne or Pierre Vadeboncoeur elsewhere. In contrast to what is usually claimed (though with some justice in other fields), it is the continuity of thought that is striking. And this is a good thing.

I believe in generations. But I believe even more strongly in the solidarity of like-minded men.

In my own generation I found there were an incredible number of my contemporaries who bored me to death and in whose company I felt a perfect stranger. At the same time I did have friends in the generation above mine (call it force of habit) and I have friends in all the latest movements. Questions of age apart, there are simply certain people who amuse you and others who leave you yawning; people you feel spontaneously in tune with, no matter what their ideals, and others who will always remain outside your world. But among the members of one family there is always the possibility of an exchange.

Certainly it makes a difference to have been young during the Depression, during the war, or during the post-war period; to have been twenty under Duplessis or under Jean Lesage; to have read Malraux, Camus, or Sartre at twenty rather than at forty. That marks you. You don't react the same way to the same facts or the same ideas. You can't possibly have exactly the same perspective on things. Similarly, a Canadian necessarily has a different outlook from a German or a Chinese; a worker's son has different reflexes from a farmer's son or a boy from the middle-class. Those are factors in conditioning. But can one ever accept being completely locked into one's class, one's culture, or one's generation?

I'm not trying to convince anyone; I'm just saying that I don't believe so; or if one can, then it's a bad sign.

So here is a new generation. It casts a greedy and yet somewhat nervous eye on the world. It wants to do things. The things that have already been done leave it cold. It's looking for new tasks. It amplifies the importance of the goals it discovers for itself, and is exasperated to be constantly told about things that are being done now, which it considers to be as good as finished. This is the way the face of the world is changed. Like all creative people, the present generation is intoxicated with the discoveries it foresees, which block further discoveries yet to be made. It seems to be at odds with everything that is not itself. And then, little by little, it begins to find friends. It finds support in quarters it couldn't have anticipated in the first place. It isn't a question of self-betrayal, it's just that it has begun to discover its roots and true relationships.

Then personalities emerge. They have little in common. The

more mature they are, the more their originality declares itself. One shouldn't think of the new generation as an enemy army destined to overthrow their predecessors, but rather as a team which, in its own way, will occupy most of the positions filled by the team they replace. And naturally, every team has, as well as its regulars, its irregulars, its latecomers, and its traitors.

It isn't so easy to understand and accept one another, even in a single generation. "We indulge in arbitrary classifications," Hubert Aquin writes about the generation that is young today, "and I know few journalists or academics who can resist being brutally guided by the impermeable authority of their ideological group." When we act this way we are being either frivolous or dogmatic. And he continues: "But it is still possible to think, and such an important act, even if it is performed by a social or political rival, should not be considered a kind of hermetic hymn accessible only to the members of the singers' cult."

It may still be possible, but it's rare and becoming rarer as the generations pass, because the young people of today no longer know the situations which were the shaping forces in their predecessors' self-definition. At least their deafness is not voluntary. And we are not going to ask them to begin all over again. They have already accepted the responsibility for their own lives—and that's a lot.

Bit by bit these problems will all shake down, and soon a new generation, the generation of children who are learning to read today, will throw them all back into question again.

March 1964

Return from Europe

I dedicate the following observations to readers who have never been to Europe, or who have gone only as tourists, or late in life at an invulnerable age.

And I address them particularly to anyone who has been put off or irritated by the snobbery or cutting judgements or negativism of young people "back from abroad".

But I should also warn that I am a biased commentator.

I was once a "back-from-abroader" myself and I often recognize, in young ex-expatriates of today, attitudes that I once shared myself.

The expression "back from abroad" has a specific meaning: it applies to individuals who have come back home after a fairly long period of study in Paris, London, or some place like that.

At the same time the expression defines a certain type of person: it means a person who hasn't completely returned, one who has left part of his heart and mind over there.

When I was very young, I knew a lot of people who had come "back from abroad" in the second sense. I was struck by the ridiculous figure they cut. As a general rule, they seemed to me to be insupportable, never satisfied with what they found back here, unjust and hypercritical, always ready to make odious comparisons. Or else they were simply maladjusted, having lost all sense of the possibilities of life here. Or else they just made a mess of things and clammed up, their only preoccupation being to return to Europe, in dreams if not in reality.

Later on I was better able to appreciate their distress. When I came back from Paris myself.

I had sworn on leaving that I wouldn't be one of them. I rejected their revolt in advance, and refused to have any part in their sterility, their eternal nostalgia, or their put-on accents. I intended to improve my own speech without catching that infectious Parisian overtone.

Once I arrived, it only took me a few weeks to become superficially acclimatized. At twenty the operation seemed relatively simple. I knew I was only going to be there for a limited time.

And it took me four or five years to become readapted to life here when I got back. Even today there are scars that sometimes reopen. Here, it's not just a stop-over, it's real life.

Generalizations are dangerous. Certain French Canadians think of a stay in Europe as an invitation to pleasure. Others, on the contrary, feel ill at ease. Europe, you could say, doesn't "take" on them. They get through their specialized studies honourably, but neither London nor Paris is a decisive experience. They remain impervious to the charms of the old world.

But let's concentrate on the first kind. In highly civilized cities—and I imagine the same would be true of certain American universities—your first reaction is to feel small and provincial. Expectations and standards are different. Thrown a little off balance, you take stock of the gaps in your own education.

Inevitably, you encounter a lot of mediocrity. There's no short-age of that anywhere. I was even very surprised to have some mediocre professors. Their mediocrity was, however, if I may say so, more competent and more demanding that the usual variety. And then there are also the real masters. They are irreplaceable. Around you there is an abundant intellectual and artistic life. There are creative people who are no better than our artists but who are more numerous, which creates an atmosphere which is not easy to explain to people who have never known it and who suspiciously ward off such explanations when you get back. In these privileged places one's spirit expands, becomes more alert, more comparative. It can also become drunk on all this, but it's a stage one has to pass through, and the milieu provides its own antidotes. All the instruments of culture are ready to hand.

Suddenly one day you realize that you too have entered this more intense kind of life. Intellectually you are participating in a society which is so much better structured and so much richer than your own, a society where thousands of intellects collaborate and compete with one another to make up one vast and endless movement of mind which is beginning to carry you on its tide.

I am not referring to human qualities. Fortunately, the exile warmly remembers the presence of such qualities at home and finds them more fraternal, warmer, solid, and comforting. But is it such a consolation? He also remembers this or that faculty in one of our Canadian universities, our theatre, our reviews that scarcely exist yet, everything that in our country remains hastily improvised and not always very happily so, intellectual "achievements" that are too quickly crowned or too soon discarded.

Intellectual ferment isn't everything. Perhaps it isn't even the essential. But he experiences or at least gets a taste of what a great adventure it is. It is a heady wine. He finds it very strong. His defences buckle on every side. He tries in vain to restructure his thoughts into a new synthesis. He gives it up as a bad job. He starts over again. He grows.

Am I trying to suggest that we are hopeless mediocrities?

I am comparing two environments with the relentless eye of a young man of twenty. In one sense he finds the comparison stimulating. He thinks of everything there will be to do on his return, of all the discoveries there are to share, of the enthusiasm burning inside him that he is going to try to communicate to others. But at the same time he is aware that he won't always find people ready to share his discoveries. He can foresee the resistance he will encounter. And he anticipates his own solitude.

The value of such a voyage does not only lie in the possibility of comparisons. It also provides an opportunity to see oneself from afar, like seeing yourself as someone else in a total context. These intuitions will have to be verified on one's return, but in retrospect, vision is set off against a background of wider horizons.

After two or three years abroad, the student can't always measure the importance of the experience he has had. It's only when he comes back that he discovers it. Even if his basic ideas haven't completely changed, he has become another person. And he has to readjust to the milieu where his roots still are.

Take an example from another generation. Edouard Montpetit, our first qualified economist, came back from Europe at the turn of the century. A brilliant student, he had graduated at the top of his class in Paris and one can imagine the career he might have made for himself in Europe working among his young peers. But he came back. He came back to discover businessmen who mistrusted intellectuals, priests who were suspicious of political economy (which they considered a science of material values, hence unworthy of the most spiritually advanced nation in North America), and politicians who were only too happy at the thought of using him. In one sense his career in Canada was crowned with success. But the man had to backtrack to the ABCs of his profession, had to justify the very existence of the discipline he had been taught, had to become, as he himself has written, a kind of Jack-of-all-trades, a handyman in his field, whose multiple activities left him nothing but the taste of ashes. Despite himself he became a pioneer and never ceased to regret the career he might have had as an intellectual leader in a richer environment.

We have covered quite a bit of ground in the last fifty years, and solid foundations have been laid in several disciplines. Still, the best of our returning expatriates, whether they are returning from the States or from Europe, know that in accepting repatriation they are amputating part of themselves. They have made their decision. But they cannot escape an aftertaste of bitterness when they find themselves hedged in by obstacles and when ill will prevents them from accomplishing even the things that are possible.

Film makers, sociologists, actors, writers, doctors, political scientists, or psychologists, they practically all feel that they have accepted a sacrifice. Often that may be an illusion. There is no guarantee that a career in Europe or the United States would necessarily have taken them very far.

But in one way or another, although not to such a cruel degree, every "back-from-abroader" feels condemned, even today, to retrace the steps of an Edouard Montpetit. When he gives in without a struggle to this discomfiture he quickly becomes apathetic. Is the fault always exclusively his own?

June 1963

A Primitive Tribe Without Education or Culture

I read in a Western paper that Quebec is "uneducated". And elsewhere, in the same vein, that French Canadians are under-developed. Or that they are without culture.

The more I hear judgements like these, the more they annoy me. For the most part they are made by people whose own personal culture is not exactly brilliant either in scope or in intensity, and even less in depth. When asked what they mean, they reply with statistics on school attendance, where it is true we rank among the lowest.

But is this equation just? Is one necessarily uneducated and uncultured just because one has quit school after the seventh year? Is one a barbarian or a dullard or a mediocrity just because one hasn't gone through high school? And conversely, is "in-struction" in the academic sense the same thing as culture?

Here I turn with pleasure to the old distinction, more and more forgotten nowadays, between instruction and education. "To instruct," says *Littré*, "is to train someone for something, to impart knowledge of various subjects to the youth of the na-tion," whereas "education" is "the act of upbringing, the formation of the child or the young man." In this sense it is true that a complete education presupposes a lot of instruction, but at the same time goes beyond it. One may conclude, and experience bears this out, that there is such a thing as a culture of illiterates, a wisdom that is passed on from generation to generation — and also that there is such a thing as the incult technician, that is, a technician who is just that and nothing more.

In the past this view of things led certain conservative minds to draw obscurantist conclusions. Since instruction wasn't everything, they decided that it wasn't worth anything at all, at least in the case of those who were prevented by circumstance or lack of intellectual gifts from pursuing it very far. This was nonsense. But we are guilty of the same stupidity when we pretend to be convinced that semi-instruction is equivalent to culture.

I have known Quebec farmers who never went beyond the rural school and who were magnificent human beings: rational, colourful, capable of assuming considerable responsibility, and penetratingly intelligent. The best had something royal about them. You could talk to them for hours and draw from their conversation a fund of human experience which they had long meditated and could express eloquently. They struck me as healthy and joyous individuals.

That doesn't prove anything; it is merely a very subjective judgement made in retrospect. Were those men really the way I imagined them, or am I just a city man dreaming his dream of the country? And if I don't in fact overestimate their merits, were they all that numerous, were they typical, or was it just chance putting in my way a few of her chance accomplishments? My own mind is made up: those men did exist, and still do. And I can't help remembering something I have often thought about them. I have always wondered how such rich personalities became transformed in our matriculation factories into such a weak-kneed "élite" who seem to be practically milked dry of all their original juice and joy. I am forced to conclude that we make a better job of our habitants than of our intellectuals.

Those farmers were far from perfect. To be precise they had two great faults. First, they were extremely attached to a certain order of things which they wished to protect at any price and thus were the natural supporters of short-sighted political regimes. Their conservatism is understandable in that it was a reflex defence mechanism designed to mask their second weakness—their reluctance to face the modern world, even in their own backyards. Nevertheless, poverty and misery forced the majority of them to sell their land and move to the cities to swell the number of unskilled labourers.

It was here that the absence of *instruction* became, and continues to be, a catastrophe, as it is today for that matter in modern farming. The judgements I quoted to start with have their bearing here. But it is not a question of education; it is factual knowledge that is needed and the basic techniques that are acquired at school.

The new school system in Quebec will help prepare young people to adapt better to the world they live in, which is, in the first instance, a purely pragmatic goal. It will also permit the more gifted of them to continue their studies and help put an end to a long-standing social injustice. In the future neither the individual's intellectual development nor his career will be so closely determined by his parents' wealth.

Those are great steps forward. It would be wrong, however, to be too optimistic. In themselves they do not constitute a flowering of culture. And there is no reason to despise the kind of popular wisdom that existed a decade or a century ago and that corresponded to a different kind of reality.

I expressed these ideas to some friends of mine the other day. They told me that I was trying to revive the old agricultural myth. That would be really ironic. Ever since Michel Brunet isolated and castigated that particular illusion, I've done my utmost to fight it.

Young men of my generation came under its sway in the cities. In my experience, "agriculturalism" consisted in this: a number of professors preached to their urban students the myth of the land and the infinite moral superiority of rural living over modes of life in the cities, the big city especially. This was the message, very often implicit, that a good many of us received in Montreal thirty years ago, that is, at a time when the majority of Québécois were already living in urban centres. The myth hadn't been invented here; our professors had imported it from Europe, but several of them were saturated with it, had assimilated it, and expressed it as the philosophy of the French-Canadian race. According to this theory, our people had drawn their strength and their moral superiority from their agricultural way of life. To abandon this would be to leave the path of history and invite the worst possible disasters. From this point of view the city appeared as sin personified, or at the very least as an error which one hoped would only be temporary. The people would return to the country and would once again learn to admire tracts of untamed wilderness. In this way they would regain their sense of vitality and truth.

We students spent hours dreaming of this and imagining bucolic lives for ourselves in which we would have a significant role to play. Consequently, our real plans for the future seemed to be morally flawed, because in the back of our minds we knew that we would go on living in the city just the same. The only result of subscribing to this mother-earth mythology was that it gave us a guilty conscience and led us to view various land settlement schemes with an obstinate optimism never justified by the facts. In this way we were lured away from real tasks and spent our time living imaginary romances.

It was a great shock, around 1938, to learn from Esdras Minville that the future of Quebec did not lie in agriculture. Little by little we had to open our eyes to the multiple consequences of this fact: to recognize that the process of urbanization was irreversible; to admit that from camping so long in the cities we had sunk roots there, and to accept that from now on we would have to set about solving for ourselves all the problems of life in the modern world. It was at this point that the nationalists split up; some of them remained devoted to tradition and passionate in their affirmation of the old values; others, recognizing how real and profound the change was, accepted the risk of the new values.

But nothing in all that leads me to endorse the claim that the people of Quebec have lived like a primitive tribe "without education or culture".

March 1966

A Rebirth of Separatism

If someone had said to me a dozen years ago, "By 1961 you'll have to take separatism seriously," I think I would probably have just shrugged my shoulders. After all, you can't go on reliving the past. The little abortive separatisms of 1900, 1922, and 1935 seemed to have been swept away forever. In 1950 the rising generation had discovered "the social fact" and joyously buried nationalism once and for all. It is this same generation that seems most surprised and scandalized today to find a bunch of young Turks shoving them in the back.

To have failed to predict the return of the pendulum should make one prudent. Yet when I hear a separatist leader announcing independence for 1967, I can't help feeling that someone is pulling my leg. And I am convinced that the triumphal bonfire built to celebrate and at the same time incinerate our detested Confederation isn't ready for the torch . . . at least not yet.

Separatism isn't—isn't so far?—a political force in the province. But it has come back to life more vigorous and better armed than ever. As a movement it influences political thought in French Canada. It has kindled a lot of excitement. (Though it is also true that, except in the armed forces, it hasn't yet kindled any strong opposition . . . a bad sign.)

But first of all, should we be calling it separatism—which the separatists don't like—or independentism, or sovereigntism, or something like that, as they prefer?

The vocabulary one uses is a question of political choice. If what strikes you in this adventure is something yet to be born, if you dream of statehood, of sovereignty reconquered, then you are an independentist. If, on the contrary, you stop short at the idea of secession, of break-up, of a country split into three parts, then you talk about separatism, and the odds are 100 to 1 that you are anti-separatist.

Where does the movement come from? It's roots go down into an old substratum of nationalism, and in this sense it belongs to a tradition that goes back to Papineau.

But French-Canadian nationalism exists in ten or fifteen different forms. And why, if it is to become active again, should it take the most extreme of these?

One theory is that the first generation to free itself from the morass of Duplessism was starved for absolutes. All very well, but why should young people seek purity and idealism under the nationalist banner? Perhaps the generation before them had broken too radically with the life forces of the nation; today's youth, rediscovering these basic values, exalts them to the point of incandescence.

But this explanation is not entirely satisfactory. So the decolonization thesis is brought out. When twenty different Asiatic and African peoples, among the weakest and most impoverished in the world, gain their independence, French Canadians who have just rediscovered their own nation say, "Why not us too?"

To this must be added the influence of the new school of historical thought at the Université de Montréal. It claims that the conquest crushed us as a people, that without our own state we will never be able to build ourselves up again, that we are therefore doomed to vegetate until a slow and inglorious death overtakes us. This kind of talk drives some people to despair. It irritates others. The man of action refuses the role of just prolonging the agony. He opts for life and for what has been described as one of the conditions of life: the sovereign state.

The historians' theory is more complex than this. For that matter they are not separatists themselves. But interpretations of history have a greater impact when they are simplified and reduced to vulgar formulas.

Today's separatism was sired by the extreme right (Raymond Barbeau). Then, a new twist, it sprang violently up on the left (Raoul Roy). Next there appeared a separatism of the centre (André d'Allemagne). So it already represents a spectrum of social and political thought, which is normal enough. The idea of independence is the motive force, but there is no unanimity on how independence should be used. This fragmentation of separatism into three groups has its disadvantages, but at the same time it permits men of the most diverse and sometimes even of opposite views to work together towards a common goal.

It is M. Marcel Chaput who has summed up in the tightest formula what makes today's separatism new. He writes of French Canadians: "We are the best treated minority in the world. But that's not the point. *We don't want to be a minority any more.*"

He spells out his thought this way: "Neo-nationalism or sovereigntism differs from traditional nationalism in that it does not seek to correct injustices but seeks to remove the French-Canadian nation from its condition as a minority group. Even the elimination of all the difficulties that French Canadians are subject to would change NOTHING AT ALL."

As a nationalist in the civil service in Ottawa, M. Chaput has himself been subject to much mischief and bullying (one incident in particular having almost cost him his job). No doubt he was exasperated. But he overcame his irritation. He considers it normal that the majority should impose their language and their views. The griefs of traditional nationalists seem to him to be useless lamentations. Majorities are just like that, he argues—and here at least all separatists concur. The majority mentality is stronger than they are. It's their inner law. They lean with all their weight in one direction. They crush the weaker element without even realizing it. It is senseless to reproach them for it. The thing to do is to break free and become one's own majority somewhere else.

I won't undertake to reply to this argument now. It contains several self-evident truths, but I reject it just the same, for it seems to me to be too mechanical, too geometrical, to be humanly true. I will return to it in another essay.

For the time being I will simply raise two problems.

Separatism is picking up strength again. Intellectually, it is fashionable to take it with a grain of salt; that's a mistake. Questions of snobbery apart, it is as good as other theories that are treated with reverence. The movement now has three or four thousand militants, a fact not to be taken lightly. But they are all drawn from the same milieu. Separatism has not yet reached the masses, and it is difficult to see how it ever will. The nationalist movement succeeded in 1933 because of the economic crisis, in 1943 because of conscription. But separatism has never even come close to results like these. Will it also have its chance in history, and if so, how?

It has been said that French Canadians have no political ideas, only feelings. Maybe that's true. It should be carefully noted, however, that in general their feelings have been reasonable and moderate. They possess a singular faculty for resistance. They bend in the storm without snapping. They have never shown any inclination to force the hand of destiny. Are they likely to change in this respect?

The second problem is that separatism until now corresponds primarily to an intention. Its philosophy is clear but a little short on facts. It has not yet explored its own potentialities, or to be more precise, the specialists have not yet set about exploring them—the economists, sociologists, jurists, experts in political action and theory, psychologists, etc. In all these fields, what would be the foreseeable results of political independence? Would it bring about a deterioration in the standard of living? Would it have the stimulating moral effect that one might expect? How would the new state effectively fight off the pressure of American influence? How would a certain measure of political independence be achieved, by what means? What allegiances and what resistance would be stirred up by this process? And so on. Of course I am thinking of an impartial examination of the separatist hypothesis in which each expert would follow the logic of his own particular discipline and not his political convictions.

To undertake such an analysis is beyond the competence of the ordinary lecturer or journalist. But until it is undertaken, or at least until its more important aspects are examined, separatism risks appearing more a kind of gratuitous revolt than a serious revolutionary act.

August 1961

Independence
v.
Federalism

Are there disadvantages to being a minority?

Good God, yes! The history of the last one hundred years is rich in instances. Still engraved on our collective subconscious are all the contradictory impulses of the minority complex:

towards love or rejection; towards cowardice or fanaticism; towards building those long-cherished walls around ourselves that must be preserved at any price, or towards closing ourselves in behind odious walls that prevent us from seeing and breathing, walls that certain of us hurl ourselves furiously against in an attempt to bring them down. . . .

To be French-Canadian is to be dipped in a good strong dye. If you doubt it, just look around at all those who wanted to bleach themselves free but could never quite make it. I can still hear a couple of New Canadians, women who are good friends, who are married to French Canadians, and who move freely in our intellectual circles, saying to each other: "If only they'd give it a rest. If only they'd talk about something else. Sure, Quebec is interesting, but it's not the only thing in the world. The poor devils have got a real fixation. They can't get over it. They keep digging in deeper and deeper, like wounded animals. . . ."

There is only one sure way to escape it: indifference. Don't fuss, just close up soul and let yourself slip gently into the American Dream. . . . If you're unlucky enough to think about it again, back it comes like the itch. It's a kind of tattoo. It's our wounds that are dyed French-Canadian.

Under any political regime where the operative hypothesis is majority rule, it's tough to be a minority. But that statement doesn't exactly cover the facts of the case. Belonging to an ethnic minority is not the same thing as belonging to an ideological minority. Cultural divisions do not separate people on every level. Socialists and Liberals, for example, are recruited in both Canadian communities. Nevertheless the two groups do not live their socialism or their Liberal ideas in the same way. So it is a complex reality we are dealing with, and the mathematicians and engineers of political theory had better be careful not to play around with statistics.

Besides, there are minorities and minorities. In some provinces French Canadians constitute scarcely five per cent of the population. But on the over-all they make up almost one-third of the country and form a majority in one of the two main provinces. The fact that they are the majority in Quebec, and the conviction that they will soon become so in New Brunswick, is a political reality whose judicial, sociological, and psychological consequences are of prime importance. As a result we are a significant factor in Canadian politics, and we know it.

Just the same, politically speaking we don't control our own destiny. Certain French Canadians have now come to pose this problem exclusively in terms of mastering their own political future. They are sick of being a minority and want to convince their compatriots to separate from the rest of the country to form a majority in an independent state.

They allow that until now we have been well treated as a minority. But is it true? That depends on how you interpret the rights of the majority.

In a book written many years ago, Prins sums up the problem this way: "With respect to the legal order, the minority must bow to the majority; but with respect to justice, the majority must bow to the common good." Does "the common good" consist in crushing or in threatening one of the constituent parties, or even in just letting it quietly stagnate?

In our system the executive function falls to the majority; it decides who will lead the country and in what direction. The majority makes the rulers, it does not make the truth. For my own part, I cannot accept that the direction of the state should be turned over to the majority unless the strictest attention is paid to the rights of others. This holds all along the line: the rights of (minority) Catholic schools in British Columbia should be as vigorously defended as those of (minority) neutral schools in Quebec. I maintain that I have the right, morally, to judge and if need be condemn the majority, any majority. Without that right, you impose a paralysing conformity upon me—that of the totalitarian democracy.

The power of the majority is limited; it does not prevent rivers from flowing, mountains from standing there, or people from being different. The majority must take the existence of rivers, mountains, and people's differences into account.

Minority "nations", for that matter, also have certain obligations of fidelity towards the state to which they belong. The right to secede, posed as a general principle—and it must be so posed if we are going to take the subject seriously at all—is a dangerous postulate. If French Canadians have the incontestable right to quit Canada whenever they want to, then why shouldn't Brittany

or Alsace quit France, the Walloons quit Belgium, and the
Sicilians or the Welsh quit Italy or Great Britain? But Central
Europe is the classical example of how the application of this
principle sows anarchy and throws every achievement into perpetual doubt. It is a kind of right to divorce by simple unilateral
decision exercised against the state whose composition is not simple but complex.

It will be objected that all this is nothing but political moralizing
and that we must face up to the facts, that rather than lose ourselves
in dreams or wishful thinking we must get down to the brass
tacks of basic social realities.

And what do they tell us? That for all its declarations the
central state (and even more significant, nine provinces out of
ten) is not *canadien* but Canadian. And also that to be incapable
of setting up our own sovereign institutions and to be impotent
in having the final say on our own political destiny is a real
weakness. This has been demonstrated a hundred times over,
and once, twenty years ago, at a time of war and conscription,
in a most serious way. However, if I had the time, I think I
could show that even on that occasion we exercised more influence
than we thought, for the events of 1917 and the fierce will of
our people in the first conscription crisis remained vivid in memory as a threat that would have to be faced again.

But fundamentally what we want is to cease being the weaker
ones. So isn't there a singular amount of illusion in the separatist
solution?

The real problem, the real anguish, comes from being a minority
in North America, a tiny minority of one to forty in the middle
of a mass civilization.

And if this minority should become a very small independent
republic on the United States border, would it really have gained
anything? It would possess new and important tools of autonomy;
there would be an upsurge of national vigour; that is true. But
as a state it would be much weaker, hence in much greater danger
of falling under the influence of American colonization. It would
have to hunt for allies elsewhere. And do we, a minority that
is not backed up in America by an immense reservoir of human
resources, really believe that we are capable of becoming another
Cuba?

What remains for us to do is to use what we have—the provincial state of Quebec—but to really use it and not just go on shouting like children about everything we could do if only we lived under ideal conditions. What also remains for us is the task of patiently widening our powers and establishing the foundations of a new federalism.

September 1961

Quebec, Capital of French Canada

Quebec has opened a *Maison du Québec* in Paris. The province has taken to acting as a state, an act which, they say, France is almost ready to recognize, and one which hasn't stirred up much enthusiasm in Ottawa. The provincial government plans to open a similar house in London. It has pledged financial aid to the World Congress of Francophone Universities, if other states are willing to participate in kind. In these ways it is playing a modest international role, doing it by way of culture, which is the proper sphere of the provincial state.

The government is also talking about giving moral and financial support to French minority groups dispersed throughout Canada, and even throughout America. Perhaps we will see *Maisons du Québec* discreetly appearing in Toronto and in other English-Canadian cities where French-speakers are numerous enough. In this way, it could be claimed, the provincial state is playing a Canadian role. These projects are initiatives of the new Ministry of Cultural Affairs, itself a creation of the electoral program of the Liberal party. In both you can see the personal influence of M. Georges Lapalme.

The key idea behind these moves is that Quebec City is the capital of French Canada. In a certain sense, and, one might say, in one sense certainly, the state of Quebec is the national state of French Canadians, and from this situation stem rights and responsibilities which we have now consciously assumed for the first time.

Is this such a revolutionary attitude?

Ontario has maintained a kind of semi-official consulate in London for years. Even Maurice Duplessis has been known to help a French-Canadian institution in another province. So precedents do exist.

For a long time Quebec has also accepted particular responsibilities on behalf of French minorities in other provinces. Quebec citizens have fought in every battle for French schools in provinces where francophones are in a minority; for example, during the First World War the campaign against Regulation XVII of the Ontario Schools Act helped aggravate the conscription crisis. But ordinarily these struggles were waged on the federal level, or were turned over to private groups. Now the Conseil de Vie Française has as its specific aim the uniting of all the forces of French Canada across the country.

Let's take a concrete example. Twenty years ago, Western French Canadians felt they needed their own radio station. They asked the federal government and were refused. They then launched a subscription campaign to which Québécois were invited to contribute. This eventually permitted the installation of four French stations in the West. In this case neither the federal state nor the state of Quebec intervened.

Now it is the provincial state that is going to take the initiative. On behalf of the diaspora of French culture, it will act, I repeat, as the national state of French Canadians, in the same way, its promoters add, that Ottawa is the capital of the Anglo-Canadian state.

This evolution begins with the refusal of the central state to act as a bi-national, or, if you prefer, as a bi-cultural state. In view of this failure in federal policy, the Lesage government has clearly set out to demonstrate that Quebec is not a province like the others.

Is this a case of abuse of provincial powers?

Quebec draws the financial backing for its political policies from taxes which it must levy "for provincial purposes". Are the new goals which the government has set itself "provincial" in a constitutional sense? Until now they seem to me to be indisputably so. The term "provincial rights" could even be interpreted more widely. But how far will it stretch?

The real problem, however, lies elsewhere. A "cultural affairs" policy, if it is to go anywhere at all, is going to cost plenty. Will Quebec have the necessary resources to carry it through? If Quebec becomes the national state of French Canadians, as Ottawa, in the main, represents the national state to the rest of Canada, it will have to do so without enjoying the same resources or the same authority. If Quebec, in its role as a province unlike the others, assumes responsibilities which have no equivalent in the other provinces, it should be able to tap other budgets or discover new sources of revenue. And in this field its prerogatives are limited, for the central state and the nine other provinces are English-Canadian.

As things now stand, Quebec citizens pay taxes to Ottawa, in return for which they do receive important services (family allowances, defence, diplomatic representation, etc.). But as French Canadians they do not obtain as much as Anglo-Canadians do, even without being aware of it, and this is even truer for French Canadians living outside Quebec.

If the situation were to remain unchanged in Ottawa and if, on the contrary, it were to develop even more vigorously in Quebec in the direction indicated, it would soon become intolerable. We would little by little become aware of the fact that our "national state" is incomplete, relatively poor, and constantly limited in its initiatives. The more it became "national" in its objectives (and the functions of the state far outstrip cultural activities), the more its weakness and its limitations would become apparent, the more it would demand power and money to pursue goals which would become ever more pressing and more clearly defined. In this way a policy designed to come to the aid of French minorities in other provinces could, in the long run, push us even closer to separatism.

You would be wrong to suppose that, because I am not a separatist, the prospect of such an evolution seems reprehensible to me. It is, on the contrary, natural and organic. Either English Canada will see the light in time, in which case it will begin to work with us towards a fundamental transformation of the central state, a development I have never ceased to hope for, or else it will continue to forget that we exist (except in Quebec), it will prevent, obstruct, or emasculate any real attempt to renew Canadian federalism, and it will remain indifferent, off-hand, distant, or scornful towards us. If it does, then one day, inevitably, we will take a stand and it will be the entire nation that will opt for another solution. It was a moderate in politics, Maxime Raymond, who, right in the middle of the war, told the English-Canadian majority: "We are perfectly willing to share the house, but it has to be a livable place for everyone." It is possible, after the experiment has gone on for years, that French Canadians may slowly become convinced that the house is not, in fact, habitable. Then, given the right international context, given (*and this is most important*) that independence has become a serious project and is not just an adventure, given that we have success-fully laid the foundations of our own dwelling, why then the will to be completely free under our own roof will become irresistible.

Alongside an official separatism which is still on its first legs, we are beginning to see in Quebec the growth of feelings that have scarcely ever been manifested before in our history and that are not easy to define. In particular there is a new kind of self-assurance that is less impatient and more realistic than it has ever been. It can be seen in men of action and intellectuals who do not willingly advertise themselves as nationalists, in men who politically may be New Democrats, Liberals, Union Nationale, or Independents. They share neither the anxieties of the old-style Quebec nationalists nor the scorn that Anglo-Cana-dian nationalists are inclined to lavish on French-Canadian society. One of them recently said to me: "For a separatist, everything begins with separation. For me, it seems possible that everything will end there; I mean that we will harvest it like a ripe fruit, if we know how to cultivate it properly."

History never moves in straight lines. Not so long ago I was baffled by a younger generation that seemed to be turning away from nationalism. Today that same generation is taken aback by the breed of young wolves who are making nationalism their career. What will the next ten years bring? What will girls and boys who are twelve or fifteen today be thinking when they are no longer adolescents but young adults?

For the time being we are extremely interested in what is happening in our midst; many of us are passionately involved in our adventure; we are less poor, less helpless; we are beginning to accomplish things; our more ambitious projects don't frighten us off any more; we are ready to discuss in public problems which only yesterday we scrupulously hid from one another. This new ferment constantly goes beyond politics but never ceases to have political repercussions. Is it just the euphoria that follows the demise of Duplessis? Many of us feel that it has become possible to be creative again. And that the only sure prescription for survival is to start to live.

November 1961

Nationalism in 1936 and 1961

Politicians in Quebec are asking themselves nowadays to what extent they should take the new wave of nationalism seriously. Is it reaching the voters? Will it ever become popular?

Some people fear French-Canadian nationalism. Others think of it as a spur. One curious turn of events is that the Union Nationale is in danger of losing its nationalist heritage. The party seems to have gone sour on provincial autonomy and, for the time being at least, has lost a lot of its grip. It hangs on, hews to its old traditions, declares itself partisan to private enterprise, denounces state intervention, and sides with those who consider our educational system untouchable. So it has become primarily a conservative party.

As for the Liberals, they seem rather wavering in their doctrinal attitudes. Doubtless they are delighted at the new upsurge of nationalist sentiment—that is, of course, as long as it remains "controllable". Which takes us back to the questions I raised at the beginning. Not long ago an old party workhorse told us: "In politics you never want to get too excited about nationalism; it comes and it goes." But sometimes it comes on very strong.

Young people are asking the same questions another way. They wonder if nationalism in the past ever reached the intensity that it has today.

How can one answer these questions? It's not easy to measure a nation's feelings. Nor is it easy to judge political movements out of their context.

In 1932-6 the backdrop to nationalism was the Depression. In 1942-5 it was war and conscription. In both cases nationalism became popular because of a state of crisis. In 1961 there is no equivalent crisis, yet nationalism is growing by leaps and bounds.

In both earlier cases nationalism sprang up *against* the party in power: against the Taschereau regime, and then against the pro-federal attitudes of the Godbout government. This time it has broken out after the death of Duplessis, and one can say that it aligns itself more or less with the Lesage government, which, as governments go, is still young.

But let's leave aside analogies that might be drawn with the war period. To me, more interesting parallels seem possible between nationalism in 1932 and 1961.

During the depression, nationalism first found its voice in various youth movements. I belonged to the first of these, a group called Jeune-Canada.

Here are the circumstances of its founding. In the summer of 1932 the Conservative government of R. B. Bennett called an Imperial Conference in Ottawa, an important event at that time. The central government commandeered the services of sixty specialists; there wasn't a single French Canadian among them. At the last minute, to save face, the government named *one* French-speaking official. That gave us a good notion of our importance in Ottawa.

A few months later a department head was to be selected for the Customs Office in Montreal. Despite a swift build-up of public opinion, a certain Mr. Laing got the post. The students took the news of this appointment as a slap in the face. They called a meeting at the Théâtre Gésu and issued a *Manifesto of the Younger Generation* on the rights of French Canadians.

So the reaction was one of wounded pride. We felt humiliated, and we rebelled at the fact of our non-existence. It was a brand of nationalism that is at one and the same time very emotional and very formalist, therefore very profound, for what is at stake is the sense of personal dignity. We felt a deep solidarity with a human group that was being treated with utter scorn, but at the same time we felt spiritually impoverished, for all our emotional response amounted to was nervous irritation and the boiling of anger.

What was the next step? Our recognition of the economic inferiority of French Canadians and the forced admission that this subordination was a grave malady. How could it be cured? For the most part we of Jeune-Canada were not much interested in economic problems, and yet we were drawn by our nationalistic fervour into this area where we were notoriously incompetent. The group accepted, almost without examination, ideas that were in the air at the time: for example, "home-market purchasing". That was a consequence of the belief that as consumers French Canadians had one sure weapon, their buying power, which they should use to nourish local industries. It was a simplistic idea, extremely inefficient, later to be linked with that of co-operative buying. Another example was the nationalization of "big trusts", a vague word which directed our revolt against large companies financed by foreign capital which were exploiting the natural resources of Quebec.

The first of these objectives favoured small capitalists in the province and won us the friendship of certain industrialists and businessmen. As far as our "anti-trust" campaign was concerned, we let ourselves be absorbed by Dr. Philippe Hamel who had launched the movement in Quebec City and got ourselves called "revolutionaries" by Premier Taschereau.

Up to this point we had the livelier type of university student with us, but we had failed almost completely to reach the masses.

None the less, at a time when radio was just beginning and TV didn't exist yet, we held public meetings that were just as animated and much better attended than those of the separatists today.

From here on the picture gets somewhat blurry, for Paul Gouin founded his Action Libérale Nationale group to rejuvenate Taschereau's party, drew up a program of reforms which had been pending for years, and came out strong against the dictatorial practices and corruption of an old political regime on the decline.

We viewed the A.L.N. with suspicion. Its reformist politicians weren't pure enough for our taste, and after all, salvation was scheduled to come from our generation. So we cooled a little towards the idea of direct action. Forced to conclude that there was no sign of a Saviour on the horizon (otherwise we would have been easily seduced by the mystique of a leader ... and what a pity Abbé Lionel Groulx was strapped into a cassock!), and disgusted by the mediocrity of our contemporaries, we sank all our hopes in education. What would save Quebec? "Education," was our reply. But by that we meant nationalist education. We reproached the public schools with being too neutral or lukewarm in patriotic matters. We wanted them intensely nationalistic, as if it was a foregone conclusion that nationalism was the final answer to all the problems that besieged the French-Canadian milieu. It was only later, and even then only in very general terms, that we were able to put into correct perspective the prime necessity of building up levels of competence throughout the whole educational system.

At the same time we read Abbé Groulx's books and the inquiry published in *L'Action française* under the title "Our Political Independence", and some of us drew separatist conclusions from them. But separatism remained a distant and hazy ideal which evaporated little by little as our own movement developed.

There were other youth groups, too, notably La Nation led by Paul Bouchard, which was unconditionally separatist and extreme right in politics (drawing inspiration from Maurras and Mussolini, never from Hitler). Here verbal violence and frenzied nationalism were the order of the day, as well as open war against the domination of Anglo-Saxon institutions and parliamentary democracy alike. La Nation was fanatic in outlook, but it had very little influence on French-Canadian nationalism. Perhaps, indirectly, it revived the idea of the provincial nation-state and in this way prepared people for a more rigorous conception of real autonomy.

But little by little the nationalist fervour died. By 1936 Maurice Duplessis's Union Nationale party was in power and his policies deflated or discouraged the nationalists. We felt that we had failed and that it would be up to a new generation to begin the adventure again. And the young generation of today has already reached the point where they are beginning to look to the youth of tomorrow.

Quite evidently there are many similarities between those times and ours. But historical parallels never coincide all along the line. The ideas that were current then were less coherent and more dependent, perhaps, on particular men and circumstances. Today's nationalism can draw on native intellectual resources. It benefits from a greater freedom of expression and can follow its own inspiration to the end.

But it has not yet won over the masses. It remains the preserve of social strata that have always been traditionally nationalist. That is why the politicians aren't seriously scared. The real test of the political future of nationalism has yet to come. It is not just a question of whether or not it will become a popular movement, but above all of what might happen if it does.

January 1962

Confederation But . . .

Should the protection afforded French language rights in this country be "put on ice" as of now?

Several recent events, ranging from the upsurge of separatism to the Fulton proposal for the repatriation of the constitution, oblige us to examine this question.

In other words, which is better, a guarantee that the status quo will be maintained, or a more flexible situation in which certain gains are conceivable? I side with those who find the status quo intolerable, although I belong to a generation that has tolerated and sometimes even glorified it.

My stand is that Confederation is better than separation, as long as it is made over. But in the domain of language rights (and this is far from being the only vital area; the sharing of powers between the central state and provincial states is undoubtedly even more important), what is implied in "making over Confederation"?

To me it seems that it consists in this: Canada proclaims itself a bilingual country, but it barely is one. It is therefore essential to make it truly bilingual. I am speaking, of course, of its political institutions and not of individual citizens.

Progress in this realm over the last thirty years has been ridiculously slow. We were granted bilingual stamps, then bilingual banknotes, then simultaneous translation in Ottawa, piecemeal concessions, all of them. After each "victory" everything had to be started all over again. We French Canadians were handed a few humiliating crumbs to keep us constantly in mind of our situation as a cultural minority.

In my opinion the question can and must be settled at one stroke—then we can get around to talking of other things.

In this perspective the country should accept frankly and without reservation in its political institutions the principle of official bilingualism. After this we should move on to an honest discussion of other projects whose realization is implied in the principle of state bilingualism. In this way a series of practical objectives would become apparent, some of which could be reached immediately, while others would require more time. Finally a time-table should be established for those measures which can only be realized slowly, and it should be followed religiously.

What measures can be taken without delay? I will give three examples: First, recognize French as an official language in all provincial legislatures; second, use both languages in all official documents (the celebrated "bilingual cheques" belong in this category, though they are just a drop in the bucket); third, complete the construction of a French-language radio network across the country so that in almost any place in Canada, French can be heard on the state radio.

These measures, particularly the first two, are symbolic gestures that the separatists will shrug off as of no importance. But I don't believe that this would be the reaction of the majority of French Canadians. The official recognition of French in Halifax or Victoria might only result in two or three speeches per year. But at least French would not be excluded from other legislatures. This would amount to a moral adhesion to the principle of bilingualism; practically speaking that is totally insufficient, but it paves the way for real reforms.

These cannot be accomplished rapidly and they require an enormous amount of good will and an imaginative approach. I am thinking, for example, of the progressive recognition of French as a working language in the federal civil service (in the armed forces in particular) and in administrative services in other provinces where the French-Canadian minority has reached a certain numerical importance. In another sphere I am thinking of the progressive and effective recognition of the right of French Canadians to be educated in their own language wherever possible and under the public school system.

How can we reach these goals? I have no global solution to offer. What I ask is that the question be seriously studied and, specifically, that a systematic inquiry be made of how the problem has been met in other states (for example, in Belgium and Switzerland). Another inquiry, as detailed as possible, should be undertaken to determine what motives prevent French Canadians at the present time from participating as fully as they should and could in the administration of their country.

It will be objected that these suggestions ride roughshod over constitutional boundaries. That is correct. For the time being I am examining what a bilingual state should be. Under Confederation its powers are fragmented. As things now stand, the proposed reforms would have to be approved by eleven governments. Isn't that as good as saying from the start that they are totally unrealizable?

Anyway, at present neither the central state nor any of the

provinces are, to my knowledge, ready to accept the idea. So the experiment might be tried in another manner.

Does there exist in English Canada a group of individuals numerous and open-minded enough to agree to study this "utopic" proposal more closely? I can imagine such a group meeting and forming, with an equal number of French Canadians, a kind of unofficial constituent body that would finally agree on a common program. Around this program a campaign of publicity and information could be launched in all parts of Canada.

Would such a venture stand any chance of success? A few years ago I wouldn't even have dared ask that question. But two developments have, it seems to me, made the experiment conceivable. On one hand, the reaction of a number of Anglo-Canadians to the Americanization of our country; on the other, Quebec separatism. These two new factors have certainly modified the opinions of at least some Anglo-Canadians. The question is, to what extent?

But suppose that the pessimists are right and that the scheme is an idle dream. Then a back-up solution must be envisaged.

If it is felt that on the provincial level the state of mind outside Quebec makes bilingualism impractical, it might be decided that each province would become unilingual. At that rate Quebec would become exclusively French. This raises the problem of linguistic minorities, and in particular that of the anglophone minority in Quebec. To that I would reply that Quebec should then model its linguistic policy on that of New Brunswick or Ontario.

For French Canadians are becoming less and less willing to pay the full price of a linguistic experiment that is already a century old. It goes without saying that to implement such a policy would require adjustments to the constitution.

There, in my opinion, is one of the meanings—in this case with regard to language—that "remaking Confederation" might have. To be sure, it should be more closely defined, and the whole problem should be examined systematically.

It's an urgent task. Events move quickly, and the concept of Canada is becoming more fragile by the hour.

March 1962

The
Anglo-Canadian Nation?

On a trip through the West a few years ago, I asked everyone
I met a stupid question. I asked them, "What is a Canadian?"
The answers I got were even less brilliant than the question.
As they began to mount up, my image of Canada began to fade
away, for they spoke of too wilful a faith in too faint an object.
Or are we to accept Pierre Berton's view of things as they
are today. He writes in the June 1963 *Maclean's*:

> Without Quebec we are nothing; without Quebec Canada makes
> no sense as a nation; without Quebec we lose the one aspect
> of our society that makes us unique; without Quebec we are
> carbon-copy Americans, lacking only a vote in Congress.

I must admit my uneasiness on reading these lines. For us
to be the sole source of originality for the rest of the country
makes even less sense than Canada without Quebec. When one
social group can define itself only in terms of its relation to another
group, that means that the first party doesn't really exist. As
for the second, it's like feeling the hand of a drowning man clutch-
ing your shoulder.

Mr. Berton is neither an historian nor a sociologist but a clever
journalist. So I look to him not for a profound analysis of reality,
but at least for an intuitive grasp of the opinion that the group
he belongs to has of itself.

Or if not the group as a whole, at least some of its more dynamic
factions. And, precisely, a little further on Pierre Berton tells
us that English Canada has a generous complement of reactionaries
who are always automatically ready to fight yesterday's battles
over again.

Often they are anti-papists of the Loyal Orange Association
variety who fear French Quebec even more than they fear living
next to the States. They mistrust the French language because
of a "mystic belief" that a child who learns another language

becomes, to a certain extent, "one of them". So in order to remain himself, the Orangeman is forced to refuse the very thing
that might give a sense of identity to English Canada: a friendly
and open co-existence with French Canada.

This kind of man, apparently, hides his true feelings behind
arguments like these:

> If we allow French to be spoken in the public schools of this
> province we are going to have other groups who want it. . . . The
> Italians could ask for it. . . . You'll have a Tower of Babel if
> you permit this.

It's an old argument that still flourishes on the Prairies, and
it's one that never fails to make us furious, for it denies the
bi-ethnic or bi-cultural character of Canada. The most recent
wave of immigration has given it new force by reminding us
that there are now not just two groups to share Canada, but
several.

And indeed, the latest census reveals that as far as ethnic origin
is concerned, Canada is divided as follows:

British descent	43 per cent
French descent	30 per cent
Others	27 per cent

Which permits the following observations: 1. That the British
no longer form an absolute majority, and 2. that the "others"
are almost as numerous as the French Canadians.

It's easy to quote statistics. But one shouldn't draw any hasty
conclusions from them, for they fall a long way short of the
truth. For one thing they do not reveal the fact that the great
majority of key posts, particularly in the economic sphere, remain
in the hands of those of British descent. And above all they lend
an artificial unity to those "others", who remain essentially
divided.

In a recent speech, Marcel Faribault pointed out that the most
numerous of these minority groups is the German (about one
million), which makes up less than six per cent of the total
population, "and no other group exceeds 500,000". To call the
totality of these ethnic groups "New Canadians" is handy but
false; many of them are third-generation Canadians, whereas hun-

dreds of thousands of Britishers (and a few Frenchmen) arrived among us only a few years ago. The only common characteristic of the "others" is negative. All they share is that they belong neither to the British group nor to the French.

Despite statistics, then, we come back to the classical division between anglophones and francophones. And a necessary second adjustment requires us to count the vast majority of "others" in with the anglophones, though on the cultural level their influence seems to have been less cohesive than dispersive.

As if to emphasize this fact, the francophone group is now more and more frequently referred to as "French Canada", while to describe the anglophones, the only possible term seems to be "English-speaking Canadians". The former group, at least in Quebec, forms a highly specific cultural entity. The latter, much more numerous and more widely dispersed, is today urgently seeking a sense of unity and identity.

Old "British" Canadians, at a time when the English ascendancy was still in force, never looked to us for aid in self-identification. They knew they were very different from Americans. Today's anglophone establishment, which coincides with its American counterpart, is anxious and leaderless, if not already assimilated. This is why they either are feverishly trying to get closer to us or, on the contrary, find in the present state of affairs additional reasons for ignoring us completely, since in what concerns them we are neither competitors nor adversaries. It goes without saying that I am speaking here of thoughtful, contemporary English-speaking Canadians, and not of any of those groups that are historically or otherwise retarded.

This is doubtless the reason why it is so difficult for French Canadians to find points of communication with the other culture.

Of the two groups, we still remain less numerous and, more significant, less powerful. Yet despite all our contradictions we know better what we want. English-speaking Canada is the majority, firmly established, and still vigorous in its grasp of reality. But it is in its will to survive that its weakness is most apparent. Its real problem is not us but its own attitude towards the United States, and it so happens that our demands aggravate this problem. It finds itself questioning whether it is really worthwhile continuing to exist as English Canada. Or if it is possible, how much it will cost. And whether it is worth paying the price.

I am interpreting here dozens of conversations, hundreds of articles, countless political speeches, all of which betray this vast collective hesitation before which we are nothing but powerless witnesses.

It is possible to imagine that to protect itself against the troubles in Quebec, English Canada might forge a new sense of unity and learn to define itself once again. Then we would have *someone to talk to* and they could talk back, and the battle would be fierce. But that would be better, it seems to me, than messing around in the kind of swamp we are all bogged down in now.

July 1963

The F.L.Q.

It's the night of May 16. At a friend's house on the outskirts of Westmount we had talked for hours about the future of French Canada. There were only three of us left. We were just about to leave.

Suddenly, an explosion, very close. We look at each other. The same thought flashes into our minds. Then another explosion.

"It's them again, the F.L.Q."

We all have the same reaction: Let's go and take a closer look. We walk towards the sound, an old army tactic, only this time, instead of marching towards the sound of the guns, we walk towards the detonations, not a very reliable guide for that matter, because the bombs are going off at random. The radio is silent. We try to telephone the newspapers, but there is no reply.

Where the hell are we anyway? It's hard to realize that this is Montreal. . . .

Finally our luck turns. We see some debris at the end of a street. A police car is parked there. Some officers are taking notes. That's about all they can do. A few people shaken out of their sleep in the middle of the night stand around looking dazedly at an eviscerated telephone booth, pieces of mail-box, and broken windows in the surrounding houses.

It's like a stupid accident. There aren't any victims, but everyone standing there is thinking: It might have been me. A taxi-cab driver is talking excitedly about another bomb that, he says, blew up a church.

We head over that way. The church isn't badly damaged. We look it over, inquisitively, but there isn't anything to understand. So we all go home.

Next morning it's reported that explosives had been planted in other mail-boxes, but their timing devices were either defective or poorly regulated, so those that weren't duds risked setting off the dynamite at the wrong time. One of these bombs exploded when demolitions expert Leja was trying to defuse it.

The terrorists can no longer plead ignorance. A few weeks ago O'Neil, the night watchman, was killed. *They* know. *They* know the risks they impose on innocent bystanders. *They* know that any one of those bombs might have killed someone—either someone out for a midnight stroll or, the next morning, children on their way to school.

Will they begin again? Who will their next anonymous letter be directed to? Whose death in the mail-box? How many of them are there? Who are they, and how do they operate? This attack on Westmount is just for show. Where will they strike next?

I think of them as dangerous animals escaped from their cages, holed up in some dark corner and threatening, if they go on, to sow panic in the city.

And then they turn up with the faces of children.

We see them in court. They might be our sons' friends, or our sons.

It was those youngsters who did it.

The apparent injustice of justice stirs our pity. If one forgot oneself for a moment, it would be easy to forget what they had done.

And yet they did it. But why? What kind of a cause do they serve?

The state defends itself. One could wish it did a better job of it. But it is normal that it should defend itself, just as it would be incongruous for it to be swayed by pity. Any weakness would be self-negation. Order must be preserved now. The whole mechanism of justice must be brought to bear against crimes in common law.

As for the man in the street, he is upset by it all and is prey to contradictory feelings which he tries to reconcile as best he can.

To be sure, there's the usual amount of sheer indifference.

"And you, madam. Does the F.L.Q. worry you?"

"Not me, young man. I sleep very well, thank you. A few bombs don't scare me. They didn't even wake me up."

Those who *are* afraid claim that there's a simple solution—that against such dangerous public enemies the police should be given unlimited powers. Acts of savagery bring out the beast in others, and the rancorous bourgeois strikes back with borrowed claws.

But the most common reaction, the one I hear from strangers who speak or write to me, runs something like this:

"Yes, it's horrible. But they're so young. And then think of their families. . . . They certainly are fearless. It's better than hanging around the streets. You really can't help being just a little bit proud of them."

So there's a kind of semi-complicity which Léon Dion analysed extremely well in *Le Devoir* last month in his article "The Aftermath of a Coroner's Inquest" (*Le Devoir*, June 21, 1963). Among the youth of Quebec there's a kind of gut sympathy. They say they don't sanction violence, but maybe that's just to excuse themselves for not having gone that far. Some of them, at least, are quite openly its exponents and theorists. Armed with some poorly digested Franz Fanon, they preach the necessity of hatred in no uncertain terms. "We have learned another language, the language of *hate*. . . . To choose to fight for the people is also to choose to hate their enemies and fight them to the end." No doubt they are quite happy to scandalize their elders. But perhaps it is true that they're just sharpening their claws. I'm ready to believe that the F.L.Q. network has been smashed, but I'm afraid that violence is here to stay.

It is disconcerting to think that violence has broken out today, when it wasn't even considered a serious possibility at the time of the conscription crisis. There were thousands of angry young people then, supported by an angry population, and besides, each of us felt personally threatened. Anyone could have set up the cry: "You might as well die here as on the battlefields of Europe."

I did hear it said. But there was no revolt. Nobody blew up any army installations. And yet we detested them as the symbol of a servitude much more real and keenly felt than today's abuses. And in those days violence had turned half the world into a blood-bath.

Today the situation is less acute. But there has developed, starting in countries in process of decolonization, a contamination of terrorism, considered to be the weapon of the underprivileged. Those who have been infected by the disease and who have succumbed to its temptations of violence do not seem to be doctrinaire fanatics but very young improvisers. I don't pretend to judge the accused, whom I do not know. But those who defend them most passionately, and who may be tempted to imitate them tomorrow, are fledgling converts to nationalism, amateurs whose convictions appear to be as absolute as they are flimsy and artificial. They are adolescents who dream of "disalienating the nation" by setting off bombs, in the same way that others of their generation dream of getting out from under the paternal roof, or still others look for violent emotions in risky sports. It's all part of the air we breathe in this modern age.

Is it a characteristic of this generation? Of our times more likely, for in the same age group there are others who revolt as strongly *against* violence. They stand for the same kind of refusal—for one that requires an even deeper conviction perhaps, because violence is more present and more seductive than ever—and they turn resolutely and totally away from violence because of the respect they feel for man.

Non-violence can be dangerous, too, since it can be a cover for cowardice. Gandhi warned of this repeatedly. But non-violent activity also carries a certain element of risk with it, especially if it is conducted outside the limits of legality. A separatist would unquestionably show more courage, or at least more considered courage, if instead of throwing bombs he refused, for example, to pay his federal income tax. Naturally, such a gesture would be less showy, and he would have to assume the whole risk for his action. The first victim would be himself; there wouldn't be any mutilated demolitions experts or children. But if the movement became generalized, the state would be more profoundly hurt. An individual performing an act like this lays himself open to prosecution by the state; he doesn't go hunting for martyrs in the street.

It's easy for me to talk, since I am neither a separatist nor a terrorist, nor am I a conscientious objector as far as paying income tax is concerned. I do know, however, what I respect and admire, and for me violence is a human regression. American blacks who let themselves be fire-hosed and insulted and bitten by dogs are, in my eyes, higher on the human scale and truer servants of their nation than bomb planters and the perpetrators of terrorist plots.

August 1963

Fanaticism

A close friend who lives abroad wrote to me last summer: "It bears repeating, even if it's a cliché, we're an adolescent people. And one of the characteristics of the adolescent is that he believes that what happens to him has never happened before. He has no sense of relativity; he sees his own situation as absolute. 'First' for him means 'unique', an absolute first. You can see this in all our major debates—on education, on separatism, etc." And my friend concluded succinctly with these striking and instructive remarks: "As a people we haven't suffered yet. We're ignorant with that particular kind of ignorance. We don't know how to hold opinions. An opinion isn't a certitude. To transform an opinion into a certitude, fanaticism is the key."

That made me jump. I had read the passage the way one often reads a journalist, that is, very fast and very carelessly—even faster and more carelessly than they write. I thought I had heard a command: "Let's give fanaticism a try!" whereas my correspondent had been describing a mental process: "For an opinion to become a certitude, and sometimes even a certitude that is ready to kill, a certain dose of fanaticism is required."

But what is fanaticism?

You will have to excuse me for taking down the dictionary again. They say that analysis is a destructive habit and that it's better to trust one's intuitions. That's all right for the creative act. But when one wants to reflect on a word in order to penetrate a contemporary attitude, it's probably not a bad idea to inquire what current meaning is given to that word.

According to *Littré*, the fanatic is, in a first sense, someone who believes he is divinely inspired. The word has now lost some of its religious overtones, and the second meaning of fanaticism, according to *Quillet* (who follows *Littré* in this), is blind and violent adhesion to some opinion. Even if the fanatic doesn't believe in God, he still thinks he hears voices: the atheist deifies his own inspiration.

Fanaticism means great disorder of heart and mind, but great strength at the same time. It is true that fanatics of different kinds have changed the course of history; whether they have made mankind any nobler or happier is another question.

The fanatic violently rejects tepidity and indifference and is right in doing so. But where does tepidity begin and end? Is it possible that intellectual vigour and strength of feeling are the attributes of certain opinions and not others? One would have to be an adolescent to believe in such exclusiveness. Just as there are fanatics of revolution and fanatic conservatives, moderation too has its share of passionate devotees.

But there is another ambiguous word. What exactly is passion?

I find in my *Littré* two quotations that point up its ambivalence very well.

The philosopher Malebranche says: "It is none the less true that passionate people interest us passionately and that they leave on our imaginations impressions very like those they have been struck with themselves."

And Philippe de Commines, the chronicler, writes: "Even the wisest often err when passion enters the discussion."

So we can say that passion is an indispensable motive force, but also that it sometimes deranges the intelligence. It doesn't matter if the passion is large or small; little passions are perfectly capable of warping little minds. On the other hand, is it possible to conceive a great work without powerful passions? Passion is beautiful, even in its wildest paroxysms, as long as it doesn't close in upon itself. To forget others and the dignity of others is a great sin against humanity and one which no one can ever completely avoid in his life's struggle. Fanaticism consists in forgetting this systematically.

That is why the most detestable kind is intellectual fanaticism—be it religious or a-religious—and I am speaking, naturally, of the fanatic who has reached the adult stage. He ends up thinking in categories; he no longer sees individual human beings; he is a paralysed spirit in what he imagines to be a petrified world, one which he judges in terms of his own fixed ideas. But basically he is more worried or anguished than most. Often he is the most self-tortured kind of person imaginable, and this is what keeps him human. But he refuses to explore these troubled regions and takes refuge instead in the fortress he has erected for himself, dragging as many of his contemporaries as he can in after him. And here he believes himself impregnable.

When he judges society around him, he has an easy game of it. I referred a moment ago to certitudes that were ready to kill. But our rotting society of "wise men" can also play the role of assassin and does it so discreetly that it is scarcely noticeable. For it is hard on the powerless — the poor, the maladjusted, the uneducated, any small human subgroup. . . . It is quite ready to crush those whose voice is too weak to be heard, and in its headlong pursuit of power it can even entertain the idea of self-destruction. Yet it is hard to say to what degree any new fanaticism is truly liberating.

What about Cuba?

I think that as far as fanaticism is concerned it wasn't Castro who started things. He harshly liquidated the residue of the Batista regime, but, considering the revolutionary context, his first acts were relatively moderate. Soon, however, foreign interests who considered themselves threatened or wronged began to cry havoc in the States and little by little various lobbies began to marshal public opinion and the American government. That's when the real excesses began. When the big bully denies the little fellow the right to breathe, why, it may not be a very pleasant sight, but it's perfectly natural for the little fellow to go mad with rage. And when the situation becomes so horrible that it compels those who are caught up in it to make a choice between servility and revolt, then I can understand the revolt. But revolution itself creates situations that are often inextricable.

When you belong to the weaker side and are hypothetically destined to remain weak, then it isn't very wise to invite a test of strength and become totally engaged in the brutal play of force and counterforce in a given situation. No matter how disgusted the weak become with the hypocrisy of the strong, they are wrong to scoff at justice, for in doing so they close the door on the one world in which they could live in liberty. It is possible to reduce human history to the simple question of a balance of power and in that way base your theory on one of the most infallible of all social mechanisms. But man is not just an animal. His moral progress may be slow and precarious, none the less it exists, and it has never, I think, been stimulated by fanaticism.

People are called fanatics not because they believe in certain ideas but because of the way they live that belief. When a doctrine springs from a narrow clique, the danger of fanaticism increases. Men who live in relative solitude feel themselves engaged in a struggle with almost the whole of society. Convictions reach their boiling point and emotions become incandescent precisely because of all the obstacles that must be surmounted and the near universal opposition that the little group encounters.

To speak more concretely, I do not identify separatism with fanaticism, although a number of separatists are fanatics of the most sombre hue. There are others among them, however, who are fighting within the movement against any hardening of thought into sectarian attitudes, and these men should be credited with great personal courage. They follow an ideal that exalts them without alienating them. Their liberal views are more praiseworthy than those held by the defenders of the status quo, for they must inevitably be maintained at the price of an inner struggle. They refuse to abandon themselves to an ideology or to the mania of some messianic creed. This is a temptation that the man in the street never has to face. It remains totally foreign to him unless he finds his own interests directly threatened.

The fanaticism of those in power is secretive. There are many ways of hiding it. It consists in not moving, in not listening, in mechanically repeating the gestures of yesterday. If a threat looms, then a spark kindles in that usually serene eye. So we must also speak of fanatics of law and order and of sectarians of moderation who remain blind and deaf to the movements of history. I can still hear ringing in my ears the voice of a big businessman, who had been as cool and realistic as you please until then, saying: "Those French Canadians should remember who won the battle of the Plains of Abraham." Even physically he wasn't the same; his features became distorted; I was looking once again into the face of fanaticism.

Invariably excess calls out excess. When the one speaks, the other wakes. Hatred settles in and the inexpiable war begins.

January 1964

We Are a Winter Race

Wintertime! Good old wintertime! Terror of intense cold, folklore of frosty weather, cordial traditions of ice and snow, deserts of solitude... But before this winter litany piles up too much, it might be wise to see just where we are. Right in the middle of it once again, that's where. Months of winter behind us, months of winter ahead. Now snow, now zero weather, and always that feeling of a bitter struggle lying in wait just on the other side of the door.

> *Mon pays ce n'est pas un pays*
> *C'est l'hiver*

I remember a long time ago, in Paris, what passed for winter was day after day of low grey sky and drizzle. The damp penetrated everything. The air was soft. There was little danger of dying from cold. But one felt a certain nostalgia. What one missed was a good snowstorm to make everything white and sparkling. Or better still, a nice sharp little cold snap with a powdering of chilly sunlight from a hard winter sun. Yes, we missed that. And the special harshness in the air. The burning in the throat and lungs. The wind that cuts right through your clothes and skin and gnaws at your bones.

But in Paris, spring suddenly arrived and that made up for everything.

The worst part of a northern climate is not the winter but the fact that winter makes such lengthy preparations and lingers on into those thankless months that we call spring.

And here we are in mid-winter, like a ship in mid-ocean. The crossing has been long, but there's as much of the journey left to cover.

I used to have a way of explaining things. When someone said, "There's no spring in this country," I would reply: "That's just because you're blind or insensitive to it. We have ten springs, but you have to know how to recognize them. When it's very cold and the sun gives nothing but light, then suddenly at noon one day you feel a kind of relaxation in the air, a respite. It's fleeting. But a little softness settles down around you. Of course the cold sets in once more, and the snow will snow and wind will blow again. But your body has understood the promise. And it will come again now and then, each time a little more potent. Those scattered moments are our first spring."

But as I grow older, I see how much such thoughts betray the poor man's predicament: the less he owns, the more he is attached to what he has, to this or that little object in particular. The fasting man finds in the plainest food a savour that the glutton forgets ever existed. These furtive springs of ours are only real for people who have scarcely any spring at all.

What transformations has climate worked on Frenchmen who came here three and a half centuries ago? "The cruel, inhuman, negative splendour of his geographical space has made the French Canadian fundamentally different," writes J. Ethier-Blais. "By his land he is different. There is not the slightest doubt, for example, that at a certain level, hidden deep within himself, the French Canadian is a better interpreter of Chekov's plays than of Racine's. He feels the Russian play more naturally, he renders it with greater visceral intensity. He discovers in it a kind of excess and an appeal to sensibility which are familiar to him and which correspond to a basic need in his nature. The North American soil has thus acted upon and, to a certain extent, has defined his instinctive reactions." The land and the cold; an immensity aggravated by winter, and winter multiplied by immensity.

This stark phenomenon is less keenly felt in the city where we live sandwiched together and safely sheltered from winter's wild whims. Less keenly felt but no less real. We know all too well where we live, and besides, we feel the call of the surrounding wilderness. We need to verify the limitlessness around us. It has marked us permanently. I know very few Canadians who do not feel at home with Russian writers and musicians. It isn't easy to say exactly why, but in this kinship a profound feeling for the land and its climate must play an important part. By a thousand signs we recognize them as our brothers. Country people here are—or at least used to be—jovial, gay, full of zest, good sense, and realism. When their sons or grandsons begin to write, the first thing they express is their solitude. Think of *Boris Goudonov*: its strange Slavic world is penetrated with rhythms and laments that a Canadian can recognize as his own. Our winter is full of violence but a violence that borders on paralysis and death.

> Late fall, winter and muddy spring
> Your sleep-inducing coils I sing
> That wind my heart and brain in gloom
> In a vaporous shroud and a misty tomb

Baudelaire's winter is foggy and soft. Certain days here, cutting

and suffocatingly cold, remind one more of the opening lines
of *The Vampire*: "You who strike like a knife..."

We should be free to leave, to follow the age-old migration
routes to the south. Life here has become too impoverished. We
need to change our skins, to switch one kind of burn for another.
Or rather we want to breathe a milder air in the midst of an
abundant nature. To rest, yes. But also to restore a certain
sprightliness to the brain.

One of the most incomprehensible phenomena imaginable is
the life of the Eskimos. Here is a race rooted in the far north
and perfectly adapted to the physical environment in which they
are condemned to live. They are one of the miracles of human
civilization. But why did they ever stay there? Were they so
preoccupied with survival that they never even thought of looking
for a more hospitable place to live? Were they not strong or
numerous enough to drive a passage south through the Indian
tribes to win themselves a place in the sun? Or was it that they
were just too attached to their own way of life, too absorbed
in it ever to accept the idea of possible change? At any rate,
they have proved that man can live in an almost perpetual winter
in a northern country in comparison to which we other Canadians
are southerners enjoying the easy climate and the soft life.

Not so long ago, when we could still think loosely about the
planets and imagine that there were wonderful worlds left to
discover, it was easy to believe in the existence of some faraway
haven in space. But now science-fiction has nothing to propose
but deserts; deserts of fire or deserts of ice. Life as we know
it can only flourish in a temperate climate; a few degrees too
much or too little and life withers.

The nobility and purity of winter, the clarity and lightness
of the air, the regal whiteness of the snow...And here we are
in mid-season doing our best to forget it, or in mad pursuit of
the pleasures it offers.

Evening falls and the snow with it. Winter becomes intimate. It
holds out the invitation of home and hearth and of sitting in
front of a wood fire watching the flames constantly changing, like
the sea.

February 1966

It All Began
in a Theatre in the East
of Montreal

I had just begun to read that huge issue of the review *Esprit* devoted to the theatre, but by the second page of the first article I was turned off. It was Camille Bourniquel writing about his childhood:

> Since I was thought to have a certain flair for recitation and since my parents were not anxious to surrender me too early to the narcotic effects of music, they found me a professor who prepared students for the Conservatory of Dramatic Art. Given ten or twelve years I might have managed to get in, if my professor had not had the singular idea of showing us the entrails of the sacred monster, taking us backstage at the Théâtre Français one day when they were giving a matinée performance of *Oedipus Rex*. That experience filled me with a lasting horror.

But what was so singular about that visit backstage? Couldn't it rather be considered a kind of test? What surprises me is that later on Bourniquel turned to the stage at all. It took him years to expiate that youthful sin, until finally the password was given him.

This is what I mean by his sin:

> To have gone through the looking glass too early, to have seen the back side of the set and what little remains of a king without his wig and regal robes, is hardly conducive to illusion. Realism and magic seemed dislocated from the start.

What *is* singular is this child's incapacity to be lifted out of himself by the reverse operation—that is, to see and feel what becomes of an ordinary mortal, when, having adjusted his wig and slipped on his robe, he steps out on to the stage and acts. Backstage is the very place this miraculous passage takes place.

But it's not something you can argue about. All I can do is oppose my own experience to his.

If I trace back the roots of my love for the theatre to its beginnings, I find them in the backstage atmosphere I first absorbed at the age of five or six—before the first sudden revelation then, before the great discoveries, before the realization or the presumed realization that one knows what it is one loves and what one is looking for.

The "entrails" of my sacred monster were neither commodious nor grand. It was a little opera house in the east of Montreal, soon to be transformed into a cinema. We used to arrive early, well before curtain time. Through the stage door trooped people I knew well, just ordinary everyday people already metamorphosed by stage fright. They would go down a dark little staircase to the basement dressing-rooms and temporarily disappear; you could hear them trying out their voices; there was a smell of powder and greasepaint. Then they would emerge, inhabitants of another age: Heroes, Scarlet Women, Bandits, the King of France and the Queen of England.... It only needed the stage lights to put the finishing touch on the transformation.

It was a game, the very stuff of childhood ("I'll be a robber and then you'll come and try to get me and I'll kill you...."), a game organized and played by adults, a serious game that required long preparation.

At about the same time I went to a fancy dress ball, in the country, on a terrace as the evening fell. The arrival of the guests was a marvellous progression. But it wasn't theatre, I felt that very clearly. Everyone was disguised, but they remained themselves and ate, drank, and danced like themselves; were recognizable by the way they talked and what they said. It was very amusing but it wasn't at all serious.

Whereas the theatre was truer than make-believe. Behind the curtain everyone would take their places. The musicians would tune up. And then, in the next instant, a transformation would take place.

I knew the melodies and the dialogue by heart. My father was in charge of voice. I used to attend performances where most of the soloists and all the chorus were amateurs. It would have been easy to sit back smilingly and demystify the whole performance. But each time it was pure magic, directed by my father's silhouette which I could distinguish in the dark orchestra pit. Somewhere down there in the blackness my mother played the piano and my maternal grandfather the bass—a real family enterprise. But the transformation was complete.

Suddenly laughter and applause would break out from the audience. The curtain would fall. Behind it stagehands would invade the set. Backstage would become bustling and noisy again. Lost characters would circulate among the canvas-backed decors, their eyes shining. They were becoming human again, and wanted to touch each other, almost too much. But after the intermission and the stage manager's *trois coups*, they would regain their distance and their truth.

That lasted for two seasons; then came the humdrum experience of school—and farewell stage, costumes, and painted sets. Fortunately, I later spent some time with the Jesuits, who had their pupils put on plays at the Théâtre Gésu, so once again I had a chance to prowl around backstage, to sniff the smell of make-up, to try on wig and cloak, to become someone else. But this time the adventure was less pure—it was mixed with vanity and calculation, and the sense of lessons unlearnt and homework neglected. Then, too, I was soon spotted for a post at the keyboard. In a college ensemble the pianist alone is at least one-third of the orchestra. Like the director, he sets the rhythm of the action; he knows that when he strikes a particular chord the curtain will go up; he enjoys the illusion that he is running the show.

Besides that there were always the holidays. And it was great fun to get a group of friends together in the country, to make an old barn over into a playhouse, to write a script, and to lose oneself for weeks on end in an incredible adventure.

But alas, one's critical faculties were beginning to stir, and one began to realize that despite all the hard work the result was pretty cheap. The cinema suggested points of comparison, but we didn't take it all that seriously, it was too different. Noble, dramatic passages and our dreams of how they might be realized on stage were a formidable enough challenge in a country where the theatre hardly existed yet. Those were the thankless years when a physical love of the stage takes possession of you and yet can never be satisfied.

And after all, what is the theatre? Nine times out of ten, a vain enterprise at best. What can be more futile than this masquerade of men and women pretending to be what they are not, before an audience that laughs at anything or is bored to tears and like as not fills only a quarter of the house? Wooden grimaces, mechanical gestures, a complex and meticulous craft, a warehouse full of technical equipment, rank amateurism unredeemed by good intentions, a hollow trade, a tiresome profession, trivial entertainment that the public is quite right not to take seriously. And then, suddenly . . .

To tell the truth, the sudden spell has not been cast all that often for me. One Musset, one Ibsen, a couple of Pirandellos, Shakespeare, Claudel, Dostoevsky, Beckett . . . plays I did not particularly choose, but which chose me, and often in the most unlikely circumstances. I remember, for example, a production of *L'Eternel Mari* played in impossible conditions above a nightclub. From where I sat the pulsating rhythm of the dance music below was louder than the music from the stage, and yet there resulted one of the strongest theatrical experiences I have ever had. At other times it is a scene, a character, a cry, or a gesture that captivates, and that is enough to put one into contact with something sacred. That is why, though it is easy to criticize what displeases you, it is impossible to define the miracle. Who has ever known how to speak about music?

We have strayed a long way from the rags and tags I began with. And yet everything hangs together. I mistrust the musician who is satisfied to be alone with a fine score, for music isn't only mathematics or architecture, it is also, originally, a fine sound brought to life through rhythm.

"Personally," a friend tells me, "I prefer to play Racine to myself, alone. In the theatre there are too many foreign elements that risk killing or overloading the poetry; one is too dependent on the actors, on the audience, or on pure chance. The classics should be read, not seen. Have you ever seen a tragedy that was completely satisfying?"

Never, I have to admit it. Doubtless it's got something to do with the actors. Perhaps it's a lost art? But surely Jean Racine wrote to be played.

August 1965

Growing Old Isn't an Art—It's a Kind of Holiness

He lives two cottages from me. I've been watching him for weeks. Such a state of acute agitation is marvellous to behold.

His wife has persuaded him for once to take a real holiday. Until now he had settled for a few extended week-ends. But he finally gave in. We won't see forty again, will we, old boy? So, why not slow down a little. . . . You've reached the age of thrombosis, stroke, angina. . . . A few little palpitations—nothing to worry about, of course, absolutely nothing to worry about—but still that was enough to break down his resistance. So he decided to rent this cottage on a northern lake miles from anywhere, in the middle of Nature, "because that's the only place I can manage to forget things." He has been here since the beginning of August and intends to stay until school starts again.

I saw him arrive. He walked around all afternoon stretching his arms and taking deep breaths.

"Talk about pure air! And those wide-open spaces! Just give me a big lake in the big woods any time! You feel relaxed the minute you get here!"

Every few minutes he would go down to the end of the dock

to relax a little. Then he jumped into a canoe and paddled around the bay, touching down briefly at our point on his way back.

"Come on over for a drink. . . . The kids are out fishing. It's nice and quiet. Bring your wife."

He looked at his watch and hurried off to his own dock as though he'd just been called to an important business engagement.

The sun sinks lower. He talks and talks. His wife sits there like a turnip. I listen to the story of a deal he has just closed that he is really proud of, and another one about some transaction in the making that he wasn't able to follow up before he left, which worries him. His wife's breathing is so slow and regular I wonder whether she isn't asleep with her eyes open.

He has already rebuilt the dock. "It's incredible how sloppy people around here are. Just look at this cottage. I'm ashamed to live in such a place. The wood's drying out and it needs a new coat of paint. . . . "

"Oh, come on, Jules! We're fed up with your painting projects . . . and anyway, didn't you come up here for a rest?"

But how can anyone rest in a house like this? A good coat of paint will spruce it up a little. He takes a quick look at his watch. What about the children? They should be back by now.

"When they're here," says his wife, "you can't stand them. They're out fishing. It's perfectly normal. They won't be back till dark. We'll put the outside light on. Let's just relax."

I look at her. She's stable, a little slow, the passive type, a bit vegetal you might say.

He paints his cottage. One coat isn't enough so he spends a week at it. Now the house stands out like a splash of colour on the other side of the bay. He's worn out because he wasn't used to so much exercise. He tried to get his three sons into the act but they have more of their mother in them; they sneak off to the beach and roast happily in the sun.

Does that mean that his wife is a slouch? On the contrary, she is exceptionally efficient. Not a wasted word or emotion. She knows what she's doing and knows how to rest, whereas her husband gives the impression of being constantly late for something and desperately trying to make up for lost time.

I watch him stretch out on a big flat rock. But he isn't satisfied with his angle of exposure to the sun; so he shifts position. He looks at his watch. He gets up, runs into the house and comes back with a large bath-towel which he spreads on the rock and then installs himself anew. Three or four minutes of immobility, which must seem an eternity to him, and he checks the time again. He goes and dunks his head in the water, a brisk rub-down, then he stretches out again with the brusque movement of a soldier springing to attention. There he is, back on his feet shouting to one of his sons; he gets the kids settled into a power boat, watches it starts up and disappear; he calls his wife; he sits on the rock.

Here she is, a calm presence beside him, settling down a little distance away and slipping into her customary torpor.

He lies down, looks at his watch, gets up, skips stones, takes up a book, puts it down, jumps into the canoe, and steams over in my direction looking around for me anxiously. What if this last distraction fails him? Aha! He discovers me and greets me ecstatically.

He's doing his best, but he just can't stand it.

"I think," he confides to me, "that the mountain air makes me nervous." Mountain air? We're at 800 feet altitude. "In the morning the crows wake me up at five. Don't they bother you, too?"

Any noise makes him jump. His holidays are wearing him out. I think he's getting more agitated than ever. But it's mainly the silence he can't get used to. I wonder if he's one of those people incapable of inner life. But could you call his wife's lethargy "an inner life"?

I feel sorry for him and say, "Let's go on a fishing trip."

He makes a face; he doesn't like fishing. But soon the idea of any activity in this desert has won him over. He decides the plugs we have aren't good enough, so he drives off to the nearest village. The flies he brings back are useless because he decides we're to fish in deep water so we can relax better. The children want to come with us; he discourages them, saying we are going to do some serious fishing. We dig for worms and in that flinty ground it isn't easy. He wants to hire a guide but can't find one. After two frantic days we are finally ready.

Here we are at the end of the lake where, the locals say, "they're really biting". We wait. My friend has adopted the theory that there's nothing like fishing to really empty the mind. Here we sit until soon we are the very image of serene and relaxed anticipation. He looks at his watch. He jerks his line. He looks at his watch. He checks his worm. He looks at his watch. I say:

"What time is it?"

He has to check it again. All those automatic little verifications didn't tell him anything. He sighs: "We've been here twenty minutes already. Not a nibble yet. Let's go further on."

But I've got a fish on the end of my line, a little trout that's fighting for all it's worth. He tries his luck once again.

"It's difficult, isn't it?" I say.

"Difficult? They won't even touch my worm."

"No, difficult to relax."

"I don't know what you're talking about."

He was at the end of his tether. But he's beginning to find his feet again now that the holidays are nearly over.

His wife comes back to life at the beginning of autumn as though she were coming out of deep summer sleep, her *estivation*, while he, I can sense, is just beginning to get control of his nerves. Why only yesterday he said, "You can smell fall in the air." He sighs. We have to go back now, back to the city, back to its hustle and bustle. He doesn't look at his watch any more. He talks fondly about our fishing trips—all two of them. He speaks of the "astonishing quiet" that we are going to have to leave.

Those painful hours he passed, hardly able to wait till they were over, the time it took to lay the fire, or eat dinner, or put the children to bed, or get up and go for a morning swim—now that those hours have at last been safely navigated, he is beginning to miss them. He oscillates between impatience and nostalgia. He doesn't know how to savour "the vivacious, virgin beauty of today".

It's a disease that many succumb to. They can only enjoy the present moment by burning it up in feverish activity. What will their old age be like when this resource is denied them? It's true that since they live so restlessly they may be spared this curse, that they may disappear all of a sudden. And just as all their lives they have eaten quickly without tasting anything, so they may disappear in one ultimate hurried spasm.

I only use the word "curse" in reference to people like them, and I hasten to take it back again because it's false. I have known a man whose old age was the most successful part of his long life, and God knows he loved every minute of it. But as much as he knew how to enjoy eating, drinking, and sleeping, and was attached to other people and other ideas, he also discovered in good time the secret of growing old. He spent hours travelling back into his past but never returned burdened down with it. The future continued to interest him passionately—the future of others, which was constantly present to his mind. For people like that, growing old is more than an art: it's a kind of holiness.

October 1965

The Churchwarden

Not long ago a local newspaper attributed the following statement to Cardinal Léger: "To be honest we must accept the fact that living in a pluralistic society means that some of us have had the courage to say that they are agnostic or Marxist."

I read this declaration with astonishment and joy. It struck me as important. I was reminded of many cases it could have applied to and one in particular which I propose to tell you about. Since then, I have been assured that the Cardinal never made such a statement and that he regrets it was ever ascribed to him, so I lose my introduction. But here is the story anyway.

Twenty years ago I was stumping the province as secretary of a new political party. My travels were usually uneventful but for someone who until then had led the life of an intellectual and who was rather intimidated by the prospect of a life of action, they were not without certain hazards.

One winter evening during the Christmas holidays, I found myself stranded in a little town, or rather a large village. I had forgotten or didn't know the names of our party militants. There wasn't a room to be had in either of the two hotels. Nobody paid any attention to me. I was thinking about begging a bed at the presbytery when a stranger accosted me. I had been drinking a glass of beer in the tavern and he had overheard my predicament.

"I'm all alone in a big house," he said. "Come over and spend the night at my place. I know who you are," he added. "You're one of the *bloqueux*." (That was what our opponents called us.)

The man inspired confidence. He was solid, very "country notary" (though he belonged to another profession), well dressed, obviously a person of some importance.

So I followed him, glad to have found a roof and a bed. The snow swirled around us, a real winter tempest. There were lights in most of the houses and you could see the Christmas trees. The streets were empty—a good subject for a picture postcard. "Christmas in French Canada."

He went ahead of me to show the way, but perhaps also to let on that we weren't together. He said later, with a good-natured laugh, "If the boys in the party ever find out that I put up a *bloqueux* . . ."

He lived in a rangy old frame house. Lighting up a wood fire he explained that his wife and children were at Saint Y —— with his father-in-law and that he was going to join them there the next day. He gave me something to eat and offered me a drink. When I excused myself for being a nuisance, he replied: "I was bored. You'll keep me company. And how's the campaign going?"

He belonged to one of the old parties but shared some of our ideas. But "You won't have any luck here," he said. "Isn't politics the art of the possible? What's happening in Montreal?"

And so it went. Two hours of commonplace conversation with this good-hearted country fellow who I will call "The Church-warden". He wasn't one any more, but he had been, and even "Chief Warden", which shows how highly the curé and his fellow citizens thought of him.

Each time he spoke about his little town it was with a heavy laugh, as if to say: "You'll have to take us the way we are." But as the evening drew on and he had more to drink, I noticed that his laugh didn't ring so true any more. Little by little I began to sense that despite appearances the man wasn't happy. I tried to probe the cause of his bitterness, with the party's interest in the back of my mind, for after the idealists, malcontents made up the bulk of our natural clientele.

He drank slowly, the same way he talked—not really to excess but deliberately seeking some other world parallel to his own, where he could breathe easier. The bitterness was only one stage towards a state of semi-drunkenness; now the tone grew more intimate, more friendly. He had read the review that I had been editing for the past six years. He read it the way country people still do—slowly, seriously—and what he remembered about it was not its nationalist policies but its views on the modern world and its references to the Catholic Left in France. ". . . What exactly did you mean when you wrote that . . . ?"

For that matter, he was widely read in many of the authors he referred to in an off-hand way; Bernanos, Malraux—and Mauriac in particular, who often writes about life in a narrow provincial society. They were favourites of mine too. He used to read at night when everyone else was asleep.

"Do you know Jules Romains?"

He led me to a bookcase which he unlocked for me, saying: "Here's my passport to hell," and I saw on the shelves the whole set of *Les Hommes de bonne volonté*, Valéry, Brunschvicg, and rationalists of smaller calibre.

He obviously possessed a vigorous intelligence.

He had ideas of his own and a habit of forming personal judgements. Why had he buried himself here? I asked. Didn't he ever feel the urge to write?

Suddenly the Warden exlaimed, "Can you even begin to imagine what it's like to live in a place like this when you've lost your faith?"

It was an abrupt revelation. All at once we had dropped into an unexpected world.

He went on talking, without admitting to begin with that he was talking about himself.

It had all begun years ago, maybe even at college. In those days he hadn't been much of a reader. Books didn't interest him. That came later along with the religious crisis, trying to get over it. He'd read them all, apologists, theologians, moralists—the works.

"But what struck me most in those books," he said, "were the objections raised against faith. *I think there are people who are born atheists.* [I am sure of that statement, word for word.] There must be a lot of them in the province. But everyone lives in his own hole. *Like rats.*"

"But if it all started at college . . . "

"No, no, nothing but doubts there, and the usual scepticism. At university I had lots of other things to think about; I was a good student and a real hellion. Then came marriage. I came back to make a life of it here where I was born. To be specific, I was born on a farm a few miles away. It seemed obvious that my future lay here. I set up practice. In those days I wasn't concerned about anything in particular, my family, my clients, a little politics. I became a churchwarden at thirty-five, the youngest the parish had ever seen. I was hand in glove with the curé. And as pious as you please. Every day I paid my visit to the Holy Sacrament almost without a second thought. And then one day after a parish retreat I began to think about it. And my doubts came flooding back all at once."

He was trying to explain to himself what had happened. A kind of reverse vocation had revealed itself. "My road to Damascus," he said, looking me straight in the eye without smiling.

"I went to see the curé. He was a good soul. 'Is it evil books you're reading?' he asked. 'No Father, there are no books of any kind in my life.' 'That's it then. Your faith is fading away. You must feed it up.' You should have seen the books he lent me. Things went from bad to worse. I began to lose weight, my appetite disappeared. My wife cooked all my favourite dishes. The curé's recipe was, 'Drive out doubts as you would drive out unclean thoughts. Pray.' Every prayer became a new source of suffering. My good books bred 'evil' thoughts. I learned every possible objection raised by biblical critics against every chapter, book, verse, and word in the Gospel. With that to build on,

I began to set up my own synthesis. I even jotted down some notes. But who could I show them to?

"Then I began to doubt my doubts. I tried a new approach and went to see my old professors, the fathers at the college. Some were consoling: 'It's temptations. And tiredness. Take a rest. Make a closed retreat.' Others, for I saw several of them, immediately became aggressive: 'What about hidden sins? You should know that a baptised Catholic never loses the Faith unless it's his own fault. Everyone receives the grace required. It's pride. Beware of committing the gravest sin of all, the sin against the spirit.'"

As he continued to tell me—his acquaintance of a bare three hours—about how he had deceived those closest to him, about his loss of faith and the lie he went on living, I began to feel like a priest and to wonder if he was going to ask me for absolution. Was his atheism as natural to him as he claimed it was?

It was during a closed retreat that he finally admitted to himself: "I don't believe any more, I'll never believe again, and I am condemned to live with this secret all my life."

This conclusion revolted me and I couldn't help asking him if there wasn't some other solution.

"Here? No. You must be pretty naïve if that's your question. Somewhere else? Move out? Start my career over in some other place? How would I explain that to my wife, who is perfectly incapable of understanding that anyone could have problems of this kind! . . . Yes, we're a happy couple . . . at any rate, she doesn't ask questions herself; for her, any kind of questioning is a sin. . . . Yes, I admit, I was weak. I should have told her about it, ruined my marriage, maybe even lost the children because pious women have such a strange sense of duty. And all that to go . . . where? To some other little burg where I would have found the same priestly domination and where I would have been a source of scandal. To Montreal? I'm not cut out for city life, and my wife even less than me. It would have made everyone unhappy. And how do you begin your career over again at forty in an unknown metropolis?

"My roots are here," the Warden repeated. "That surprises you, does it? The people around here don't interest me particularly, but I can't get along without them any more.

"The only thing was . . ." said the Warden and the tone changed. Until now he had spoken calmly, rehearsing for me arguments he must have gone over night after night, but suddenly the tone changed and his features became drawn. "The only thing was that I had to take communion at Easter in front of the whole parish. That disgusted me. What drove me to it? A remnant of faith? A sense of self-respect? Respect for the faith of others?"

"You were deceiving them anyway."

He took it as a criticism.

"What would you have done in my place? I'm just a common atheist, not a hero. . . . So as often as possible I arranged to be away at Easter. It's not easy in my profession. And then my wife was insistent. Everyone does their Easter devotions in their own parish. That way it's easier to check up. . . . The first time I thought I was going to be sick. I couldn't swallow the thing. I felt myself becoming unclean. . . ."

And that's how he came to be Chief Warden.

I have suppressed all the details. The man's region, his age, his profession, his party. And I won't say when he died—doubtless after having received the last rites.

The motives of his disbelief and the system of thought that he adhered to would undoubtedly make young agnostics or Marxists smile today. Though he was a cultivated man, a nationalist, and quite conservative in his opinions, he wasn't interested in Charles Maurras. A-religious but not anti-clerical (except for a few outbursts due to bad humour more than anything else), he was interested in mystical phenomena, which he spoke about in his country-notary style as though describing the habits of a colony of ants. He had had to piece together his own philosophy, but in the worst possible circumstances—without ever expressing it openly, without airing it, without having it shaped by discussion and exchange of views, without ever going down as deep as he could into himself.

Notice that he had to operate under two different systems: the orthodox one, which he knew better than most of his fellow Catholics, and the other, his own, the one that spoke from his innermost heart. The result of this secret effort was far from impressive. "Growing older, I've become a sceptic," he said sadly. God knows there was reason enough.

At the time he gave me the impression of a man buried alive. Alcohol helped a little to dull the pain of his spoiled life. The man must have possessed considerable vigour just to be able to keep up appearances when he was such a mess inside. Watching him I had a sense of terrible loss, of an impoverishment of himself and the society he lived in, of a stupid and useless sacrifice. And I wondered how many "rats" like him there were in our French-Canadian society, each buried in his own separate hole.

It is quite possible, after so many years, that I have invented part of his character, that I have added traits observed elsewhere, for others, somewhat like him, have also confided in me. But the Warden sticks in my mind as the choice victim of a closed society.

I was better able to understand the urge that had driven him to confession much later on when I reread *Les Deux Sources*. Bergson writes that anguish is a disturbance in the relationship between the social self and the individual self. He analyses this disequilibrium "in the soul of some great criminal" who hides his act as much as he can, but must also live alone with it. He is regarded with awe but he "knows what he is and feels more isolated among his fellow men than if he were alone on a desert island." For he is cut off from society and cannot rejoin it except through confession. Sometimes, without going so far as to give himself up, "he will confess to a friend or to any good person. In this way he rejoins the truth, if not in the eyes of the public at large, at least publicly for one person, and he is reunited with society at one point, by a single thread. . . . "

I was that point, that thread. The Warden's sin was, in his own eyes, not to have ceased to believe, but to have presented a false image of himself to his fellow citizens. In the end someone had to know what he really was, and chance had made me that necessary witness.

Was the intolerance of his milieu in fact as formidable as he thought it was? As far as he was concerned, it was doubtless wrong to hide his disbelief, but he was not wrong to fear scandal and society's vengeance.

For what must be stressed is that social intolerance is the profane order taking upon itself the functions of the sacred. As a non-conformist, the Warden would have been rejected by any narrow and homogeneous community. His small town was not exceptional in any way; it was the very incarnation of the law that a society closed in upon itself lives by. What we are dealing with is not a specifically religious reaction but a social instinct which in this case focussed on a question of faith. One might even say, without stretching the point too much, that it is almost the same impulse that leads the respectable father to forbid his daughter to marry a black or a non-believer. The father feels threatened in his integrity as a white or a Catholic. Of course this is just an analogy and there are closer parallels to be drawn. The bond which ties this type of believer to his church seems, at least from the outside, to be the same as the one that ties the militant to his party. His membership in the church no longer means primarily and essentially the free circulation of inner life and spiritual values, but first and foremost his adhesion to a visible social group and its commandments, to its rigid disciplines, to its human successes and its human failures. The missionaries count their converts and any defection is treason. Where then is the Gospel in all this?

I write these lines in memory of a poor devil who was swallowed up in this swamp and was never able to free himself from it, in memory of a provincial dignitary who was carried high in the esteem of his fellow citizens because he agreed not to contravene their laws—having previously committed a careful, studied self-emasculation.

We parted early the next morning. I caught the first train with a crowd of congenial and colourful people on their way to celebrate the holidays with their families. New snow dazzled in the bright sun. I had come back to the land of the living and that evening spent with the Warden could now retreat like the memory of a nightmare.

But I have never been able to look at this society in the same way since.

May, June 1964

Must We Kill the Killer
to Prevent Crime?

It is the spring of 1857 and Leo Tolstoy is in Paris. He is twenty-eight. He hears talk of a public execution. His curiosity gets the better of his revulsion. It is still night when he sets off for La Place de la Roquette where the guillotine is already set up. He is not alone; there are some 12,000 spectators, many women and children among them, who have left their beds to witness the spectacle, and they crowd and shove in order to "see better". The local cafés are serving wine.

The execution takes place.

The same day Tolstoy writes to a friend: "I have seen plenty of atrocities in the war and in the Caucasus, but if I had seen a man drawn and quartered before my eyes it would have been less revolting than that elegant precision instrument which in one second takes the life of a strong, fresh, healthy human being. In the former case there is at least the paroxysm of human agony; in the latter a frightful calm pushed to a point of extreme refinement, a kind of comfortable assassination, nothing grand. . . . And that horrible crowd! A father was explaining to his daughter the neat and clever mechanism involved. Etc. . . . "

Later on, in his *Confessions*, he sums up his impressions this way: "When I saw the head separate from the body and the two pieces fall away each on its own side with a dull thud into its receptacle, I understood, not by reason but with my whole being, that no rational doctrine of human progress could ever justify this act; and that if all men living in this world, or all who had ever lived since the beginning of time, concurred, by invoking various theories, in stating that this execution was indispensable, I would know that it was not indispensable but that it was evil." (Quoted by Henri Troyat in his *Tolstoy*.)

Our civilization in the last one hundred years has at least become more discreet. For a long time now we have guillotined, hung, shot, electrocuted, or gassed people behind closed doors. The trial and the sentencing are public, but the criminal "expiates

his crime" before a few chosen witnesses only. A brief announcement in the newspapers informs us that justice has been done.
That's all.

But what "rational doctrine of human progress" can long continue to justify such semi-secret acts?

Raise the question with the man on the street, especially if
it's just after a trial which has dealt with some ghastly crime,
and you soon realize that in the eyes of the average man the
most horrible kind of punishment is justified. "Make him pay",
that's the *leitmotif*. Often one has the impression that it's vengeance
that's involved more than punishment: "An eye for an eye".

Those who defend capital punishment cite the principle of
using it as a deterrent. The execution of a murderer, they say,
dissuades other potential murderers from yielding to instinct or
self-interest.

In that case, what justifies keeping the death of the criminal
discreetly veiled? What kind of an exemplary punishment is it
when it is kept hidden as much as possible? What real faith
does the public have in the value of a "lesson" which is never
spoken of in polite society and which takes place in the presence
of a handful of specialists?

The reply to that is that there are many perfectly legitimate
acts that are not performed in public. Undoubtedly, but does
the public consider such acts to be exemplary? A surgical
operation, one might say, must seem to be regular butchery to
someone who doesn't understand it. But the reasons it is performed out of the public eye are professional and are not simply
to protect the sensibilities of the masses; indeed, television occasionally does permit the public to witness some of the more spectacular surgical interventions. Yet it remains unthinkable today
to give television coverage of capital punishment.

In the past it has been noted that sometimes a public execution
caused a crime wave, just as some suicides set off an epidemic
of suicides. Respect for human life is still an extremely fragile
thing. The picture of a real assassination, albeit legal, risks
stimulating a murderous reflex in certain sick minds. Yet once
again, what is the value of an example that one keeps hidden
as if ashamed of it?

It could be argued that a general and abstract acceptance of the principle is enough; that it should be sufficient in a given society to know that every murderer runs the risk of ending his days on the scaffold to prevent would-be assassins from killing. But the facts prove the contrary; abstract acceptance is not enough. Well, then, if force of example is necessary, shouldn't it be driven home with a heavy dose of publicity? Shouldn't such cases, despite the objections of delicate sensibilities, be given the fullest public exposure as often as possible? At this suggestion we all draw back and feel extremely ill at ease. Is this a sign that dissuasion by example is effective after all?

Those who are won over to the cause of capital punishment as a deterrent are people who have never themselves entertained the idea of killing someone. They are convinced that if ever faced with such a temptation, the idea that they would have to pay by the rope or in the chair would be enough to shock them back to normal. They think they are speaking in the name of good common horse sense. But what do they know about it? The maniac or the sick-minded man is governed by other laws. Crimes of passion by their nature defy rational explanation. People who are described as anti-social or professional killers are certain in their own minds that they will escape justice.

Can one go so far as to say that the threat of capital punishment has never stayed the assassin's hand? Certainly not. But it is also possible to state that torture has forced witnesses to reveal what they know, and who among us is ready to reintroduce that method of extorting evidence?

If all human life is worthy of respect, then why treat the policeman as especially privileged and reserve the death sentence exclusively for the individual who kills an officer of the law? In absolute terms such a position seems indefensible, yet it is easy to see how certain people have come to rationalize this decision. The policeman hunts down the criminal and in doing so takes risks which none of us would accept. He therefore expects to enjoy a special kind of protection. If he does not, he may feel abandoned by the very society for which he risks his life, and this attitude may undermine his morale. That, basically, is the point of view that M. Claude Wagner expressed in the incredible statement he made on January 18. You will remember that the central government had just commuted the sentence that had been brought down against one John Colpitts, condemned to hang for having killed a prison guard at the Dorchester Penitentiary in New Brunswick.

"Those Ottawa types are really hopeless as far as justice is concerned," the Quebec Minister was reported to have told the newspapers, and this is how M. Wagner explained the origins of his strange outburst of anger: "You might just as well say the federalists have signed the death warrant of another guard, for if Colpitts didn't hesitate to stab one of his guards when he was already serving a ten-year sentence for armed robbery, what won't he do now that he knows he's got to spend the rest of his life in the pen?" M. Wagner forgets that this young man stabbed the guard despite the threat of capital punishment, which was still in effect at the time he "didn't hesitate to stab one of his guards". Therefore, under the mantle of capital punishment, the guard was guaranteed a protection which proved to be illusory. M. Wagner's naïvety is disarming but unconvincing.

The one thing that we can retain from his remarks — and all citizens can agree on this — is that the criminal must be prevented from doing harm. The death sentence, obviously, achieves this by suppressing the guilty person. But it remains to be seen whether it is socially necessary to have recourse to a method that is so radical, violent, and repulsive.

In other words, it is not enough just to suppress the death penalty, we must also set up mechanisms that will prevent the occurrence of second offences. In this respect our system has already shown itself to be inefficient on several occasions, which has given new arguments to those who advocate capital punishment.

April 1966

Why Keep Reminding Us That He's a Jew?

There are eight of us at table. He is the most brilliant of the guests. Like most of the others he is a businessman and an anglophone, but he speaks very good French.

We have been invited to a club and I don't like these premises for males only. "Tavern" rhymes with "cavern", and I don't expect dens for females only are much fun either. Anyway, this time it's a men's club, the food is good and the company pleasant.

He is sitting beside me. He speaks well and amusingly and is enjoying himself. He has the ease and assurance of wealth.

And yet quite often he lets drop remarks which seem to me to be out of keeping, or at least unnecessary. For example he says "Being a Jew...", which comes as a surprise to me for I hadn't caught his name the first time. Did he have to say he was a Jew? Once that's established, does he have to underline it a few seconds later: "As a rich Jew, I..."

What's got into him? Nobody here is hostile. Why does he have to remind us every time he draws breath that he's a Jew?

Ten minutes go by. Speaking of something else, I suddenly hear myself saying: "Of course, I am a French Canadian." This time I surprise myself. Everyone knows I am French-Canadian. But my neighbour insists too much. Even given his type, he overdoes it... "Though I am a Jew... A Jew, you know..." Finally I can't contain myself any longer and I challenge this near-stranger with: "You seem very conscious of the fact that you're a Jew."

He laughs it off in the same easy manner. "You noticed that, did you? Yes, it must be some kind of tic. But aren't you conscious of being French?"

And he drops the subject to take part in the general conversation again. But without his knowing it, I've harpooned him. He comes back at me shortly after with an answer to my question, or rather we are all treated to it, for, disregarding conversational transitions, he suddenly attacks.

"My neighbour here finds me very self-conscious about being a Jew. He's right. I practically never forget it. I'm quite ready to accept the fact, but I never forget it just the same. And in the circumstances I'm hardly likely to."

He was a rich man's son. He went to the rich man's schools. He knew he was a Jew but it was the other boys who taught him that to be Jewish was to be an oddity, if not an anomaly. Some of them let him know this without malice aforethought, others never missed a chance to tease, like children who torment a fat boy, or a hunchback, or someone with squint. But you learn to take it. You tell yourself: "All right I'm a Jew, I'll always be a Jew." And you learn to live with it.

Then comes university. And you discover that being a Jew excludes you from belonging to such and such a fraternity, and that revolts you. "They're my classmates. Why can't I be like them, why do they reject me?" Later the same polite exclusion is firmly maintained elsewhere. You want to join a certain club? Unthinkable. You're a Jew. These select clubs that ordinarily only open their doors to the rich remain closed to the rich Jew, just as they remain closed (and this is directed to me) to French Canadians. "You are French Canadian. I am a Jew. That's the way it is. Only don't be surprised if I don't forget it. The others keep reminding us of it constantly—even perfect gentlemen, even those who denounce racial prejudice, even those who consider it 'improper' to make the slightest allusion to religion. For that matter, they know that I don't go more than twice a year to the synagogue. But in their eyes I am irredeemably marked."

His eyes shine with indignation. He masters his voice, his gestures, his facial expression — everything except his eyes, which remain young, which say, "This isn't the normal state of things," which protest against the injustice that is being practised against him. For there is a secret place within him that has never ceased to suffer. And it made me thank God that I wasn't like those racists who deny the universality of mankind.

As dinner was finishing, however, and even as I was praising myself, as well as the Lord, a memory came back to muddy my clear conscience.

It had happened a couple of months earlier. The election campaign was in full swing. Daniel Johnson was making up to Réal Caouette and the Créditistes. I was at dinner again this time (I know, but one has to eat to live), and I was anxious to take advantage of the fact that my neighbour was an anglophone to ask what the English were thinking about the provincial election.

"I don't suppose you've been following the election campaign? . . ."

"On the contrary . . ."

In fact my neighbour was deeply interested. It frightened her. For M. Réal Caouette had declared, a short time before, that his political heroes were Mussolini and Hitler. Now that Daniel Johnson was buttering up the Créditistes, it meant that M. Caouette's preferences didn't scare him. Therefore, the two were alike. And if Johnson came to power, what would happen? It was an urgent question, for my neighbour was a Jew.

"I told my grandmother, who is eighty-four, 'Grandmother, this time you've got to get out and vote. It's important.' And she replied, 'In 1932, I was in Germany, they told me to go and vote, and I voted. But it didn't make any difference. I'll vote anyway, but I'm afraid it won't make any difference.'" The young woman spoke in a low voice, very slowly, choosing her words.

"Did your grandparents live in Germany?"

"Yes. After the election, when Hitler was gaining power, my grandfather said, 'This time we'll have to leave.' His friends told him, 'There have been others like this man before, things will work out in the end.' But grandfather was intransigent. He knew that this time things wouldn't get better. So he took his family to Holland and later to Canada."

I watched her as she was speaking. Suddenly the reality of what she was saying struck me. If in late 1932 or early 1933, I told myself, that German Jew hadn't decided to leave his German homeland, my neighbour wouldn't be sitting there beside me. She couldn't have urged her grandmother to get out and vote, and the whole family would have perished in the gas ovens.

I was alive in 1933. And what were we doing here in Quebec when that German Jew set out on the road to exile?

I belonged to a group of nationalists, a bunch of young Turks who called themselves Jeune-Canada.

At the time, Jews the world over were protesting against the treatment they were getting in Germany. They held a meeting in Montreal in which certain politicians participated, among them Senator Dandurand, so we staged a counter-demonstration. I can remember down to the last detail how we got the idea for each of our political meetings, except for that one in particular, which we baptised "Politicians and Jews". I wonder to this day who or what inspired it. But we held it just the same, because a cloud of anti-Semitism had polluted the atmosphere. It was Depression time, everyone was hurt, and everyone was looking for a scapegoat.

I was one of the speakers at that meeting, and I spoke a great deal about politicians and just a little about Jews. But it was still too much. For our speeches were dreadful. One of us went so far as to proclaim: "You can't tramp on the tail of that bitch Jewry in Germany without hearing it yap in Canada."

"Forgive them, Lord, they know not what they do." And, really, we didn't know. The speeches of twenty-year-old youths reflect ideas that are current in their milieu. And the ideas that were floating around then weren't always very lucid or beautiful.

But that's exactly the frightening part. Take my four friends, the speakers that night. They were nice guys, all of them. None, as far as I know, has turned bandit or Jew-baiter. They were sincere and ardent.

At the very time that Hitler was getting ready to kill 6,000,000 Jews, they could speak very sincerely about "alleged persecution" and "so-called persecution" in Germany, which they contrasted to the bad treatment, "very real — by contrast", which French Canadians were subjected to here. I can still see myself and hear myself braying with the best of them at that meeting, while in another part of the world a German Jew, by accepting exile, was snatching his family from death. . . .

How many things are there today that we refuse to believe and yet are true? Six million victims haven't rooted out anti-Semitism. There are days when the progress of the human race seems dismally slow.

February 1963

Jesus, Mahomet, and Marx Reconciled in Chaos

First of all, here's what inspired the following remarks: a war film seen on TV late at night when the mind's defences are weakest against the assault of violent images.

The subject is trite. We are supposed to sympathize with a bunch of soldiers through a close-up view of their lives. They're wounded and are fleeing before the Japanese invaders somewhere in the Pacific. Finally a ship comes to evacuate them from the combat zone. But the sea is rough. And then enemy planes come in flying low and strafe the decks of the ship. The photography is good and we feel the terror and hatred of the machine-gunned passengers. We detest these inhuman robots who take wounded soldiers, women, and children as their target. We detest the horrors of war, the stupidity of such senseless massacres, and the perversion of the highest of human faculties for the arts of carnage.

But now the Japanese planes fire a final burst and stream away. Another squadron has appeared in the sky — American this time. The survivors can breathe again. Their saviours have arrived. It's the same mechanical apparition, the same brief overflight, but this time the infernal racket has a fraternal sound, this time we cheer on those brave automatons whose only aim is to save human lives. In the background, martial music swells up "to the glory of arms deployed in a just cause"—those same arms that would have been just as happily deployed in machine-gunning other women and children and wounded soldiers, if only a Japanese ship had appeared on the horizon.

A trite film inspires trite thoughts: by playing up the horrors of war it is likely to turn on your pacifist sentiments—if doesn't stir up your belligerent instincts.

Getting up from the television my eye happened to fall on an open book, a history of the crusades in which René Grousset movingly recreates the story of those wars of conquest that were waged in the name of the Cross. The techniques are necessarily more primitive. We regress in the arts of carnage to swords, lances, arrows, and torches flaming over the heads of the massed armies.

Even with these crude weapons it was still possible to kill and wound astonishing numbers, not to speak of pillage and rape. Christendom spread throughout the Moslem world, and in order to reconquer the land where Christ had given up his life, Christians lopped off as many heads as they could. "After the final assault," writes Grousset, "Jerusalem presented a spectacle of such slaughter of enemy warriors bathed in such an effusion of blood that the conquerors themselves were seized with horror and disgust." It is true that when he was proclaimed king of Jerusalem, Godfrey de Bouillon refused "to don a crown of gold when Christ had worn only a crown of thorns". It was a noble gesture, but it didn't ressurect any eviscerated Arabs.

We have done better since, and pacifist propaganda has given us our fill of the holocaust of Hiroshima and the death ovens, the technological carnage of an industrial age. At least in the days of hand manufacture, to kill a man required the human agency of a hefty blow, or maybe even two.

This excursion into the past reminds one of the scandal of the human spirit which develops in two directions at once, in the arts of progress and in the arts of destruction—a scandal which has led to a long series of wars from biblical times. This prompts some people to detest the military profession, which particularly embodies this contradiction, for it is a profession essentially linked to destruction, yet one which always claims to be associated with law and justice. (By their works shall ye judge them.) Writing this I treacherously recall a phrase from Péguy: "There is only one thing in the world that has caused more wars than Injustice; and that is Justice." Treacherously, because Péguy admired the profession of man at arms.

A frequently quoted passage of his runs as follows: "The spiritual sleeps at night in the camp bed of the temporal." That's done it; now that I've taken down my Péguy I feel like just keeping still and listening.

Here's the thesis he develops about Rome in *Argent Suite*: "... the incredible need of the temporal that survives in the spiritual; the incapacity, the absolute incapacity of the spiritual to do without the temporal." And more concretely: "It is the

Roman legion, it is the Roman soldier, it is Caesar himself who sets aside that quantity of the world where the Latin declension rings out, and Latin conjugation, and Nisus, and Euryale, and the descent into hell. For everything was forced to wear the Roman mantle and thus, in a certain sense, everything was forced to wear the military mantle."

Europe and Christianity, as Péguy saw them, go back to Rome. French Canada goes back to Rome, back to the Roman legions. "Military arms are the cradle where customs, laws, the arts, and even religion, where language and race... lie down at night."

Think of the French expansion in America in the eighteenth century. Think of the French retreat of 1760 which left behind the little uneasy nation of French Canadians that we are, and then read these words: "The soldier measures out the quantity of ground where one language is spoken, where certain customs, where a certain spirit, soul, and race holds dominion. The soldier measures out the quantity of ground where a soul can breathe. The soldier measures out the quantity of ground where a people does not die." But before closing the book—because there are still more atrocious realities that must be considered, and there is a limit to what we can quote—let's have one last look at what Péguy says of Caesar's legions: "If Virgil is in Racine and in Hugo, and Homer is in Racine, and the Virgilian is mixed with the Racinian, not like a foreign text learned in the classroom but like a brother and like a father, it is not Virgil who did this, it is the Roman soldier who did it."

In short, on this earth of ours, the soul has not yet learned to do without the body. But the reverse is also true.

It is a closely woven fabric. And human history lies so close to the history of men's wars that the angels themselves would be hard put to imagine a history free of carnage.

And man continues to say to man: "Throw down your weapons first and then I'll throw down mine. But even if you say that you have abandoned yours, I won't believe you. And even if I see you throw them far away from you, I won't believe my eyes, I'll know that you have a hidden cache somewhere that you can find again when you need them." Americans, Russians, Chinese, not to speak of the underworld, all continue to believe, in some hidden recess in their minds, that the last scene in the human drama is always a test of strength, and history has never ceased to prove them right.

At least until now.

Would it have been possible, even yesterday, to imagine that a weapon could dictate the vital necessity of peace?

But already the warrior of the nuclear age can no longer measure "the quantity of ground where one language is spoken, the quantity of ground where a soul can breathe." From now on, he must measure in terms of the quantity of ground where neither speech nor breath will survive. From now on, he must measure in terms of a space where human life will be impossible. Impossible for any man, whatever language he speaks, whatever the colour of his skin. His dominion, from now on, is only over the flat egalitarian zone of death.

And who says so? The mystics? The poets? No, the scientists.

Neither Homer, nor Virgil, nor Racine will mix spiritual blood on this deadly desert. No more Latin declensions, nor Germanic, in this warrior's bed where flesh and bone and granite will dissolve. And the followers of Jesus, Mahomet, and Marx will be reconciled in chaos. There will be no friendly planes, nor even any hope for the generations to come, for the life the survivors pass on will be terribly diminished.

Humanity is slowly becoming adjusted to this idea. The speed with which it will penetrate men's brains and the conclusions that will be drawn from it will govern the future of the planet.

December 1963

Journalism's Duty To Probe the Unknown

Do there exist ideas and attitudes which are extremely widespread and yet get no public hearing? That is exactly what *Le Magazine Maclean* suggested in its inquiry last June into the possibility of economic union or even political union with the United States. The exact percentages needn't detain us, they are always a little suspect, but the fact that there is a real annexationist tendency in the country, particularly in Quebec and the Maritimes, seems irrefutable.

I don't intend to debate the question of annexation here. The thing that interests me is that an idea shared by millions of people should never find its way into the political arena. It is all the more surprising when one remembers that the idea of annexation is older than Canada itself, and that hundreds of thousands of Canadians, French Canadians in particular, have personally acted upon the idea by emigrating with their families to the United States. Furthermore, I don't imagine that annexationism is the only idea that has failed to gain political favour despite the fact that it has millions of supporters. A little research would undoubtedly turn up others. What's the explanation? Could it be that certain concepts survive better in the dark, like temptations, and are destroyed by light? Could it be that they are such a corrosive menace to the society in which they develop that society rejects them as soon as they take form?

Take annexation for example. It has never, as such, had any real success politically. But the idea doesn't disappear for all that; it lives on underground.

This is very strange, for most opinions that have even a modest circulation usually find some formula for expression, whether it is sincere or not. And others, even less widely held, stimulate a taste for novelty, and flourish as exclusive fads. Ideas that are difficult to realize and have been dormant for long periods, like separatism for instance, are revived by the confluence of various factors and stir up a multitude of interpretations. And yet attitudes which no observer had really anticipated break out all of a sudden—for example, the profound dissatisfaction of certain important regions of Quebec, which explains the unexpected success of Social Credit theory in the province. It's like proving the law of motion by walking. How many proofs of this kind remain to be discovered?

The recent film made by the Liberal party on the youth of Quebec, *Jeunesse année zéro*, doesn't prove anything at all. But it captures a disenchantment, a scepticism, and a lack of faith which run exactly counter to the ideology and the dynamism of present-day Quebec. It certainly isn't the first time the public has mocked or insulted its politicians. Slogans such as "The more they change the more they look alike", and epithets such as "self-interested, clownish, dishonest, and lazy", were frequently used to describe Members of Parliament thirty years ago, a fact any of my contemporaries can vouch for. It comes from an old attitude of contempt combined with the wish to milk the M.P. or the government to the last drop. So while patronage inspired scorn, in return it was a kind of personal recompense for having put up with the system.

Nothing is less democratic than to expect little from general laws and practically everything from small favours curried here and there. This means living as much as possible on the margin of political institutions (just as the average citizen tries to live on the margin of floods, epidemics, and pollution), instead of considering them as useful instruments.

Now, to judge by the images shown in this film on today's youth, their attitude is not only widespread but is becoming virulent. It is accompanied by a monumental ignorance of men and facts. It makes no distinction between governments and politicians. As far as one can define it, it seems to be a kind of political agnosticism. On the one hand it is, by its very nature, calculated to be the despair of even the best-intentioned political party, for it either asks for nothing or asks for the moon. On the other, long-range solutions not only leave it cold but, to come right down to it, simply do not exist. The only political policy that they are ready to grant the privilege of existence is one that would guarantee them permanent employment.

If these images faithfully represent relatively large sectors of the young generation, then democracy here will soon find that its foundations are not very solid. Boys like the ones shown in this film are ideal material for anyone wanting to establish a dictatorship. Youths like these would rather form gangs or fascist squads than hang around day in, day out, not making any money.

They are the living witnesses to a collective failure. Neither the politicians nor the labour leaders, the clergy nor our intellectuals have been able to get them involved. It seems that they refuse to recognize the validity of any authority, and will accept neither group nor leaders to represent them. Many of them are poorly equipped for life in the modern world. They are not happy with their parents, whom they consider to be completely out of touch with events and blind to the real necessities of life. In addition, they seem to be closed to spiritual values of any kind and treat them as a joke or consider them to be lies and hypocrisy.

Is this another case of attitudes that no one will be able to formulate in political terms? Or are they skin-deep feelings that will disappear after the age of adolescence and unemployment? Or will they go on existing at some of the lower levels of society? And can they do so without affecting the collective health of the nation? Anything is possible. But for all their disenchantment, these young people are not submissive. Some of them, who don't seem at all like fanatics, have spoken of the kind of joy they felt on hearing the bombs go off. They have even said so publicly, with a curious kind of bold-facedness and without a second thought for the risks that such a manifestation of moral solidarity might incur. In short, while the means of communication have multiplied in our age, communication itself remains capricious and incomplete. We know about the assassination of President Kennedy half an hour after it happens; but things that have been going on in my own city and my own province remain completely hidden to the news media or are only discovered after a prodigious time lag. When phenomena like annexationism or the disenchantment of part of the younger generation are suddenly detected, certain journalists discard the evidence as doubtful, while others play up their discovery at the expense of all other factors involved. Some kinds of news, and this kind in particular, are difficult to verify and evaluate.

That is why the question of defining, let alone that of achieving, real objectivity in journalism is such a touchy one, unless you restrict yourself to reporting public events such as traffic accidents, crime, statements by political parties and their leaders, and so on. But the opinions, attitudes, and daily experiences of whole segments of society are also facts, and to discard them *a priori* is to opt for conformity. Trying to disengage such facts often means, in the long run, taking sides, a risk that in my view is necessary, a prerequisite of true journalism, yet one that must be weighed judiciously, for otherwise you end up taking your own opinions for important news.

It is convenient to assert that a newspaper must reflect the society that it serves. But does that mean that it is almost entirely restricted to reporting statements made by the establishment? In that case what becomes of those parts of the body of public opinion, often very large parts, which remain silent, and what about critics whose quality is superior to their social prestige? Can we always be sure that on specific questions a Member of Parliament represents majority opinion better than a university professor or a member of a trade union? No matter how legitimate its claims, or how rigorous its public conscience, authority all too often has too much to gain by keeping silent on any number of matters so that it has the last word by default. Our duty is to help it discover the multiple facets of a society that thinks it knows itself but only perceives its image in simplified terms and tends to grow in upon itself.

January 1965

You Must Drink Your Own Prose to the Dregs

Ours is a garrulous world. I talk, you talk, we all talk; radio and TV jabber on, the newspapers gabble on, but who listens? Sometimes, in the midst of all this racket, one feels more solitary, more locked up in oneself, than if one were alone in the bush.

How *can* one escape from the prison of self?

"If only I could get out of my own skin for an hour or two!" writes Musset in *Fantasio*. "If only I could be that man passing by there! . . . I'm sure that he has a thousand ideas in his head that are new and strange to me, that he is a wonderfully singular human being. But alas, the words men say to each other are always commonplace. . . . And what solitudes are contained in all those human frames."

Yes, all those words and all those people paid to talk, and so little real communication.

"So what can you do about it?" Fantasio asks his friend Spark. "Do you see this smoky old city? There isn't a square, a street, or an alley in it that I haven't prowled through a score of times. . . . I can't take a step without retracing my steps of yesterday. Well, my dear friend, that city is nothing compared to my own brain. Every last cranny of it is a hundred times more familiar to me. Every street and every rut in my imagination is a hundred times more footworn. I have walked them all countless times, up and down and every which way. . . ."

If one could, in fact, be "That man passing by there", one might be keenly disappointed. Is it true that the landscapes of the mind would all be new, that one's feelings would be essentially singular and different? And what if one found oneself perfectly at home there in a quarter of an hour? When the soul goes into eclipse all souls begin to look alike. Might as well simply go on talking. . . .

And yet, how can one completely come to terms with this dilemma?

Sometimes the worst thing is not to have to put up with the

incessant clamour, but to have to participate in it yourself, to be obliged to speak when you feel you have nothing to say. That's the kind of profession I've been practising for twenty years now.

It does have its moments of exaltation. It gives the person who follows it seriously the impression that he is serving others. It allows him to express his feelings and ideas. And then, all of a sudden, nothing.

"So why not just shut up?"

Easier said than done. There's a column to fill. You are morally bound to have something to say five times a week. The copy editor is waiting, the typos are waiting, the compositor, too, and maybe even, at the end of the line, the reader. But in the pressure of the moment what the reader expects hardly counts. You have to fill up a certain corner on a certain page like a house painter who has to cover a certain surface. The hovering hand knows it. The racked brain knows it. The hand covers the page with little mechanical doodles, the brain flounders. . . . And all for nothing, for nothing comes.

"But there's no shortage of subjects."

There are hundreds, thousands of them. It's not for want of a subject, it's just that you're not there any more. You haven't got one feeling, opinion, or idea to rub against another. Your mind is a blank. And no one will take this excuse seriously. When your body is sick, everyone urges you to go to bed. But brain and soul haven't got the right to be sick. Silence is an oasis that exists in dreams only. You must keep on talking, like the witness who doesn't know any more but is still mercilessly challenged: "Confess!"

Confess the emptiness? Resort to lies? Trot out the gimmicks, the whole professional bag of tricks?

I remember a story that Father Paul Doncoeur used to tell about the Blessed Ruysbroek. Every morning crowds of people used to come to listen to the old hermit talk. And every morning, "about ten o'clock he would open the window of his hut and speak to the assembled pilgrims about the things of God that had been revealed to him in his contemplation. And the good folk would go away carrying his words with them like a priceless treasure."

So far, the story is quite dull. Not even a miracle. But here is the wonderful part:

"Now it seems that on certain days old Ruysbroek would open the shutter and say, 'Today, brethren, there's nothing.' And with a kindly smile he would dismiss the crowd and close the window. And it is said that on those days the people were more delighted than ever and went away repeating on all sides, 'He is a true saint!' So while many virtues were attributed to him by popular acclaim, the rarest of all his titles to sanctity was that when he had nothing to say, he said nothing."

Imagine a public figure or lecturer who would dare do that. Imagine a journalist, responsible for a full page, saying, "Tonight all I've got for you is three little paragraphs." Maybe in time he would gain a reputation for holiness. Meanwhile he'd be tossed out on his ear.

One evening you have a lot to say. It sometimes happens. But the radio only allows you six minutes of air-time.

"Six minutes! That's not nearly enough!"

"All right, ten seconds more."

At six minutes and ten seconds the guillotine falls. But the next day you're coming into a dry spell. For a start, the sound of your own voice is unbearable. To tell the truth you're a commentator with nothing to communicate.

"Six minutes is much too much."

"All right, let's say five minutes fifty."

What can you do? At least the listener can turn you off if he finds you stupid. But that's a consolation forever denied you. You must drink your own prose to the dregs.

If it was only the question of this momentary humiliation it wouldn't be so bad. But to speak out, to address oneself to one's fellow men, when one is totally without a message is an imposture. The words one utters are without substance. The public's attention is aroused to no purpose. One becomes a contributor to universal hubbub and chaos. The human spirit becomes a machine for the propagation of noise.

"Stepping out on to the Town Hall stage in New York," writes Dhan Gopal Mukerji, "and looking into the faces of my audience and into my own heart, I discovered to my dismay that I was a man *totally without a message*. And I clearly heard a voice within me saying: 'Go back to India, back to the wellsprings of sanctity, and restore your soul.'" This is exactly the danger that lies in wait for anyone who agrees to speak too often without having anything to say; the soul slowly but surely withdraws into inaccessible regions, the eye dulls, and words crowd forth onto one's lips. To give back to human speech its primal fullness one would have to institute a reign of silence.

We accept the empty words in hopes of discovering someone new—"that man passing by there". But he will go on passing by, forever just out of reach, in all the normal circumstances of our daily conversations. The effort we make, actively or passively, to escape from ourselves by pretending to speak to or listen to others carries us constantly up to the surface of ourselves where there is nothing—neither the self, nor the other—nothing but a little noise, increasingly vain and irritating. The monks of contemplative orders have been telling us this for ages, but the truth they embody has nothing religious about it; it is part of the human condition. And how tiring it is ever to be digging deeper and deeper into oneself; but what a desolate fatigue comes from never trying to dig at all. A man becomes lonely because he has never consented to be alone.

And that brain of his! "Every last cranny of it is a hundred times more familiar to me than the closed city that I live in. Every street and every rut in my imagination is a hundred times more footworn. I have walked them all countless times, up and down and every which way. In this dilapidated brain of mine I am the sole inhabitant. I have caroused in all its cabarets. I have rolled through it like an absolute monarch in a golden coach. I have trotted around it like a fat bourgeois on a sleek mule. And now I dare only enter it like a thief in the night with a dark lantern in my hand."

There is always that solution as a last resort; once the assassination has been committed, never set foot there again; let the corpse rot; always run off somewhere else; speak, but never commit yourself; never believe in anything beyond the latest superficial sensation; follow the rockets where they burst, despairingly.

Is that possible? I doubt that death is real. One always runs the risk of a resurrection.

November 1963

INDEX